D1204765

THE PEOPLES' COOK BOOK

THE PEOPLES' COOK BOOK

Staples, Delicacies, & Curiosities
from the Earth's Humble Kitchens

Huguette Couffignal
Translated and Adapted by James Kardon

Additional Recipes by Marlene Anne Bumgarner and James Kardon
Illustrations by Susan Marsh

St. Martin's Press   New York

A French edition of this book was originally published
© 1970 Robert Morel Editeur
This expanded English translation and adaptation,
including all new material, is Copyright © 1977
by St. Martin's Press, Inc.
Illustrations © 1977 by Susan Marsh
All rights reserved. For information, write:

St. Martin's Press
175 Fifth Avenue
New York, N.Y. 10010

Manufactured in the United States of America
Library of Congress Catalog Card No.: 76-62756
Cover and book design by Susan Marsh

Library of Congress Cataloging in Publication Data

Kardon, James.
The peoples' cookbook.

Translation and adaptation of
La cuisine des pauvres by H. Couffignal.
Includes index.
1. Cookery, International.
I. Bumgarner, Marlene Anne, 1947-
II. Couffignal, Huguette. La cuisine des pauvres. III Title.
TX725.A1K26   641.5′9   76-62756
ISBN 0-312-60007-0

To those who consider life something other than a monstrous belly with a
  golden navel for all to worship;
To those who have tasted and preferred renunciation,
  simplicity and freedom;
To those who make an art of living;
To those who cultivate poverty as a spiritual exercise,
  whatever their religion;
To those who find in each moment a life to live for;
To the unwilling poor, victims of society, property, climate, injustice,
  ignorance, overpopulation, stupidity, evil or dumb pride;
Because it is clear that peoples' kitchens all over the world have learned to
  adapt to what's available and from the nearly nothing at their disposal
  make something more than just enough to live on, make sturdy, simple
  pleasures and elemental feasts.

Thanks to:

The Chinese, Japanese, Puerto Rican, Korean, Italian, Arab, Greek, Turkish, Indian, Israeli, Filipino, Caribbean, Thai, Mexican, Natural Foods, Mixed, Corporate and Cultish shopkeepers of New York who provided and explained the ingredients and utensils used in the recipes in this book, and who make it possible to eat the way the world eats in a single city.

Special thanks to: Paul T. De Angelis and
Annette Kardon, Nataline Kardon,
Frances Gross, Steve Dembski,
Susan Leidner, Karen Kaye,
Kusum Joshi for checking Indian recipes,
Paula Bailey, Eleanor Gold,
Jackie Blatt, Allison Lynde, Nancy Minchenberg,
A La Bonne Cocotte, Aphrodisia,
John Ottomanelli, Katsu, Carol Kendrick,
J. Le Papier, Nancy Rosenberg,
Fred and Cynthia Smith, Margaret Fong,
John Griffiths, Joan Throckmorton
and the many who tasted the tested recipes
and gave a considered opinion.

James Kardon

Contents

The Peoples' Cooking

This book is a catalogue of information and recipes from simple peoples' kitchens around the world. It has been assembled in a spirit very different from the usual collection of international specialties and gastronomic palate ticklers. You will not find any recipes for caviar, for paté, for truffles, or fine cuts of veal in this book. Nor will you find suggestions for huge roasts or fancy stuffed birds. What you will find is an introduction to the unpretentious, delicious, and natural cooking prepared in modest homes and inns, in huts, and over open fires from Peru to Pakistan to Polynesia. The peoples of these countries can teach you how to eat well and festively for practically nothing.

Most of the world's people are poor by Western standards. This has not prevented them from making use of the resources at hand to fashion cuisines that are almost always fresh and filling and often rise to true culinary distinction. As food prices rise, as land resources dwindle and population grows, more and more affluent nations look to peasant, ethnic, and Third World cooking for inspiration.

In this book we have not attempted to cull only the highest points, the most exquisite achievements of native cuisine—the court banquets and huge feasts served only on days of great celebration. We do not believe that Western cooks want to prepare huge banquets every night and doubt they have the five cooks and fifty kitchen helpers available at an Imperial Asian court. We also believe that one can have as much reverence for a humble breakfast as for a ceremonial feast: both are life-sustaining acts of different but equal import. Cooking is an attitude and a way of life. The spirit of simple cooks lies in their knowledge that they are not simply pleasing palates but also filling a basic function that is part of the will to live.

You may not be able to duplicate the flavors of foreign foods as the indigenous people know them. It is not just because some ingredients are hard to get—in fact, more and more of them are available in ethnic or natural foods markets, and many can be easily grown in a garden. What comes naturally, almost intuitively, to a native cook is difficult to teach yourself consciously. A sense of balance, the personality of flavors, and a relationship to the food are learned as you grow, like your accent when you speak or knowing when to smile or cry. Many foreign dishes will never seem like home cooking. An American will not be able to get the taste of Easter from Greek *mayeritsa* the way he can imagine Thanksgiving just by looking at a pumpkin pie. A bowl of millet may never taste like a satisfying meal to you, and it may be hard for you to appreciate the intense luxury of an onion. But as you learn new possibilities, some will almost certainly find their way into your own native style of cooking, especially as you realize the exciting tastes, nutritional values, and huge economies to be realized in peoples' cooking. Rice and beans, beancurd and *miso* soup are not only a lot cheaper than steak, they are often a lot tastier.

The Peoples' Diet: Famine and Feast

There are only two families in the world:
those who have and those who have not.
Cervantes, Don Quixote

Is there a life less enviable than that of the Mexican peasant woman, up with the dawn and quickly dressed in her cotton *rebozo* to spend her day finding and preparing food for her family? Making enough *tortillas* for a numerous household is hard work. She throws nothing away, using old tin cans not just to save bacon grease, but also for dishes, pots, and to store water. She can't buy in wholesale quantities because there's never that much money on hand. She has to market meal by meal. When someone aches she even buys aspirin pill by pill. Her life is constant work and care.

"Does the head cry for flowers when the belly cries for rice?" is an Indian proverb of universal truth. Eat; eat or starve. Necessity is law. The problems of enough *tortillas,* water and pesos, and too much hard work in the fields dog the Mexican peasant family from dawn to dusk. What is food to them? Usually food means morning *tortillas* washed down with a brew made from roasted corn because real coffee is too expensive; then at noon, *tortillas* with rice and tomato sauce, washed down again with corn coffee; at dinner, *tortillas* with rice and beans, spiced with the aromatic herb *epazote* and traditional chili sauce. If the man works near the house, his wife brings him dinner at four o'clock: *tortillas,* beans, sometimes meat in tomato sauce and a pint of cactus beer known as *pulque.* Supper that night consists of corn coffee and milk before bed.

Large meals are reserved for holidays. On November 1, All Saints' Day, Mexican peasants set up a feast on the altar amid flowers and candles: loaves of pink and white sugar, cakes or *dulce*, cups of hot milk and rice, bread, *tortillas*, bananas, lemons, succulent *jicamas* and milk, milk! When the feast candles are blown out, hunger returns.

It may be true that some who have nothing lead a simple, not miserable life—contemplative, without ambitions but with elemental happiness. "Let us suppress misery and cultivate poverty," said Lanzo del Vasto, placing value on simplicity while fighting deprivation.

One example of this simple life can be found among the Brazilian *caboclos*, a people who mix and remix their Spanish, black, and Indian blood from generation to generation and who seem to live freely and without care. Rough but meditative people, musicians as well as dancers, the verve of their stories gave rise to a form of picaresque peasant literature, found notably at a popular little theater in Rio de Janeiro, the Casa de Caboclo. On the coast, the *caiçara* seem to live well, satisfied with fish, manioc, and the wild fruit which usually abounds in tropical countries. They pass the time as easily as in a Polynesian paradise.

Such happy cases, if they really are happy, are bound to disappear as the modern world draws everyone to its way of consumer happiness. The other picture is one of forced indolence with its corollary, omnipresent hunger for the great mass of the world's people. There may be more free time, but how different it is in spirit. The same rhythms that delight the *cabocle* may be mere escape from misery for others, helped along by coca, *chicha*, and *pulque*—drugs and alcohol.

The descendants of the great Incas drown their hunger and weakness in pints of foamy *chicha* drawn from an earthen vat. This seemingly mild corn beer may reach a strength of 36 percent alcohol—a stupefying drink. Such hunger-cheaters seem almost more common than food among the poor of all latitudes.

All over the world various leaves are chewed to ease hunger pangs. Little bags of dried coca leaves are offered in every country store in South America. The Indian chews the leaves all day, adding a little bit of mineral lime to draw out the alkalinity. Close to 10 percent of the world's population chews betel—betel palm nuts wrapped in betel pepper leaves, also accompanied by lime—just to have something to chew.

"The Otomi Indian lives and works for *pulque* alone," goes a Mexican saying. Whatever the basic reason for this, the one advanced by dieticians is no less true. This drink which is fermented from *aguamiel*, the juice of the maguey plant (a type of agave cactus), has nutrients and vitamins otherwise missing in the daily diet. *Tezquino*, spirits made from fermented wild grains and sprouted corn, similarly compensates for common protein deficiency. *Jiculi*, brewed peyote, has much the same properties, in addition to its mystical virtues.

Maguey, a useful plant whose fibers can be woven and whose leaves provide good animal feed, comes in two varieties. One, with gray-blue pointed leaves, furnishes *mezcal*, another hunger-cheater which produces psychedelic side effects. The other, with supple dark leaves and known as *Agave americana*, can be made into *pulque*. Some plants may produce up to 250 gallons of *aguamiel*. Consequently, maguey fields are often called the Mexican vineyards.

The origins of *pulque*—called *neutli* by its inventors, the Aztecs—are known only from a legend in which the poor inventor's daughter becomes the beloved of the King and the mother of the "Son of the King," who in turn becomes King. It was, however, the conquistadores who named the drink *pulque*—Spanish for bitter—in the process of stripping the native

Indians not only of their gold but also of their language.

Legend and dreamy idleness are not enough to mask the sordidness of want. Such is the case in the United States, where misery has a bitterness far removed from the apparent ease of tropical life. In a land of general abundance, extreme misery exists under the shocked eyes of those who "would never believe it." Misery is seen in the vacant stare of a blond child standing in front of his shack in Kentucky, with skeletal arms and legs and a belly protruding under his only clothing, a shirt. Around him are scattered empty tin cans from beans, soup, condensed milk. Beans are always an essential resource of the poor. The same misery can be found all over the Deep South and Appalachia, in New England, and in all cities—for instance, in Minneapolis old people live as best they can on milk, crackers, and canned soup. White, black, and Indian children suffer the same diseases—true equality before the law. These children eat beans, only beans, or potatoes and meat once a week, if they are lucky. Meat is not guaranteed. In Washington, D.C., 70 percent of the children treated at Children's Hospital suffer from malnutrition. In New York City alone, almost a million people live on welfare. Most poor families live in cities, half in the South. One quarter are families headed by women, one-third by people over sixty-five years old, and 30 percent have no head of family. There are children in the Appalachians who have never seen a pencil or a sink.

Among some people in the United States, as well as in South America, Africa, or Asia, the specter of starvation never departs, even when the daily scramble to survive keeps poverty above the level of total misery.

Famine is an ancient companion of mankind. In China alone there have been no less than ninety-one important famines per century over the last two thousand years. How many victims were claimed in all that time? India has suffered one fourth of all recorded famines. Europe, with its sauerkraut, pasta, and French cooking, has been more than once reduced to eating rats, bark, and even human flesh. The ogres of fairy tales owe their name to the hordes of Hungarians who swept down on Europe from their Asian steppes without our familiar notions as to what is food and what is not. The story of Hansel and Gretel, abandoned in the woods by their parents and almost eaten by a witch, may have similar origins. France, for all its fine sauces, had fifty famines from the sixteenth to the nineteenth centuries.

During the revolution in China, the people had nothing to eat but leaves, bark, and clay. Leaves sold in the market for well over a dollar a pound, During Mao Tse-tung's famous Long March, soldiers had to be satisfied with a bowl of millet and a little cabbage, or occasionally some rice with corn bread. Some soldiers were noted for pot-bellies, due not to good living but to the swelling caused by their grass diet. When the grass was exhausted, they were reduced to eating mud to fill their bellies, mud that also caused a swelling that could prove fatal.

Geophagy is a last resort all over the world; it is practiced by natives of

America, Guiana, Venezuela, Siberia, New Caledonia, Thailand, Indonesia, and sub-Saharan Africa. Sometimes the earth—usually clay or chalk—is prepared according to a recipe, as in the East Indies where it is mixed with water and shaped into cakes that are then roasted over a fire. A certain swamp clay mixed with fruit juice serves as jam. Thais appreciate a curious edible earth made up of silicates, aluminum, and water, colored according to the proportions of certain metallic oxides in its composition, proportions that vary from place to place. They mix the clay with water then cook it.

But earth has always been part of the human diet. The Romans at their peak were so fond of *alica*, a porridge of coarse grain mixed with a kind of earth called *creta*, that Augustus was said to have paid 20,000 sesterces for a monopoly on the product. The earth, which could be clay or chalk, came from between Naples and Pouzzoles. Equally mystifying seems the report that black people in a certain region in Texas eat, apparently for pleasure, a particular kind of red clay.

Dietary deficiencies are inextricably involved with the problem of hunger. Such enfeebling deficiencies may result from the routine seasonal gaps between harvests. In a temperate climate, the critical period is from the end of winter well into the spring; in tropical lands, the problem is worst at the end of the dry season. Even if provisions are not exhausted, there are likely to be deficiencies due to a lack of vitamins in the stored foodstuffs. This is aggravated by the fact that the best and richest foods tend to be eaten first.

If the population is basically agricultural, as in the Far East and parts of Africa, even the usual diet is deficient. Farmers tend to limit themselves to high yield crops although variety is necessary for a balanced diet. In such cases, a famine may actually balance their diets by forcing them to eat ordinarily disdained worms, insects, small animals, berries, roots, and greens. Those who live exclusively on grains may make up chronic deficiencies of vitamins and proteins with these varied foods obtained by hunting and gathering. Aberrations in diet which inspire disgust, such as eating earth, carrion and even excrement, not only serve as palliatives but also help a starving person's stomach draw the maximum from meager rations.

Deficiencies are often the result of habits or prejudices. Such is the case in the Orient where polished rice is preferred, though it lacks vitamin B1. Such is the case among many fishing peoples who throw away fish livers. These prejudices sometimes come from outside. Some people starve today because changes were forced upon them by the white men who had little idea of nutritional balance in spreading "civilization." When Africans ate millet, sorghum, manioc, yams, and varied local products, they did not suffer from dietary deficiencies. Now that they have assumed a Western life-style, working in factories instead of in the fields and farming only cash crops, they suffer from malnutrition. In Ceylon before World War II, the people ate an average of eighteen pounds of meat per year; in 1950, the average was down to six and one-half pounds. On the other hand, Canadians consume over 130 pounds and Argentinians close to 300 pounds of meat per year.

In this connection we must remember that at least seven vegetable calories must be consumed to produce one animal calorie. An acre of land may yield 160,000 calories in the form of beef when it could have produced 10 million calories in the form of sugar beets and their by-products. Using this factor, a comparison of two extreme diets—the average Korean diet consisting of 1,900 calories including 110 animal calories, and the average New Zealand diet of 3,250 calories including 1,000 animal calories—leads to the conclusion that "one New Zealand belly is worth four Korean bellies." For each Korean count seven times 110 animal calories plus 1,790 vegetable calories for a total of 2,560 calories. For the New Zealander, count seven times 1,000 animal calories plus 2,250 vegetable calories for a total of 9,250 calories. Thus the ratio of daily consumption which appears to be only 1.7 to 1—3,250/1,900—is more truly represented as 3.7 to 1—9,250/ 2,560.

It is easy to understand why the Chinese live almost exclusively on vegetables: animals consume too many scarce resources for what they yield. Milk returns 15 percent of the energy consumed; eggs, only 7 percent. Beef returns scarcely 4 percent, truly a luxury item. This explains the importance of pork in Asia. The return of energy is about 20 percent, and pigs can be fattened on garbage—vegetable calories not otherwise useful. Pigs make up one quarter of Asiatic livestock, the rest are made up mostly of work animals.

The alimentary geography of our planet seems to reflect the division of the world into two great systems of thought, Christianity and Islam dominate the area of meat and bread consumption, and Buddhism and Hinduism predominate in the region of boiled grains and vegetarianism. Alexis Carrel proposed a theory that carnivores are dynamic and bellicose, and vegetarians are weak and peaceful. "Man is what he eats," is a Hindu proverb. The effects of the difference between the two diets may be seen clearly in the contrasting sizes of pastoral, meat-eating peoples and sedentary vegetarians. In India the Sikhs are taller and stronger than the Hindus. In Africa the Peulhs, Berbers, and Saras are often six feet tall, towering over the Bochimans who average only about five feet.

Almost nowhere are diets based on nature's bounty alone balanced between meats and vegetables. One or the other almost always predominates, apparently according to whether the climate is hot or cold. Yakuts in Siberia live on reindeer meat, usually boiled and eaten with bread but without greens or fruits, which are very rare in the Arctic zone. They get their short rations of vitamins and cellulose from tree bark, the meager harvest of the short summer, flowers, and sometimes predigested lichen from caribou stomachs, a great delicacy. Contrary to other Siberians, Yakuts eat their meat raw because they think cooking destroys the soul of foods. When weather and earth allow some gardening they are quick to cultivate or gather cabbage, lettuce, turnips, blueberries, arbutus berries, and fucus, a seaweed that grows on rocks. Porridge, served hot like the other vegetables, is also a luxury. It is made from plantain seeds gathered by hunters from field mouse burrows.

Shepherds of the world get little variety in their meaty diet. Some variation does come in the form of cheese and butter, usually stored in goat stomachs, which contributes to their strong smell. The milk is bitter. Sometimes there is bread and, as in the Kashmir, some *chang*, barley beer, to brighten daily life. Among the Mongolians and other pastoral peoples of the high central Asian plateau, the herd furnishes all their needs: food, clothing, fuel (fat and dung), tools (bone), and cord (tendons). Indians in America used hollow horns for goblets and used brain to tan leather for clothing and tents.

Sedentary farmers, no poorer than the shepherds, survive on different fare. Korean farmers make do with rice and corn, usually mixed and sometimes eaten with bean curd soup. Happily for them, soy, from which they make bean curd, is very rich in proteins—an excellent substitute for meat. A fair ration of meat is the biggest problem for most sedentary people. To meet this dietary requirement they eat the most varied animals, from birds of all kinds to rats and other little creatures, whatever can be found in barren regions. Pygmies delight in carrion worms, which may seem unpleasant, but supply good quality protein. Elsewhere fish supplies the protein. For instance, in Portugal the per capita fish consumption is 100 pounds per year, and along the Asian coast rice and fish is a staple. Insects provide protein as well, as does seaweed.

Rice here, corn there, millet, sorghum, or rye—cereal grains feed the world. Northern Italians eat an average of 240 pounds of bread a year. Many live on cereal prepared even more simply, boiled as porridge. The same gestures, the same attitudes, practically the same tools are used everywhere to prepare cereals. In Asia, Africa, and America, the woman usually does the work. When a Mexican woman grinds the corn needed for the family's daily tortillas on her *metate* (a rectangular stone set on little legs on which she crushes the grain with a smooth stone roller), she repeats in all details the movements of a Ndebele woman performing the same task in Africa. Only the clothing is different. This feminine occupation is taken very seriously, even included in initiation rites, since the life of the clan depends on it.

When stones are rare or too heavy for nomadic life, as in the Hoggar in Algeria, they still use a stone roller but crush the millet on a sheepskin instead of a millstone. The peoples of Black Africa and Indonesia crush millet and manioc in hollowed tree trunks, churning with strong pestles as big as an arm.

Not all dietary imbalances or deficiencies are explained by climate and geography, or by dearth or relative abundance. There are other causes, equally disturbing, such as discrimination: not racial discrimination but discrimination within the society and within the family. In many societies the men eat first, often leaving little for the women and children. In India, Africa, and Mexico the women must sit respectfully removed from the men's table. Sons wait until their father has started eating. Young children eat alone by the hearth. Later women eat the leftovers. In India, according to Lanza del Vasto, "a woman eats squatting on the ground. . . . She dips her fingers in a bowl of rice and peppers and dextrously stuffs four fingers into her mouth, pushing the handful of food between her teeth with her thumb. She dips a copper cup into a large basin of water from time to time and drinks . . ."

Even the changes of modern life have not overturned these traditional imperatives. The taboos remain, strictly observed on boats, in trains, and at home. These traditions are not merely a picturesque detail of underdeveloped countries; such taboos may be found in our own societies. What can we make of a society that insists that women perpetually reduce their eating, sometimes to a point of malnutrition, for the sake of some standard of beauty?

The opposition of nomadic, herding cultures and sedentary, agricultural peoples is illustrated by the dietary restrictions imposed by each group. The shepherd, afraid that the farmer might acquire some of his characteristics by eating from his herds, tries to impose on the farmer a taboo against eating beef and mutton, meanwhile prohibiting farm meats like pork and rabbit for himself. Elsewhere, herding societies deny themselves other agricultural products, especially those that have been preserved. Fermented products in particular are sometimes forbidden: cheese, breads, and drinks. Some shepherds, according to J. Claudian, "have always been wary of the suspect magic represented by certain fermentations."

Perception of magic is one step from the religious idealization of certain foods, occasionally leading to prohibitions such as the sacred cow of India. The notable examples for Westerners are bread and wine, already sacred to Osiris in Ancient Egypt before becoming part of the cult of Dionysus among the Greeks, and reaching us in the form of Christian communion.

Prohibitions and taboos seem to peak in a practice rare these days, cannibalism. Cannibalism is usually a ritual act. By absorbing the dead man, one hopes to impregnate oneself with his qualities and virtues. Is it perhaps for the sake of such philosophical considerations that certain destitute peoples in the Matto Grosso in Brazil throw their dead into great ponds to be eaten by large crabs that are eaten in turn?

To cure the disease of poverty, humanity must make tremendous efforts. Unfortunately this effort is too often confused with the supposed amelioration of the human lot brought about by the exportation of modern civilization—capital, microbes, and anxiety—destroying any life styles that cannot compete. Perhaps the hope is that by spreading industrial society, our familiar industrial misery will have company.

The most important problems in combating poverty are climate and geography. More than half of mankind lives between 20° and 40° north latitude (not including Europe), precisely the same zone as the greatest area of desert. Deserts and arid zones are not likely to produce soon the miraculous harvests Israelis have coaxed out of the Negev Desert or to blossom with the roses proudly displayed in Saharan oil fields. Of 35 billion acres of land including 7 billion arable acres, man cultivates, often wastefully, only 1.3 billion and uses only 2.3 billion for even poorer pasturage. Add to that these problems: rains that fall or do not fall, such as the dramatic Asian monsoon on which the lives of so many depend; rivers that should flood, like the Nile, or should not flood, like the branches of the Orinoco, driving herders and their herds to leaner and leaner forage; impenetrable forests and high mountains where man lives only with titanic efforts.

Complicating a situation already made difficult by soil and climate are the systems of agricultural production developed by peoples all over the world. These systems also contribute to impoverishment. Although geographic conditions are not always worse in India than in many other countries, India languishes because their farms yield only 22 bushels of rice an acre. Under similar conditions in Surinam an acre yields an average of 40 bushels, and in Egypt, close to 50. Archaic techniques, mediocre seeds, lack of fertilizer, and inadequate agronomic surveillance all contribute to the disparity.

On the edges of jungle in Latin America, parts of Black Africa, and in Ethiopia, farmers strip corners of earth, and farm without fertilizer until the soil is exhausted. After a few years when the harvest gives out, they move on—slash and burn, with no possibility of improvement. The tenant farmers of Brazil are even poorer. They do not even own the land they work and keep moving with their families and meager belongings, hoping to find land that may stay good for a few years. They find an arable patch, clear it, plant, and soon move on again. However, they first sow grass that will permit the big landowner to continue to reap profit by raising cattle on land now too poor to raise people.

Adding to the misery, poor nations must often export their chief agricultural wealth in order to function in the world of commerce, while their masses die of hunger. The poor do not have enough money to buy on the world market. The only remedy is to fight ignorance and use intelligently the available resources of nature.

The world's land is poorly cultivated, and, except in Asia, the sea is also neglected. Only 1 percent of man's food and 10 percent of his animal protein come from the sea. Asiatics long ago solved the problems involved in using and preserving ocean products. However, we are wasting the wealth of the sea faster than we can learn how to cultivate and profit from its flora and fauna.

For many "primitive" peoples of the world, hunting and fishing complement agriculture. But for some, like hunting for the Eskimos and fishing for some Japanese, these methods supply the only source of food. Most peoples have more sophisticated tools than the Punans in Borneo who hunt wild pig with blowguns or the Tonga islanders who capture sharks by lasso. Even so, the techniques are often insufficient to provide enough food to feed a large population. The yield from most hunting and fishing is miniscule when compared to the effort required for the activity. How do you fill the fish baskets if you fish only with a trained cormorant, a technique very common in China and Japan? The Amazon River teems with fish, but those who live on its banks starve because they lack adequate techniques. The *rotos*, the very poor of Chile, live on 5,000 miles of coastline but eat only ten pounds of fish per year because they do not know how to catch them.

Sometimes however, archaic techniques are models of efficiency. For instance, leaves of appropriate size and strength, such as those of the banana tree, serve very well as disposable plates, pot covers, and even pots for cooking on the coals. Few modern cooking techniques are very distant from traditional grills, coals, and heated pits lined with stones and sealed with earth. There is even a technique that we have lost—cooking by dropping red hot stones directly into liquid food, a highly efficient method. American Indians who cooked this way needed only simple baskets lined with clay or well-washed bison stomachs. There was no need for clumsy pots because the vessel was never heated over a fire. A similar technique is used in Corsica to make the finest *brocciu*, a creamy goat cheese.

Of couse not everybody has, as do the Maoris, hot springs close by in which to poach dinner, prepared simply in a net. At the other end of the thermometer, the mountain people of Lebanon store snow in stone reservoirs for use through the summer.

What is most extraordinary in all this is that in spite of such meager resources, workers and peasants—and more especially their wives—have had the talent, ingenuity, and good spirits through the ages to develop simple means of preparing foods. Their preparations respect the natural tastes of foods far better than the complex, overwrought recipes of rich cuisines and mass-marketed products. Their recipes have a simple gusto which reflects the taste of food to the hungry, and is often more appealing than refined dishes. A hungry person may know better what good food is than a person with a jaded palate. These recipes help millions make feasts in the midst of want.

The Peoples' Resources

Man has learned to adapt to his environment the world over and perhaps never more so than in his ability to shape valuable foods and utensils out of his natural habitat. Many peoples' staples seem unlikely or even repugnant to the Westerner on first mention, but, seen in context, they are the natural products of man's inventiveness and economy. Below we list many of the foods not commonly employed in the modern Western kitchen but which are basic resources in the world's fight against hunger. Recipes using many of these foods can be found in the recipes section.

Tropical Trees and Plants

THE COCONUT PALM   The uses of the coconut palm are as "numerous as the stars in the sky." Coconut palms supply materials to build a house, then furnish it with everything from tables and chairs to cups, saucers, rugs, brooms, and soap, and finally food for those who live in the house. The shade of these trees brings relief from the heat, or the trees can be burned for heat! A palm wick, burning in palm oil, in a lamp made from a coconut shell provides light. Palm fibers can be woven to make clothing. The trunk can be hollowed out for a boat which is then fitted with sails, rigging, lines, and nets made from fronds and fibers. Palm trees also provide material for a wide range of industrial uses. Eleven million acres are planted with these palms, and at least 2.5 billion coconuts are used each year.

   Although lacking branches and growth rings, palm trees reveal their age in the number of scars from fronds that have fallen over the years. A coconut palm reaches maturity, that is, full reproductive capacity, at thirteen years of age and continues to bear fruit well into its sixties, when it begins to decline. It dies in its eighties or nineties, a life span curiously

parallel to that of man. On the average, a coconut palm produces 70–120 nuts per year.

Coconut palms usually grow near rivers or by the ocean. This fact gave rise to the theory that the tree spread around the world from its original home in Southeast Asia as the nuts were carried by waves and currents across the oceans. Palms have also been found 200 miles from the ocean, in Guiana. In Brazil they grow in the arid Ceará in the northeast; even more amazing, they survive at almost 2,000 feet above sea level on the dry Borborema plateau.

Most fruit trees yield only one annual harvest, but the coconut palm provides twelve different products at any given moment. At the top the bud, which resembles cabbage with its bouquet of ivory leaves, is sometimes harvested and sold as heart of palm, which has a very fine taste. However, when the bud is cut, the tree dies. Coconut palm flowers are protected by an envelope of fiber that can be made into shoes, hats, or sun helmets. Blossoming, the flowers exude a nectar with a very special taste, beloved of bees. The nuts take about ten months to develop if the flowers are not used first for other purposes. When the heads of unopened flowers are bent back and crumpled, a sweet sap flows, at a rate of up to four quarts per day. This amber liquid, with no taste of coconut, can be boiled like maple sap for syrup and crystallized into a red sugar. The sap will also ferment rapidly, changing within several hours into a robust drink with up to 8 percent alcohol. This drink is popular under many names throughout the tropics: *toddy* in India, *tuba* in the Philippines, *tuwak* in Indonesia, and *bangui* or palm wine in Africa. Allowed to sit for a few weeks, the sap turns into an excellent vinegar.

The coconut palm provides well—there are always enough flowers to produce coconuts as well as all these other riches.

After a soaking in salt water the fibers that cover the nuts, known as coir, can be woven into cloth, twisted for rope, or used for insulation or cushions. Automobile manufacturers cover the fiber with latex and use it for seats. The shell itself, hard and fine grained, can be used in many different ways. A half-shell is a convenient cup. Add a handle and it becomes a ladle. Many uses are possible: spoons, ash trays, handles, toys, buttons, lamps. Charred shells are valuable not only as charcoal but also as air filters for gas masks, submarines, and cigarette filters.

A five-month-old coconut contains 2 big cups of a fresh, and sweet, crystal clear liquid which is rich in vitamins and minerals. During World War II, military doctors, both American and Japanese, used this pure and sterile liquid in place of glucose solution for intravenous injections. The meat, gelatinous at first, slowly hardens. After a year it is fully ripe. The natives grate the meat to a pulp which can be soaked and pressed in cloth to yield coconut "milk" for cooking. When heated the meat yields oil for cooking, lighting, and—mixed with ash—soap.

Copra, an important item in commerce, is made by drying halves of the shelled nuts. Copra oil can be extracted from the copra, the residual material going to enrich animal feed. Copra oil has many uses in soaps, and diverse toilet articles, lubricants, hydraulic fluid, paints, synthetic rubber, margarine, and confections. Copra oil finds perhaps its most important application in India in the vegetable shortening *ghee*, the principal cooking medium for the large vegetarian Hindu population.

None of the coconut palm is thrown away. The fine strands from the fronds are woven into clothes and textiles. The stems can become skewers, arrows, or brooms as needed. The trunk, although mostly fibrous and particularly so at the core, can supply a few solid planks. The roots can be chewed for dental hygiene, or their extracts can be used in dyes and stomach medicines.

And there are no coconut trees without crabs—enough crabs so that their meat may be a staple to some. The crabs are enormous and meaty. Coconut crabs display unusual intelligence in climbing the trunk, pinching a nut from its bunch, shaking the stem to make the nut drop and burst. Then the crab climbs down and feasts. When men want to catch a crab, they tie a belt of grass high on the trunk. The crab, crawling down the trunk after knocking off a coconut, lets go when he touches the grass, thinking he has reached the ground. Stunned by his fall, the crab is easy game for the hunters.

THE DATE PALM   The date palm is the mainstay of arid countries and equals the coconut in the variety of its uses—360 of them according to a hymn sung by Mesopotamian farmers. Dates can be eaten plain or made into honey, wine, and vinegar. Dried pits are used for fuel or crushed and added to animal fodder. The tree trunk is used for small boats and lumber; the fronds, for brooms; and the fibers may be woven into baskets, nets, and cords. As always, the bud is a delicacy for fine salads. One pound of dates contains 1,300 calories: 70 percent sugar, 2.5 percent fat, and 2 percent protein.

OTHER PALMS   Palm trees make up a vast family. Some species, such as the central African oil palm (Elaesis guineensis), are grown for their oil. The carnauba, or wax palm (Copernicia cerifera), is a useful tree. Its seeds take the place of coffee for the poor of Brazil. The wax that seals the vast frond fans is highly prized by industry, particularly record manufacturers. Cut regularly, the fronds renew themselves after six months. The fruits are used for animal feed

Sugar palms are distinct too. All palms yield sweet sap for palm wine, but some species are richer in sugar. Notable examples are the Borassus flabellifer of India and West Africa, the Arenga saccharifera of tropical Asia and Indonesia, and Nipa fruticans from the shores of the Far East.

The starchy marrow of the Sago Palm (Metroxyla), when crushed and washed, is a staple through much of Southeast Asia. Reduced to starch, this pith is used in puddings and stews. The fruit, cooked and roasted, can take the place of bread.

The Mauritia palm from the savannas of South America, and the Coripha from Indonesia and Malaysia also yield starch.

Betel palms provide the nut that when dried, sliced, and wrapped in leaves of the betel pepper plant is chewed daily by millions as a mild stimulant.

KARITÉ (BUTYROSPERMUM PARKII)   This tree of the African savanna, typical of the south Sudan, bears a fruit resembling a prune which when boiled yields a valuable vegetable fat known as karité butter. In Sudanese markets the butter is usually sold in five- or six-pound chunks still retaining the shape of the calabash in which it was prepared and packed in thin baskets of plaited grass. It is used not only for cooking but also for soap, light, medicine, and beauty cream.

CACTUS   We have already noted the maguey, the Mexican agave used to make a bitter beer called *pulque* (see page 4). Another cactus resource is the *opuntia*, or prickly pear *(Ficus indica)*, with its very sweet, juicy fruit. Once the spines are singed off, the lobes are eaten by people and animals. Opuntia is assiduously cultivated all over Latin America. *Xique-xique*, with its long arms bristling with spines, is used in the same ways.

BREADFRUIT   This originally Polynesian fruit—known as *meis* in the Marquesas, as uru on Maupiti, and more simply as *Artocarpus* among the botanists—provides an exceptionally valuable food for tropical populations.

The attempted transport of breadfruit trees was the mission of the voyage recounted in *Mutiny on the Bounty*. In April of 1789 the plants were, with less dramatic shipboard incident but greater nutritional impact, finally imported to the Caribbean. It was hoped that breadfruit would help alleviate the perpetual famine and dietary deficiencies that afflicted the poor inhabitants of the Antilles, the West Indies, Barbados, etc., as a result of the abusive monoculture of sugar cane. These poor people had to be maintained at least minimally to work the plantations and keep the profits from sugar cane, a cash crop, pouring in. Captain Cook, the first European to discover the prolific breadfruit, had become excited at the possibility that it could serve as a cheap way to feed the plantation populations. However, breadfruit kept the Polynesians healthy and strong only as part of a diet that included fresh fish and varied fruits and vegetables, unavailable in the crowded Caribbean. Breadfruit alone turned out not to be a balanced diet, and it would be some years before profitable sugar cane land would be idled to insure a wholesome diet for the poor.

Breadfruit, despite its insufficiency as the sole food of an entire population, is a very useful plant. Like the palm tree, the breadfruit tree provides material for everything from food to roofing, clothing to cooking pots. The flowers are prized as bait by fishermen and as garments by the beautiful young *vahinees*. The seeds, too, are highly valued. They resemble chestnuts in appearance, taste, and preparation. The fruits themselves stay fresh for as long as eight months.

TARO   Taro (or colocasia), with its large round leaves swaying at the ends of long stalks is a common plant in the tropics. The starchy roots are another of grainless Oceania's staple foods. Taro has the same uses as breadfruit, and is used to make one of the most famous of the Pacific region's staples, *poi*.

Insects

Insects are sometimes a usual feature of diet and often a last resort in famine. There are peoples in Ethiopia who live solely on grasshoppers. No doubt we Westerners should learn to use insects for food—not only to rid ourselves efficiently of what are otherwise pests but also to utilize very nutritious substances. Crickets are 20 percent protein raw and 50 percent protein when cooked. By comparison, beef is only 17 percent protein.

Insects have long been considered good food, even a delicacy. In Leviticus 11:22, Moses details which varieties of locusts are proper to eat—*locusta, bruchus, ophimacus,* and *attacus.* The gospels of Mark and Matthew say that John the Baptist lived solely on locusts and wild honey when he was preaching in the Judaean desert. The word *entomophagous*—insect-eating—comes from the Athenians, who, although speaking with disdain of "barbarians, cricket-eaters," used to munch on grilled cicadas. Grasshoppers, termites, caterpillars, larvae, worms, and so on are sought out by peoples all over the map, both "civilized" and "primitive."

Arabs boil locusts in salted water, then dry them in the sun. The Tuareg eat them raw or crushed into a fine powder. South American Indians skewer and roast locusts. Others mash them into a smooth paste. Japanese, Chinese, and Vietnamese eat them roasted, fried, in a sauce, or sometimes in pancakes. The Burmese can boast of the supreme refinement: stuffed locust.

North African couscous, now often served with meat, was originally made with locusts. The preparation of this dish was quite involved. First the insects were shelled, removing head, legs, and wings; then they were crushed, salted, spiced, and worked into a paste with the couscous grains. The whole mixture was then set to "cook" in the sun in an earthen tub and stirred from time to time until a nauseating fermentation began, initiated by yeasts on grasses in the locusts' stomachs. When the fermentation was complete, the thick, odorless paste was spread on a mat of braided rushes and shaped into breads or pancakes, to dry in the sun. The locust breads hardened and had to be soaked before eating.

Crickets and cicadas are valued as toys as well as food. Often sold in braided reed cages in China, they are the joy of children—a sort of live transistor radio.

In Mexico unfortunate giant beetles may be eaten or sold live as toys, heavily decked with decorative stones. They provide sport as they try to escape and hide in every little corner. Beetles are also used for medicine—in Malaysia, every housewife keeps some dried in a jar as a remedy for sore throats.

Sweet fat worms from palms and agaves are treats not only for the Jivaros in the Amazon jungles but also for Mexicans in cities. They are fried and sold on street corners in paper cones like hot chestnuts.

In China, land of silk, people eat the chrysalises of silk worms. Ethiopians tear the wings from giant mosquitoes and other flying insects with bodies sometimes as big as half a thumb, impale the bodies on twigs, and roast them over coals. The whole family, from nursling to grandfather, enjoys this treat.

Termites are also prized. In India queen termites with enormous abdomens are considered a delicacy. Amazon Indians make whole meals from soldier termites. In Africa queens, workers, and soldiers are considered equally good fare, raw or cooked. The Pygmies like termites roasted black in a clay pot perched on stones over a fire. Termites are sometimes used with various caterpillars (themselves occasionally used for porridge) to enrich snail stews, heavily spiced with wild red pepper and salted with the ashes of aquatic plants.

The Bochimans gather termites artfully. Women watch from day to day for the moment of swarming, when harvest is best. They scratch up a thin layer of earth to show where the termite corridors are, and poke little wooden plugs into the holes, which are removed when the swarming begins. Then the proprietor of the termite hill surrounds the place with his family, often building a shelter in which to wait. Swarming begins at twilight. A fire is lit under a roof of leaves and branches next to a trench dug around the termite hill. When the insects take flight they hit the roof, fall to the ground, crawl toward the fire and fall into the trench. The Bochiman woman then has only to gather them up with a scoop, lay them in a basket, and cover them with fresh leaves.

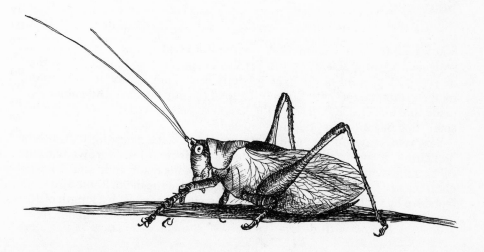

Another harvesting method is even more curious: the simulated rain method. The termite hunters, having noted that termites leave their nests in great numbers when it rains hard, fool the insects by imitating the noise of rain. To do this they station themselves around the termite hill, which may be as tall as a man, and beat on pots. The patter must be gentle. Termites expecting a downpour stream out of their holes and are drawn to lamps held by the hunters. The hunters grill the insects with straw torches as they come out, or knock them into tubs of water with great beaters.

Grilled, crushed, shaped into sausages and rolled up in banana leaves to be poached, these insects form a "termite sausage." Pressed and twisted inside a sack, they yield a useful oil.

The Kapapalo Indians catch butterflies, pull off their wings, and munch the bodies raw like peanuts. They prefer the meatier varieties. The lice from their unkempt heads are also appreciated.

Bees, wasps, dragonflies, crickets, ants, cicadas, and more—from one corner of the earth to another—insects are a public feast. In Columbia, for instance, no one shies away from a dish of soft, fat ants, fried in butter, and served with an aperitif or whisky—a replacement for olives and other snacks. People in less exotic countries sometimes think along the same lines. A French army survival handbook counsels: "If you find yourself lost in the wild without weapons, tools or provisions, eat ants, grasshoppers and termites. These insects are edible." Astronauts may soon be insecti-vores; the scientists who develop their diet are studying water fleas, which are easy to grow, cook, and eat, and are a complete food. Other scientists recommend grinding insects into powder to distribute as a dietary supple-ment to underfed populations.

Seaweeds

Many people do not know that seaweed is good to eat, but varieties of seaweeds are appreciated in the Far East, especially in Japan, where they make up 25 percent of the average daily diet. They can be used in many recipes, often mixed with flour and added to soups or rice, and sometimes made into noodles. For dessert, the Japanese may serve *kakimochi sembei*, small rice biscuits wrapped in seaweed.

Sargasso seaweed, a yellow brown algae with seemingly limitless branching, floats on the ocean by means of air nodules. It grows without roots, at the whim of the currents. Other seaweeds reach great size, like the giant seaweeds of the California coast, sequoias of the deep. Rooted 50 to 60 feet deep by suction cups, the soft but solid stems may reach a length of 150 feet. Their "leaves" are thick and heavy, recalling those of rubber trees.

Double ranks of air nodules, sometimes with a buoy the size of a grapefruit, keep them vertical and floating. Some are long-lived, but others are annuals, reaching monstrous size within the space of a few months. These huge seaweeds form submarine jungles, supporting a host of parasite plants.

The seaweeds called wrack and goemon (*fucus*) are used as fertilizer in Brittany, for example. There are several types: flotsam goemon, which is either ripped loose by tempests or comes in the form of a loose-floating annual and so is easily harvested; black shore goemon, harvested live by shore communities from flats and rocks exposed by the receding tide; marl, the accumulation of certain calcareous seaweeds, dredged up and then plowed into fields; and bottom goemon, growing 90 feet deep, harvested year round as a cash crop with varied industrial uses. American seaweed farmers have even developed an underwater harvester, with a 10 foot blade to cut the seaweed and a conveyor belt to carry it to shipboard.

Edible species of seaweed are numerous. In Japan the *asakusanori*, from the Tokyo bay area, are among the most prized. This red porphyra seaweed is commonly called purple laver and cultivated in fields 6 feet deep that are uncovered at low tide. They can be gathered at any season. It is indigenous to North American as well as Japanese coastlines. Their floating "leaves" are dried before packing. They are prepared by strong heating to harden them; in the course of heating the color goes from red to very deep green. This and other laver or nori seaweed are used primarily for wrapping sushi, as garnishes or to flavor and enrich soups, sauces, and varied dishes.

Another type of nori, amanori (Gelideum corneum), gathered in Yeso and Wayahama bays, is dried on the spot, then quickly taken to factories in the interior to be processed. There the seaweed is washed, pounded, and spread outside, even on dry winter days, to bleach in the sun. Then it is boiled at low heat until mucilage rises to the surface. This is skimmed off and cooled. The result is a translucent, thick gel which can be cut into ribbons, shavings and flakes, not unlike tapioca and used in the same way. This amanori is used in desserts under the name kanten. It is also known as agar-agar and, in Japan, thao. (Agar-agar is also sometimes made from kelp.) Amanori is used by the Asian swift to build its nest, the same nest used for the famous bird's nest soup—so it is easy to guess how agar-agar can be used to counterfeit this precious dish.

Kombu, dried kelp, is also prized in Japan (and also common off North American coasts). Gathered, washed, dried, and cut into thin noodles, kombu can be eaten dry, as is, or tenderized in hot water. Other preparations may use the same name—kombu comes in many forms. Sometimes these kelps are soaked in vinegar before drying; sometimes they are "peeled" with a knife. The dried pulp may be pulverized or just cut up. In Japan kombu is used in soups and stews; its "heart" is used as a seasoning. Kombu can even be brewed into a kind of tea.

Wakame, or lobe-leafed seaweed, is enjoyed as a main ingredient in Japanese soups and stews.

Other peoples besides the Japanese use seaweed, though not so extensively. There are old Breton recipes for dried seaweed ribbons cooked in milk or stock. The Scottish, Welsh, and Irish continue to prepare sea cabbage (Ulva lactuca); and Irish moss, also known as carrageen (Chondrus crispus), is appreciated by "Downeasters" from the state of Maine. The Welsh use seaweed to make very filling laver bread. The sweet, cartilaginous stems of Scottish badderlocks and Irish murlins—members of the Alaria family, common in the North Sea—are also eaten. Iridaea edulis or dulse has also been eaten for centuries by the Irish. It can be eaten steamed, or sautéed with other vegetables, or served raw in salads. Chileans also appreciate seaweed, especially a variety called cochayuyo. They gather it on tidal flats and prepare it in every which way: in soup, fried, pureed or in paté.

Herds and Game

MUTTON, YAK, CAMEL, AND COW   In Mongolia, a land of yurts (felt tents which are the homes of nomadic, pastoral people), the staple is meat. This diet is common among all pastoral peoples. Mongolian sheep and yaks furnish the daily foods of meat and milk.

A fat animal is the choicest. It is cut in two, boiled without being boned or butchered, and served with knives. When time and weather permit, the animal is spitted whole and grilled over an open fire. Blood is collected and dried in a sheep's intestine, then cut into slices, fried, and served. This preparation is also common in the Chinese Gobi. Extra meat is dried. In this form, called *bortse,* it is served as an appetizer before the boiled meat, along with *shinju,* peppers preserved in bitter brine. The meat is washed down with gulps of *airag,* fermented mare's milk. A bowl of *sootei tsai,* a mixture of tea and milk simmered long by the dung fire, warms the winter chill.

In Tibet every part of a sheep is prepared to best advantage. The stomach is boiled and sliced into ribbons, seasoned, and served as a salad. Kidneys are grilled whole and unopened on an open fire, without cutting away the fat. Lungs, a delicacy, are fried.

Cooking in Tibet, as in Mongolia, is done with yak butter, preserved in sheep stomachs and sold by the slice. This strong butter is used to flavor tea. Tibetan yak liver and meat, like the best parts of a sheep, are grilled or roasted.

In Ethiopia much of the population subsists on grains, but there are Ethiopian herders who live mainly on meat. A sheep is roasted, whole or quartered, on a bed of *teff* (a type of millet) pancakes which soak up the juice. Eating beef raw is not an oddity for the cultured Ethiopian palate—it is a regular feature of their wedding feasts. Even the viscera of cattle are eaten raw. Camel meat, however, is roasted, and the blood adds its savor to the sugared and peppered wedding cakes.

As a consequence of eating raw meat, Ethiopians often suffer from tapeworm. The *kusso* days of rest are observed religiously to combat this parasite. For two days a month the Ethiopian herders rest and take the dried flower of the *kusso* tree as a purgative.

SEAL, CARIBOU, AND AUK   By necessity, the Eskimos are meat eaters. They generally eat animal flesh raw—narwhale blubber, for instance—cutting off chunks at their lips with a hunting knife.

Seal liver is served sliced and smeared with fresh grease. The intestines and stomach may be grilled. Even eyes are prized. The heart is boiled—the same preparation used for snow hares, bear, and some caribou meat. Aside from meat and innards fit for eating, seals and walruses furnish fat prized as a source of oil to burn in lamps. The Eskimos pass their rest periods comfortably installed on seal skins, munching slices of walrus which had been dried in the sun months earlier on simple lattices of branches raised on stakes. Chunks and slices thus preserved are laid away in a reindeer skin sack until a time comes when they will be appreciated.

When hunting is successful, Eskimos eat caribou. Boiled leg of caribou, swimming in grease and served on a wooden plate, with its hot bones cracked for the marrow, is a real feast. Dried meat, marrow, and caribou make up a three course banquet. Caribou also furnish dessert. Their stomachs are often filled with a green gray mousse of partially digested lichens, which can be eaten as is or with some frozen berries.

The hunt is not limited to the same sempiternal beasts. Sometimes, with luck from the weather, wild geese fly by; they're delicious when roasted over oil lamps. Sometimes auks arrive in great numbers. Some are eaten alive, but the rest must be preserved for the difficult season ahead. The birds are wrapped in fatty seal skin and buried under a pile of stones. In the spring the "preserves" are ready to eat. The decomposed birds come out soaked in seal fat; they are purple, strong-smelling, and taste something like strong cheese. The Eskimos also eat frozen duck eggs.

ELEPHANT   Along with monkeys, buffalos, and antelope, elephants are an excellent source of protein when people can find them. Not only are elephants a protected species so that usually one is allowed to kill only three a year, but they are also hard to catch. Not all people hunt with guns—some Africans still use ancestral methods. The hunters, smeared with elephant dung, encircle the huge beast. At the psychological moment they run under the elephant and jab at his entrails with keen poisoned lances. They then trail the elephant as he runs berserk in his death struggle.

The animal is usually butchered on the day following the kill. The intervening time is spent driving stakes and trimming palm branches to erect wide racks three to four feet from the ground for the elephant barbecue. The barbecue itself takes at least two days. Seven or eight racks are necessary, with good sized fires underneath each one, to cook a ton of meat. The trunk alone may weigh well over 200 pounds. The fat, particularly from around the heart, is precious. It is essential for cooking during the long months before the next successful hunt.

The scramble begins: cut, hack, and slice. So many hands and legs are working and climbing over the bloody mass that much is butchered at random. Machetes fly, flies swarm. In the torrid heat the stench rises to fill the jungle. Other men, called by tom-tom, arrive to barter chickens, rice or maybe tobacco, for the meat. Worms thrive. Before laying the meat on the smoking racks, packs of worms have to be knocked off with a machete. Multicolored viscera spill from the opened carcass.

Roast or boiled meat, raw or boiled manioc, then more meat—20 pounds of meat per person per day per glutting: a good hunt.

Small Animals

GUINEA PIG   Guinea pig, or *cuy*, is one of the meats of the poor in Latin America. It is sold already roasted in the markets of Cuzco either in a very hot tomato and pepper sauce or with sautéed onions. Often *cuy* is served with rice. Everyone raises chickens and guinea pigs in his backyard, the way rabbits are also raised for food in many parts of the world.

HEDGEHOG   The *niglo*, a hedgehog coated with clay and baked between hot stones, is practically the Gypsy national dish. When cooked, the hardened clay shell can be cracked with a stone; the animal is ready to serve, skinned with no effort. Gypsies use the same procedure for chicken and other fowl. Chickens need not be plucked because the feathers will come away with the clay shell.

In Argentina both male and female hedgehogs are valued. Gutted, then marinated without being skinned, the hedgehog is cooked in its carapace. When it is done, even the spines can be eaten.

LIZARDS   Like all things that live and move, lizards can satisfy a hungry person. Australian aborigines grill lizards by a campfire.

The fat lizards of North Africa, the *dobs*, are a delicacy for children, who pick out the meat with their fingers after opening up the belly. These same *dobs* also furnish eggs—there are no chickens in the Sahara. In Malaysia they grill lizard eggs and serve them with pepper. These eggs, called *tjitjiaks*, taste as good as any hard-boiled chicken eggs.

Natural Fermentation

INDIAN MASATO OR MANIOC BREW   Among others, the Indians of the Amazon enjoy this special drink. The women prepare it.

First manioc is cooked. The women sit in a circle around a calabash and chew the manioc, mouthful by mouthful, then spit it into the pot. The mash is left to ferment until the festival day, when it is welcomed by all.

KAVA   The natives of the Windward Isles in Polynesia use the same process as the Indians of the Amazon above, replacing manioc with *kava*, the root of the pepper tree *(Piper methysticum)*. The preparation of this precious liquor is not relegated to the women but is a job for men, and young men at that.

The kava roots are soaked in water. The youth of the village sit in a circle and chew the roots as long as possible, often for hours. The well-salivated mash is then spit into a tub. They add water and continue the mashing by hand, then filter it through a clump of fibers. The fermentation begins and continues until the drink is ready.

CHICHA   A similar process, starting with corn, is used in Latin America. The Indians chew the grains of corn, then spit into a bowl set in the middle of the chewers. The corn mash is then left to soak for 15 days. The resulting foamy chicha is bottled in jars, corked with mint leaves, and served in Andean casitas, local taverns, usually in rough pint glasses. Fermented twice, this liquor sometimes reaches 36 percent alcohol content. Its appearance resembles beer.

There is also a darker drink, chicha morada, made from sweet violet corn called morado.

BAIGA   This northern Chinese drink from the Gobi Desert is very strong. It is made from curious ingredients: millet and pigeon droppings. These are mixed together and heated in little metal pots. After fermentation, the mixture is very alcoholic.

Baiga is better if the pigeons have been well fed. It is the feast beverage that washes down the New Year's chiao-tzu or dumplings.

Guide to Ingredients and Utensils

Grains

All grains can be eaten whole, cut up small, or ground into coarse or fine flour. Whole grains keep well over long periods of time if stored in a cool, dry, ventilated place, free from rodents. Stored in plastic, they may mold or mildew. Whole grain flour and polenta do not keep well beyond a few days and should be refrigerated. Refined white flours, such as are available at the supermarket, keep almost indefinitely but are not as nutritious and are relatively expensive in a world where white bread is unknown or a luxury. Whole grain flours have a fuller taste, more appropriate to the simple dishes in this cookbook. Refined flour will do in any recipe calling for flour, but, if possible, use flour that you grind fresh yourself. You can buy good quality whole grain flours of almost every kind at health food stores, but make sure it is fresh.

Grains are ground in order to shorten the time needed for cooking and to make a softer end product. Grinding small quantities of grain is not difficult. A mortar and pestle—among the first of man's tools—will do the job but with more than a fair amount of hard work, particularly with corn. The ideal process uses a grain mill with stone or steel grinders, but a blender or coffee grinder will do the job as long as you carefully supervize the operation. Use small quantities so as not to strain the machine and not to heat up the grain too much by long grinding. It may be necessary to sift flour or meal made in a blender. It will not have as even a texture as if it were ground in a grain mill. You can cut up wheat for bulgur by grinding it for a few seconds in a blender or coffee grinder.

Grains can be grown in any garden except the postage stamp variety. Ask a gardening friend or your county agricultural agent for advice about what seeds to plant, when and how to cultivate, harvest, and winnow.

Legumes:
Beans, Peas, Soy, Peanuts, and Lentils

Beans and peas are the cheapest protein available. Since long before the word *protein* was known, they have formed the basis of most poor people's cooking, along with grains. Soy beans feed the Chinese, peas and lentils (called *dhal*) replace meat entirely for vegetarian Hindus; Africans depend on the peanut and black-eyed peas; Latin Americans, on beans and chickpeas (garbanzos); the people of the Middle East survive on lentils and beans; and Europeans and Americans fall back on beans and pease porridge when meat is scarce. Beans, peas, and lentils are available in good quality and variety at supermarkets. Raw peanuts (best for cooking) and soy beans can be found in oriental markets, health food stores, and sometimes supermarkets that have health food sections. Middle Eastern markets and Indian markets stock the greatest variety of beans and lentils—Esau sold his birthright for a mess of pottage resembling *ful medames* (see p. 164).

Beans, soy beans, and peas are commonly reduced to flours and ground in the same way as grains (see above). These flours can be used to enrich breads, soups, and puddings.

Beans and chick-peas should be soaked overnight, which reduces a long cooking time—1 to 3 hours depending on the size. They should also be rinsed and picked over for stems and stones before cooking.

All legumes are easy to grow and, in fact, enrich the soil with nitrates. Choose seeds on advice of your county agricultural agent, or just save and plant the beans from your larder (split peas do not grow).

Soy beans, lentils, whole peas and, best of all, mung beans can be sprouted to make a crunchy, delicious fresh vegetable. Soak a small quantity (2 to 3 tablespoons) overnight and drain. Let sit in a gauze covered jar in a warm dark place for 3 to 6 days, rinsing and draining every day, until completely sprouted.

Milk, Cheese, Curds

Milk from any animal is a rich colloid of fats and proteins. Natural ferments, rennet—an enzyme from calf's stomach—or an acid like vinegar, can precipitate most of these particles as curds, which separate from a rich clear liquid called whey. Natural ferments and acids produce a soft curd fairly slowly, which can be drained to make fresh cheeses such as cottage cheese, farmer's cheese, and some ricotta. These cheeses are often salted or enriched with cream. Rennet speeds the curdling process and produces a harder curd that is generally used for aged and cured cheeses. These curds are generally cooked slowly at low temperatures and drained before being used simply, like mozzarella; or they are left to ferment quickly like Camembert or cure slowly like Emmenthaler. Taste and texture depend on the milk, the method of curdling, the kind of cooking and pressing, the cultures used, and atmospheric conditions.

Whey can be used in breads or in making whey ricotta or gjetost, a Scandinavian cheese with an unusual taste.

Farmer's cheese is generally satisfactory when a recipe calls for fresh cheese. Hard cheeses of any kind can be used when grated cheese is called for, although these cheeses come in a wide range of tastes and textures. Where specified, use the cheese recommended. Avoid processed cheeses, such as American cheese or cream cheese, and mass-marketed packaged cheeses. Fresh mozzarella picked out of a tub of whey in an Italian market makes a better pizza than the plastic-wrapped cheese sold in supermarkets.

The Indians often cook with curds made simply by natural fermentation—they let milk stand warm for a few hours until it sours. They use it as is or drain it in cloth to separate the more solid curds from the whey. Pasteurized, homogenized milk, which is all you can buy in most stores in the United States, does not sour naturally—it only spoils. It can be soured by adding some acid such as vinegar or lemon juice—about 1 tablespoon per cup—and letting the mixture sit ten minutes or so. (Soured milk should thicken to about the consistency of buttermilk.) This procedure is adequate for making sour milk to use in baking but is not suitable for making curds, since they will be too sour. The simplest procedure for making your own curds is to add 1 tablespoon of buttermilk to 1 cup of boiled milk and let stand at room temperature until it reaches the approximate consistency of yoghurt. This mixture is identical to "clabbered milk" (see "Drinks and Desserts" section). To obtain curd suitable for crumbling or frying, drain this liquid mixture through cheesecloth.

Raw milk, available on prescription from health food stores, will sour naturally.

Buttermilk, originally the liquid produced in churning butter, is made nowadays by souring milk with bacterial cultures. It can be substituted whenever curds or soured milk is called for, but it should be added at the last minute because it tends to curdle further and settle out if heated too much. Yoghurt, another good substitute for curds and important in its own right in Near and Middle Eastern cooking, is made like buttermilk by adding a bacterial culture to milk and incubating it. The taste and texture depend on the culture used and the conditions of incubation. Yoghurt is a true health food. Its role in the good health of Balkan and Caucasian mountain people led to the discovery of several important vitamins. The bacteria apparently aid digestion too.

All milk products can be made from the milk of any animal that gives milk. The majority of common cheeses and soured milks are made from cow's milk; but sheep and goat cheeses are useful and readily available here, especially Greek goat cheese, like feta, and fine French cheeses.

Meat and Fish

The meats available in wealthy America and Europe are not the same as those that most people eat from time to time. There are animals we do not eat, such as lizards, guinea pigs and turtle doves; animals we do not eat often, such as rabbits and game; and parts of familiar animals we do not prize, such as lungs and chicken feet. Even familiar meats are different— our grain-fed beef has a different texture and taste from the meat from the poor cattle slaughtered by the poor; and American hormone-puffed chickens are a different bird from the scrawny yard-fed birds familiar to Africans and Italians.

A good butcher and most supermarkets can usually supply on request all kinds of organ meats and soup bones, but these items are a major stock in trade in Latin and Chinese markets. Unusual, cheaper cuts and organ meats are flavorful once you get to know them.

Italian and Chinese butchers are likely to stock rabbit. Fine butchers stock game, but it is very expensive, and really only qualifies as people's meat if you hunt it yourself.

The kind of fish used in the recipes of different peoples depends on what is plentiful off nearby shores. Americans tend to confine their taste to a fairly narrow range of fish, but almost all fish and sea animals are edible and eaten somewhere. A Greek fishing village dines on whatever they catch that day. Small fish, dried or fresh, can be used to enrich a soup or season a sauce.

There is little reason to be shy about eating every soft part of seafood. Fish cheeks generally have a taste finer than that of the fillets, and the Chinese prize fish eyes.

In American cities Chinese markets carry a wider and more exotic assortment of fresh seafoods, including eels and sea cucumber, than average seafood markets. Japanese markets carry very fine seafood for their raw fish luxuries. Italian and Latin markets always carry *bacalao* (dried cod), but Chinese markets offer a far greater variety of dried fish. Fish that you catch yourself taste best because they are absolutely fresh.

Animal Fats and Vegetable Oils

Animal fats and vegetable oils account for much of the taste and character of different nations' foods. They are also an important element in nutrition—fat is a concentrated form of energy for people who do not overeat.

Olive oil is vital to Italian, Spanish, Greek, and Middle Eastern cooking. It is more expensive than other cooking oils, but without it Mediterranean dishes lose much of their character. Note that the olive oils of different nations have different tastes. Olive oil does go stale when exposed to air so buy it and store it in small bottles.

Peanut oil does not have a strong taste but is generally the best choice for frying, especially Chinese foods. Other light vegetable oils can be substituted freely.

Ghee, either clarified butter or a shortening made from coconut and other vegetable oils, is an important component in many of India's regional cuisines. When we refer to *ghee* in the recipes in this book, we are talking about the shortening which is sold under that name in Indian markets—it is also more widely used among the average people in India than butter. Fine and rich, this shortening gives body to the lively spices of curries. If the shortening *ghee* is unavailable, you could substitute a mixture of coconut and peanut oils, or plain peanut oil, or indeed, that other form of *ghee*, clarified butter.

Sesame oil is more truly a flavoring than a cooking oil becaue it is so strong and so expensive. Use it sparingly, but use it, especially in Chinese food and also in some Middle Eastern and Mexican dishes.

The animal fat most commonly used in cooking is *pork fat*, either in the form of *lard* or *bacon drippings*. In Mexico, South America, and Europe it is the most inexpensive and consequently most popular shortening. Lard is rendered fresh pork fat and is available in most supermarkets or at your butcher's. Bacon drippings are the grease left over from cooking bacon or other salt pork.

Many peoples, especially Moslems and Jews, have dietary laws against eating any part of the pig, thus *mutton* or *lamb fat* and *chicken fat* take the place of lard in their cooking. Hindus cannot eat any animal fats and replace them with vegetable shortening or oil. In the United States many people use vegetable shortening or oil in place of lard or any other animal fat because it is lighter, keeps well, and does not burn as readily. However, lard and bacon drippings, and indeed chicken and lamb fats, have their characteristic tastes and should be used if called for to better approximate the taste of certain dishes.

Recipes from pastoral areas such as the Middle East and central Asia often call for mutton or lamb fat. Mutton is not commonly available in the United States, but what we call lamb is much older than what a shepherd generally chooses to call lamb. With either mutton or lamb, simply use the drippings from roasts, chops, or stew meat or render pieces of fat cut from the meat or bought from your butcher. To render fats, chop the fat into small pieces and heat it over water, occasionally mashing until most of the fat has melted. Strain out the membranes and fibers.

Chicken fat, obtained either by skimming soups, collecting drippings or rendering the pieces of fat generally found alongside the backbone, is often used in Eastern European cooking, particularly by Jews whose dietary laws prohibit the use of lard and milk products such as butter with meat dishes.

Suet, rendered beef fat, is common in British cooking.

Butter varies in taste according to the breed and diet of the animal that supplies the milk. However, because it is perishable and subject to strong health regulations, there is relatively little variety available in the West. Clarified butter, melted butter from which the sediment has been removed, is also good for general cooking purposes because it does not burn as readily.

Spices and Herbs

Spices and herbs are what give markets, except for supermarkets which are scented at best with aerosols, their characteristic smells. Along with cooking oils, spices and herbs also supply much of the characteristic national flavor to dishes. Historically used as preservatives they are employed most freely in the cooking of tropical countries such as India, Mexico, Africa, and the Middle East, where foods spoil most readily and where most of the sharpest flavored spices happen to grow. Using spices and herbs well is a question of experience and imagination. You must learn what harmonizes and what the dishes should taste like, remembering that on native tables some exotic blends are as familiar as salt and pepper.

Herbs are unquestionably best when fresh, and they are generally easy to grow on the borders of gardens or in window boxes. Thyme, marjoram, mint, tarragon, basil, parsley, sage, rosemary, and dill are standard garden herbs. Fresh coriander, also known as *cilantro* or Chinese parsley, with its highly distinctive, somewhat bitter flavor, is important in Indian, Mexican, and Chinese cooking, and is available in ethnic markets. It is also worth cultivating, as is *epazote*, a Mexican herb. Both can be grown from the seeds that are often available in herb and spice stores or ethnic markets.

Spices, like herbs, are best when fresh, but the freshest you can usually get them is "fresh" from the store. They lose their fragrance over time and in the air, especially when ground, so it is best to buy spices whole and in small quantities. Herb and spice dealers, who have a good turnover, such as

Aphrodisia in New York, are probably the best suppliers. In addition, their stores are exciting places to visit; you will never smell more variety.

For maximum freshness, grind whole spices each time you need them. The traditional tools for this are a mortar and pestle. These can be bought at any kitchen shop or at ethnic markets, where they come in a fine assortment of shapes and materials. You can grind large quantities with less effort in a coffee grinder or a blender, but most whole spices are soft and easy to crush by hand.

One of the most important spices is hot pepper, the usually dried fruit of *Capsicum* bushes. The hottest pepper is *cayenne*, a small red pepper, usually powdered, and used, for instance, in African cooking. It also serves well in Indian curries, although Indians generally prefer hot fresh green peppers. The Mexicans are the greatest experts on hot peppers, called *chiles*, which can be ground, used whole or prepared for *mole* (see p. 225). Seeds and inside membranes should always be removed before use.

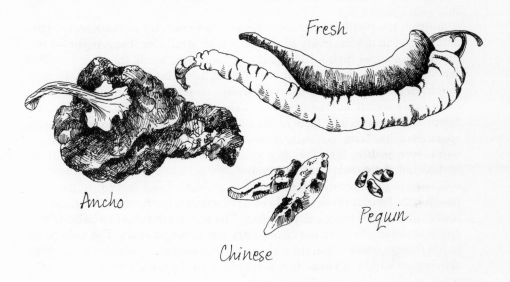

Fresh

Ancho

Pequin

Chinese

Mexican *chiles* vary greatly in taste, ranging from the sweet *ancho chiles* to very hot, very small red *pequins*. Any of the hot *chiles* are appropriate in recipes calling for powdered chiles. Commercial chili powder is a blend of ground hot peppers and cumin or oregano; it is not recommended. Such blends are not very fresh and you can control the taste of dishes better by crushing chosen *chiles* with other spices yourself. For a fuller discussion of Mexican uses of *chiles*, see Diane Kennedy's *The Cuisines of Mexico* or Elizabeth Ortiz's *Complete Book of Mexican Cooking*. The Chinese make their dishes hot with fresh hot green peppers (sold in Chinese markets) and with ginger. They also use a milder spice, not related to these *Capsicum* peppers, called Szechuan pepper, which has overtones of anise. All *Cap-sicums* can be grown from the seeds fairly readily in your garden, but they tend to cross fertilize, so that results are unpredictable, and your *anchos* may come up hot.

Curry powder is a blend, usually stale. It is not used in India and is not recommended. Make your own curries starting with cayenne (if you like hot food), turmeric, cumin, and coriander, then adding fenugreek, anise, cardamom, cinnamon, clove, and ginger as desired and as appropriate. The blend should match the dish. Some of the spices have a bright, sweet aroma, such as cardamom, cinnamon, clove, and ginger. Others are slightly sour, such as turmeric and fenugreek. Cumin and coriander have solid, full tastes. You do not need to use much, no more than 1 or 2 tablespoons of ground spice blend in a dish for four people, to get a distinctive but still delicate taste. Indians generally fry the spices when they begin cooking, which changes the flavors—but be careful not to burn the spices as they may get bitter. For Malaysian curries add lemongrass (*sereh*) to the seasoning.

Saffron, the pistil of the crocus flower, is important in Spanish cooking and is used in almost every other country as well. Use it sparingly—3 to 4 pistils for a usual dish—and grind or soak it first, using the liquid, so that the taste and color are distributed throughout the food. Pistil saffron is much preferred to the powdered variety, which is often adulterated.

Garlic is a critical part of many dishes. Use fresh garlic; it has a finer flavor. Its characteristic taste need not overwhelm a dish—it often serves to spark the other tastes. Usually it is browned whole or chopped in oil in the pan before adding the other ingredients; sometimes it is chopped finely and added at the very end of cooking.

Ginger is also much better fresh, or at least dried whole, rather than powdered. Two or three thin slices give a fine edge to many Chinese and Indian dishes and practically any fish. The succulent roots can be bought at any oriental market and many ordinary vegetable markets. The only problem is their tendency to mold and spoil. To preserve a ginger root, scrub the skin with a stiff brush and store submerged in dry cooking sherry in a cool place. It should keep well for weeks.

Special Products

Soy sauce is made from soy beans fermented in water, aged, and mixed with sea salt. There are three kinds available: thin, stocked by most supermarkets and on the table in Chinese restaurants; thick, which is stronger, heavier, and less salty and available mainly at oriental markets; and tamari, which has less salt and a stronger soy flavor and is available at health food stores and Japanese markets. Quality varies according to the quality of the mash and length of time aged, so it is worthwhile to experiment. Thin soy sauce is what is most commonly used and is appropriate for the recipes in this book. Soy sauce should be added shortly before cooking is done, as too much heat affects the flavor.

Tahina, or sesame paste, can be made by crushing hulled sesame seeds in a mortar and pestle and adding a little sesame or olive oil to give it the desired consistency. It is bottled and available at Middle Eastern and Indian markets.

Coconut cream, the concentrated extract of coconut meat, can be used as a substitute for coconut milk when thinned with water (see "Basic Stocks and Sauces"). It is available canned, bottled, or frozen in Indian, Filipino, and some oriental markets, as well as in some supermarkets on the west coast of the United States.

Water chestnut powder is used by the Chinese instead of cornstarch to thicken soups and sauces.

Peanut paste or *butter*, made by crushing plain roasted peanuts, is used as a flavoring and a cooking medium in Africa and other regions. Commercial peanut butter is crushed peanuts mixed with hydrogenated peanut oil and tends to have a more cloying taste than the natural paste.

Dried mushrooms, used extensively in European and Asian cooking, are available in far greater variety, and are often more fragrant than fresh mushrooms. The most aromatic dried mushrooms come from eastern Europe, with the Italian ones not far behind. Use them in dishes of appropriate nationality. Chinese and Japanese mushrooms tend to be more delicate. Some, like Japanese black tree fungus, are prized mainly for their texture. Prepare dried mushrooms by soaking them until soft. If the mushrooms are cut or broken up, soaking for 30 minutes may suffice, but soaking

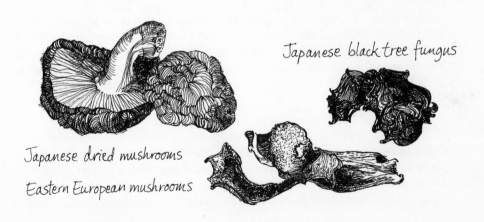

Japanese black tree fungus

Japanese dried mushrooms

Eastern European mushrooms

overnight does not hurt. Use the liquid in which they soak, too. Italian and sometimes Japanese dried mushrooms are available in most supermarkets, but the best selection and quality can be found in herb and spice stores and in Italian, Chinese, and Japanese markets. Dried mushrooms have a different texture and should not be substituted indiscriminately for fresh ones.

Most people who depend on fish have developed techniques for preserving them since they spoil quickly. The most common method is drying. *Dried fish*, like dried mushrooms, do not completely replace fresh fish, but have characteristic tastes and textures that are good in their own right.

Cod, one of the most plentiful seafish, is one of the most common dried fish. Also known as *bacalao*, dried cod is often sold in Italian, Latin, and Oriental markets as well as in supermarkets. To use dried fish soak it in cold water overnight or, depending on size, a few hours, changing the water from time to time. Drain, add cold water to cover, heat to a boil, and simmer gently for 15 minutes. Drain, saving the stock for use in sauce. Fry the fish and cook in a sauce. Oriental markets stock many other kinds of dried seafoods prized for their more concentrated taste. All are prepared by soaking thoroughly, which may take as little as 20 minutes for small shrimp, to overnight, depending on thickness and toughness.

Like Portugal, Japan is a maritime country and a great consumer of fish. Since transportation and conservation are crucial problems, drying is a very useful, if unvarying, way to treat fish. Cleaned, dried *bonito*, a variety of tuna, are opened like books to dry gently in the sun; they can be seen strung on cords in the markets ready for sale. These bonito, known as *katsuobushi*, are grated and added to soups and sauces for flavor, body, and a lovely yellow color. The dried fish is also used for fish sausages.

Dried meats, such as jerky or *charqui*, can be: 1) crushed and used as a flavoring and enriching agent in sauces; 2) eaten plain and salted; 3) cooked in sauce like chipped beef; 4) eaten as a salad with oil and vinegar like Swiss *Bindenfleisch*. Dried meats can be found in specialty or ethnic markets, but it is not difficult to dry meat at home, for example, on a porch. The finer raw hams, like *prosciutto crudo*, are basically dried and salted pork with concentrated taste and a tough texture that necessitates thin slicing or grinding.

Dried seaweeds are vital components of Japanese soup stocks and stews, serve as flavoring agents in rice dishes, and are often used as garnishes. There are three main varieties of Japanese dried seaweed available in oriental (and some health or natural foods) stores: *kombu* or kelp, which is used in stock and for flavoring; *nori* or laver, used for wrapping *sushi* and as a garnish; and *wakame*, a lobe-leafed seaweed used as an ingredient in soups and stews.

Irish moss or *carrageen* is a dried seaweed used by New Englanders, the Welsh, and the Irish. It can be found in health food stores.

Utensils

The most useful foreign utensil called for in this cookbook is the famous oriental *wok*. Made from heavy iron, it is a wide, round-bottomed pot with handles. The *wok* is well adapted for sautéing or Chinese stir-frying, deep frying, and boiling rice. It can be fitted out with bamboo trays and a high cover for steaming. It is best to buy a *wok* at a large Chinese market, as it is likely to be cheaper than in a kitchen supply store. Be sure to choose an iron *wok*, usually sold coated with grease to prevent rust. Stainless steel or aluminum *woks* are not as satisfactory. Fourteen inches is a good size.

To prepare a *wok* for use, remove the protective grease with detergent, and dry well. Then carefully wipe on a thin coat of cooking oil, heat for 10 minutes in a 400° F (200°C) oven, wipe with a damp cloth, dry, wipe on another thin layer of oil, and heat again. You can then cook in the *wok*, which will blacken after repeated use. Never wash a seasoned *wok* or other iron pot with detergent. Simply brush out, rinse with hot water, then dry quickly with a towel or over heat. When cooking in a *wok*, use wooden utensils such as chopsticks instead of metal spoons or forks which may scratch the seasoned surface. Use a wire mesh ladle for deep frying.

Chinese and Japanese cooks also pride themselves on their good knives, which are usually heavy, rectangular, very sharp carbon steel implements. Hold the vegetable or meat to be cut with your knuckles and cut by chopping gently, pivoting the knife forward from the heel of the blade, guiding it with your knuckles. Do not chop hard or saw. Like *woks*, these knives are quite useful for all kinds of cooking.

Other oriental utensils of note are Chinese clay soup pots for slow, even cooking and Japanese iron pots, used for the same purpose. Note that clay, unlike metal, does not impart a metallic taste to the food. It is, however, fragile and susceptible to cracking if heated or cooled rapidly. Clay pots also must be seasoned because otherwise they will give a clayey taste to the food. Heat them gently with oil or fill with a mixture of 2 parts water to 1 part vinegar and heat gently until the liquid boils away. Clay pots should generally not be used over an open flame.

Useful Latin American utensils include the *molcajete*, a large, rough stone mortar good for grinding grains, beans, chiles, and spices; the *comal*, a flat, seasoned iron or clay griddle for cooking tortillas or other pancakes; and the wide deep clay dishes used for paellas. A tortilla press, like an Italian pasta machine, saves hand labor and produces a more even product.

The Indian *tawa* (or *tava*), a concave iron disk, is recommended for cooking flat Indian breads.

Electric appliances, such as blenders, should be used according to instructions. In particular, when blending pastes such as *hummus*, be sure there is enough liquid so that the blades do not get stuck. In grinding grains, take care that the grains and the blender do not heat up too much.

RECIPES

Unless otherwise indicated, most of the recipes in this book will yield approximately four servings. We have not usually specified the number of servings however, because (1) most of the dishes do not easily divide themselves into categories of "entrées," "appetizers," "side dishes," and so on; and (2) it is in the nature of most simple foods to be easily and almost infinitely expandable. Leftovers from almost any recipe in this book will be good the next day, or usable in new, equally delicious dishes—bread or grain puddings, refried beans, and so forth.

BASIC STOCKS AND SAUCES

Tomato Sauce

The following is a basic recipe for tomato sauce. Vary the spices and vegetables to match the other tastes in the recipe in which it will be used. For a stronger tomato taste you may want to add tomato paste, but in that case be sure to simmer the sauce longer than you would otherwise.

    1 carrot
    1 onion
    1 celery stalk
    2–3 cloves garlic
    Salt, pepper, thyme, and basil
    1 lb. (500 g.) tomatoes (imported, canned Italian plum tomatoes
        usually taste better than the tomatoes available fresh out of season)

Chop the carrot, onion, celery, garlic, and herbs, and brown in oil. Add the chopped tomatoes and simmer very gently for 40 minutes. Add salt and pepper. Strain and mash. Makes about 2 cups.

Stock

Soup stocks contribute mightily to the character of dishes.There are two ways to approach the use of stock: one is to make a standard, flavorful stock (see below) wherever stock is called for, using familiar vegetables that may not be a part of every country's cooking; another is to make a simpler stock that can be flavored to harmonize with a particular recipe.

STANDARD MEAT STOCK

> 1 chicken, cut up, or 3−4 lbs. (2 kg.) chicken backs, necks, and feet
>   or 3−4 lbs. (2 kg.) short ribs of beef
>   or 5 lbs. (2.5 kg.) marrow and knuckle bones
> 2 stalks celery
> 1 large carrot
> 2 onions
> 2−3 cloves garlic
> 1 small turnip
> 2 bay leaves
> 6−8 peppercorns
> 4 cloves
> A pinch of whole mace
> Marjoram or thyme
> 3−4 qts. (3−4 l.) water

Cut up the vegetables; the onions and garlic can be left whole. Put all the ingredients into a large, heavy stock pot. Add water to cover. Bring to a boil slowly and let simmer gently and evenly, without interruption for 2½ hours. Drain carefully.

Store in refrigerator, protected by the fat that solidifies on the surface, or freeze. Skim the fat before using. If you want to store stock in the refrigerator for a long time, boil it up every few days.

This standard stock is good for European, East European, and Mexican recipes. For Middle Eastern, African, and Asian recipes make a simpler stock using only the meat, adding, if desired, a few vegetables or spices that will match those of the planned dish or will at least mesh well with the taste of that country's cooking.

Vegetable stocks should also be varied according to the nationality of the cooking you wish to approximate. Here is a standard recipe:

STANDARD VEGETABLE STOCK

3 stalks celery
2−3 onions
2 carrots
1 turnip
1 parsnip
2−3 cloves garlic
1 bay leaf
6 peppercorns
1 pinch mace
Thyme or marjoram
3 qts. (3 l.) water

Chop the vegetables; the onions and garlic may be left whole. Put ingredients into a heavy stock pot. Add water to cover. Bring slowly to a boil and simmer 1½ hours. Drain and use. Vegetable stock is generally not stored, but if you need to store it, freezing is the best method.

Other vegetables, such as cabbage, leeks, cauliflower, squash, chickpeas, and grains such as wheat and barley, can be used for stock, as well as other spices, but cooking times vary. Note, too, that starchy vegetables, like potatoes, peas, and beans will thicken stock considerably.

Coconut Milk

In many Third World cuisines, coconut milk serves the same function as soup stock does in Western cooking—as the base for soups, stews, and main dishes. It is an essential ingredient in Southeast Asian, Pacific, and some African and Latin American cooking, and if you are at all interested in the food of these regions, you should not neglect learning how to make and cook with this extremely versatile, flavorful milk. Making it is neither difficult nor expensive and will prove rewarding.

Coconut milk is made by soaking grated fresh coconut meat in water and pressing it through cheesecloth to extract the flavor, nutrients, and oils from the pulp. The first step in this process is opening the coconut. Puncture holes in two of the three "eyes" of the coconut by hammering an ice pick or screwdriver into them; extract the liquid sap inside (this is not coconut milk but almost pure water; it can be added to the soaking water or served as a drink as is); then pound the shell of the coconut with a hammer or the back of a cleaver, constantly rotating the shell until it cracks. A messier way is to start in with the cracking process right away, keeping a bowl nearby to catch the liquid as it spills, although sometimes you may be fortunate enough to remove the cracked outer shell without actually breaking the inner nut.

Pry off the coconut meat from the hard shell by inserting a screwdriver between the two. Take the inner meat, cut or break into pieces, and peel off the brown skin with a vegetable parer. Now either grate the meat by hand, put it through a vegetable chopper or grinder (easier), or use a blender (see complete blender instructions below). There are three methods of soaking:

> Soak the grated meat in 2 –3 cups (500-750 ml.) water and coconut sap for an hour at room temperature.

> Pour 2 –3 cups (500-750 ml.) boiling water and coconut sap over the grated meat and let sit for 20 minutes.

> Pour 2 –3 cups (500-750 ml.) cold water and coconut sap over the coconut meat and bring just to a boil, remove from heat, and let sit for 20 minutes.

The blender method is as follows:

> Place whole pieces of peeled coconut meat into blender along with 2 –3 cups (500-750 ml.) water and coconut sap (heated or not). Blend at high speed for a minute, then scrape down sides of blender, and blend again. Press through cheesecloth, as below.

The last part of the process involves pressing the coconut/water mixture through cheesecloth. You will want to squeeze hard, since the last drops are the richest ones, so a double or triple layer of cheesecloth is essential. Discard the remaining coconut pulp—it is now tasteless and without nutrient value. Coconut milk keeps for about five days if it is covered and refrigerated.

Coconut milk, like fresh cow milk, separates if it stands a while, and a rich coconut cream rises to the surface. You can skim and save this to use as a flavoring in soups and stews or to make candy. Or mix the cream back into the milk.

You can make a thinner version of coconut milk using dried grated coconut bought in markets, but you will have better results buying canned or frozen coconut cream (available at Indian, Filipino, and some oriental stores) and thinning it with water.

When cooking with coconut milk, heat gently and leave the pot uncovered, otherwise the milk may curdle.

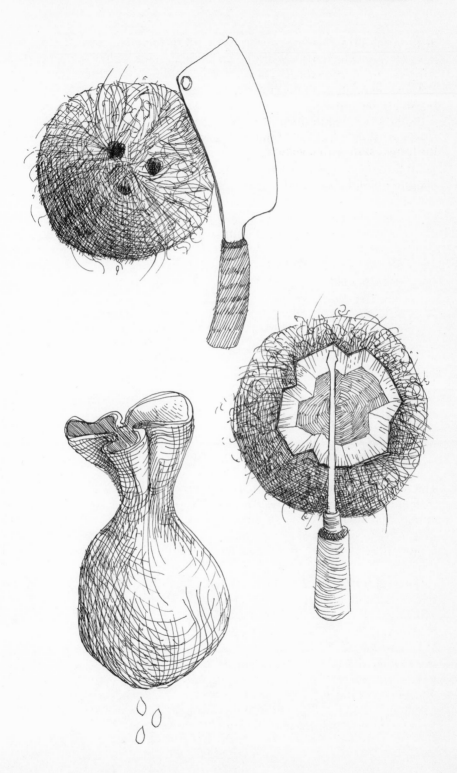

BREADS
AND
PANCAKES

Indian Breads

Contrary to some Western assumptions, India is by no means strictly a rice-eating country. The use of cereal grains varies considerably according to available water: rice is the grain of wet regions, while wheat and millet are staples in dryer areas. Indian "curries" are served with rice in some places and with diverse breads in others.

These Indian breads, like most breads from the Third World, have little in common with Western breads except the name. There are three main types: *chapatis, parathas,* and *pooris.* There are also breads made from peas and beans.

Indians use two kinds of wheat flour: *atta* or whole wheat flour; and *maida* or white flour. In the south breads are made out of rice. Both Moslems and Hindus make whole wheat *chapatis,* with only slight changes. Both cook the rolled (or simply clapped) thin cakes on a *tawa,* a gently curved pan without a handle; but Hindus use the *tawa* convex side up, and Moslems use it convex side down.

The most common stove, the *enghati,* is portable so that *chapatis* and other dishes can be prepared as easily on the road as in the house. The fuel can be coal, charcoal, or dung. The fire is fanned with the aid of a leaf of the versatile palm tree, cut with the handle about 2 feet long and the leaf about 3 feet long, then folded like an accordion, bent over, tied back on the handle. Modern stoves, particularly electric stoves, do not perfectly replace the traditional *enghati* since *chapatis* must be grilled, in part, over an open flame. An open gas burner will serve the purpose, however.

Wheat Chapatis

> 2 cups (250 g.) *atta* (whole wheat) flour
> Approximately 1 cup (250 ml.) water
> Salt

Mix and knead into a firm dough. Let sit ½ hour. Divide into 6−8 egg-sized pieces and roll thin. Cook quickly on both sides on a hot ungreased *tawa* or heavy griddle, over a high flame. Then grill quickly on both sides over an open flame, using tongs, so that the *chapatis* puff up.

Rice Chapatis

 2 cups (250 g.) rice flour
 Approximately 1 cup (250 ml.) boiling water
 Salt

Use the same procedure as for wheat *chapatis* above but with boiling water, and let sit 1 hour. Divide into egg-sized pieces and roll thin between folds of linen or other clean cloth. Cook as above.

Parathas

 4 cups (500 g.) *atta* (whole wheat) flour
 ½ lb. (250 g.) *ghee* (see p. 31) or butter
 Salt
 Approximately 1−1½ cups (250-400 ml.) water

Mix the flour, salt, and a tablespoon of *ghee* or butter with enough water to make a firm dough. Knead and let sit ½ hour. Divide and roll out, as with *chapatis*.

 Brush each cake with melted *ghee* and fold over on itself. Brush with *ghee* again and fold over once more into a quarter circle. Roll thin (pancakes should retain the triangular shape), and cook on ungreased *tawa*, or thick griddle, over a high flame.

Stuffed Parathas

 Uncooked *parathas*
 Cooked, diced vegetables—one kind or mixed (zucchini, celery,
   cauliflower)

Place vegetables or other filling on a *paratha*. Cover with another *paratha* and pinch the edges closed. Cook several minutes on both sides.

Dhal Bread

Dhal, a general name for several varieties of peas and beans, is used in India in many ways: dry, whole, cracked, milled, etc. *Dhal,* a popular food, is often used in breads, mixed with spices and condiments, minced onions and peppers, or even asafetida, one of the strongest and strangest of the Indian spices. The method is the same as for *chapatis,* using equal measures of flour and *dhal,* and mixing in the other ingredients.

> 1 cup (200 g.) *dhal* (or dried split peas)—or 1½ cups (200 g.) *dhal*
>   flour
> 1 cup (100 g.) flour
> Salt, pepper
> 1 tsp. (2−3 g.) anise seeds
> ½ tsp. (1−2 g.) cumin
> Approximately 1 cup (250 ml.) water

Soak *dhal* 6 hours, drain thoroughly, and mash (or use *dhal* flour). Add the *dhal* mash or flour to the other ingredients and work into a firm dough. Roll small pieces of dough very thin and fry.

Dosa
Rice and Dhal Pancake

This very popular south Indian dish is served all over India.

> 3 cups (750 g.) rice
> 1¾ (400 g.) cups *urid dhal* (white, unshelled *dhal*—see p. 285)
> Salt

Soak both the rice and dahl for about 3 to 4 hours. Wash well and blend in a mixer (or mash in a *molcajete* or other stone mortar) until very fine. Add water to make the paste the consistency of milk.

Let the dough sit overnight to rise (or add 1 teaspoon yeast). Add salt to taste. Make a very thin pancake on the griddle or *tawa.* Serve hot with chutney (see below).

Coconut Chutney

1 cup (100 g.) shredded fresh coconut
2−4 fresh or dry, soaked hot chiles
1−2 slices fresh ginger to taste
½ tsp. (5 g.) salt
1 cup (250 ml.) yoghurt

Mix coconut, chiles, ginger, and salt together with the yoghurt in a blender, or mash the dry ingredients first in a mortar and add to the yoghurt.

Pooris

2 cups (250 g.) *atta* (whole wheat) flour, or *dhal* (see p. 28) flour mixed with white flour
Approximately 1 cup (250 ml.) water
Salt

Knead together into a firm dough, divide, and roll into thin discs, slightly smaller than *chapatis*. Roll even thinner.

Deep fry in very hot fat, basting the top side when the *poori* floats. Fry only about 30 seconds, turn and fry another 30 seconds. Serve hot.

Khasta Pooris

2 cups (250 g.) *atta* (whole wheat) or *dhal* flour
4 tbs. (60 g.) butter or *ghee* or oil
Approximately ¾ cup (250 ml.) curds (see "Ingredients") or yoghurt
Salt

Mix and knead into a firm dough. Roll and cook like *pooris* above.

For less rich *khasta pooris,* reduce the amount of butter and mix water with the curds or yoghurt.

Malay Bread

2½ cups (300 g.) flour
1 egg
Approximately ¼ cup (75 g.) lamb fat
Salt, water
Lamb fat or vegetable shortening to fry

Make a hole in a mound of flour. Break an egg into the hole and work it into the flour. Add salt, moisten with a litle water, and knead to a firm dough. Divide into 3 pieces. Roll out into thin discs.

Brush the discs with melted lamb fat. Stretch the dough even thinner by hand, until transparent. Fold and refold the edges into the center. Roll out into a long rectangle. Roll up the band of dough on itself, then roll out thin again.

Cut into 6 inch discs and fry on both sides in hot fat or shortening.

Chinese Breads

The Chinese cook the greatest variety of breads, using many grains in different ways: baked in ovens, steamed, grilled in pans, browned in oil, or braised. The breads take many shapes, from large loaves to *brioches*, and are even stuffed with widely varying ingredients: pork, soy noodles, dates, etc.

The peasants in the regions bordering the Gobi Desert eat large, round and flat wheat loaves called *gaokwei*. Little more than an inch thick and almost 1½ feet in diameter, sometimes sprinkled with *colza* oil (the common oil in northern China), this bread needs very little cooking. First the peasants mix up a big pile of dung and straw on the bare ground. They fire the pile so that it smolders overnight. The next morning they put the dough in special molds that fit together and close tightly. The molds are then slid into the cinders and buried. Cooking takes about an hour, and one oven can cook seven loaves. The principle is not unlike that behind the French *pain de mie*.

Man t'ou
Chinese Steamed Rolls

It is in this very filling form that wheat most often takes the place of rice in northern China.

> 4 cups (500 g.) flour
> 1½ tsp. (15 g.) yeast
> 1½ cups (400 ml.) warm water

Mix the yeast with the water. Add the flour, kneading into firm dough. Divide into approximately 16 pieces, and shape into balls. Let rise 40 minutes, until they feel light. Range on a metal or bamboo steamer that fits into a pot or wok. The Chinese use a cauldron fitted into a sort of stove built into the ground with an opening at ground level for feeding the fire. Whether using such a stove or an ordinary cooking stove, the pot, cauldron, or wok should be tightly covered. Steam 20 minutes.

VARIANT   Stuff dough balls with dried pork or ham and minced garlic. Steam as above.

Chinese Pancake

> 2 cups (250 g.) flour
> Salt
> Approximately 2/3 cup (180 ml.) water
> Sesame oil
> Garlic shoots or scallions

Mix flour, salt, and water. Knead. Divide and roll out into large, thin pancakes. Brush with sesame oil. Cook on both sides on a heavy griddle. Wrap around garlic shoots or scallions and eat.

Rice Pancakes

These are a Chinese specialty.

> ½ cup (125 g.) rice
>   or 1 cup (125 g.) rice flour
> 1 cup (125 g.) wheat flour
> Approximately ½ cup (125 ml.) water
> Salt

Soak the rice 12 to 36 hours, changing the water from time to time. Drain and dry in the sun or in a low oven. Then mash or grind the rice.

Add the wheat flour. Salt. Moisten slowly with the water to make a dough that can be rolled. Roll thin, cut into 8-inch discs, and steam 5 to 10 minutes.

(Prepared rice pancakes may also be bought in oriental groceries. They must be moistened before use with beaten eggs or a sprinkling of water.)

The pancakes may be stuffed and rolled and sautéed in oil in a heavy frying pan.

Latkes
Potato Pancakes

These pancakes are a traditional Hanukah treat.

> 1 lb. (500 g.) potatoes
> 1–2 onions, chopped
> 1–2 eggs
> 1 carrot, grated
> 1 tsp. (5 g.) baking powder
> Salt, pepper
> Vegetable oil

Grate the raw potatoes coarsely and mix with the onions, eggs, carrot, salt, pepper, and baking powder. Fry on both sides in a little vegetable oil.

Serve hot with apple sauce or sour cream. Potato pancakes are usually served directly from the pan to waiting plates, so each batch is different. The best is the one currently being eaten, and the worst is the one when you ate too many.

Manioc Pancakes

These large pancakes, made in all manioc countries from South America to Oceania by way of Africa, take the place of bread, sopping up sauce and filling stomachs. Manioc is also commonly known as cassava or yuca, and is available year round in Latin markets. Manioc flour is available at Latin specialty stores.

Some types of manioc have roots that can be eaten directly after roasting. Others require additional preparation of the roots which would otherwise be poisonous. After preparation the roots are grated and left to ferment, then pressed. The pulp is used for large cakes.

The juice yielded by pressing manioc drops a sediment of starch grains, used familiarly as tapioca.

> ½ cup (65 g.) manioc meal
> ½ cup (125 ml.) water
> 2 tbs. (30 g.) vegetable oil
> Salt

Mix manioc flour, water, oil and salt into a thick batter and pour carefully onto thick griddle over a medium-high heat. The pancake should be about the size of a lily pad. Brown on both sides. Africans and Jivaro Indians of the Amazon cook these on an earthen plate supported over the fire on three well-chosen stones.

Buckwheat Flapjacks

These are an old American favorite.

> 1 cup (125 g.) sifted white or whole wheat flour
> 3½ cups (500 g.) buckwheat flour
> 1 tsp. (5 g.) salt
> 1 tbs. (15 g.) active dry yeast
> 4 cups (1 l.) warm water (110°F or 40°C)
> 3 tbs. (45 g.) dark brown sugar
> 1 tsp. (5 g.) baking soda
> 1 tbs. (15 ml.) vegetable oil

Combine flours and salt. Dissolve yeast in ¼ cup warm water; dissolve 1 tbs. sugar in remaining 3¾ cups water; cool to lukewarm. Add liquid mixtures to flour, stir well and leave to rise (several hours or overnight) at room temperature. Make sure the bowl is large enough to handle the batter doubling in bulk.

When ready to cook pancakes, stir down batter and add remaining sugar, baking soda, and oil. Blend and bake on lightly greased hot griddle. Brown on both sides, turning only once. Serve hot with butter and honey or molasses.

Yufka
Nomadic Turk Pancakes

> 1 cup (125 g.) pastry flour or fine semolina
> Approximately 1 cup (250 ml.) water

Mix the flour with water by hand on a small, smooth table to make pancake batter. Cook on an ungreased heavy griddle or frying pan. In Turkey these fine flour pancakes are prepared on an earthen disc heated on the coals of an open fire. In Iran they put the batter into an oven which is little more than a hollow in a stone, heated red hot. The pancakes cook almost instantly and come out like fine crêpes.

Taguella
Millet Pancakes

These flat cakes of millet, or less often wheat, replace bread in parts of the Sahara.

> 2 cups (250 g.) millet flour
> Approximately 1 cup (250 ml.) water
> Salt

Mix flour, water, and salt to make a firm dough. Knead well. Divide and flatten into thin pancakes. Grill on both sides on an ungreased heavy griddle.

Ethiopian Indjera
Millet Pancakes

These large gray cakes are made not with wheat flour but with a flour made from *teff (Eragrostis abyssinica)*, a kind of millet peculiar to Ethiopia. The *teff* is harvested by sickle and laid up in stacks which are protected from the "evil eye," and perhaps the wind, by cattle hides draped over stakes. The harvest is threshed by treading oxen, and winnowed in the air in the ancient manner.

Indjera is the Ethiopian national dish.

  2 cups (250 g.) millet flour
  ½ tbs. (8 g.) yeast or baking powder
  3½ cups (875 ml.) water

Mix the flour with water to make a semiliquid paste. Let sit one hour if using yeast. Cook on a heavy, ungreased griddle or frying pan. The cakes will rise as they cook, and bubbles will burst on the surface.

Indjera are enjoyed most when torn up and dipped in a pot of *wot* (see p. 165) placed in the midst of the diners.

Mexican Tortillas

This staple of Mexico is eaten at every meal. A man going off to work in the fields may eat 25 for breakfast. Since most households are well-populated, the cook has to prepare more than a hundred at the start of each day. At other meals fewer tortillas are eaten if other foods, such as vegetables and sometimes meat in a sauce, are available.

The corn meal is usually milled the evening before because fresh meal does not work as well. If the cook has a hand mill, she does not have to work as hard as when she has to grind the grain on a *metate*, a rectangular millstone with a roller. The dry grains of corn are boiled with lime before milling. Even those who can afford to buy ready ground meal prefer to make sure of the quality by grinding it a little more themselves on their *metate*.

  2 cups (250 g.) *masa harina* (fine corn meal)
  1 1/3 cups (350 ml.) warm water
  Salt

Mix the *masa harina* and salt with enough water to make a dough that can be shaped into a ball. Knead until it is no longer sticky, at least 5 minutes. Divide into a dozen equal pieces and let sit 20 minutes.

Flatten the pieces into pancakes either by slapping them between your palms, Mexican-style, which is difficult and takes practice, or with a rolling pin on a table dusted with flour, or with a tortilla press. Pare the edges. Cook on both sides on a *comal*, a flat earthen plate, or in a heavy, ungreased pan or griddle. The *comals* made by the Tarasque Indians are exceptionally beautiful.

The poor use simple tortillas like the ones above. It is possible to make richer tortillas using half wheat flour, half cornmeal flour, egg, oil, salt and water. These tortillas are cooked in the same way as the plain ones.

STUFFED TORTILLAS   These can be found in almost any Mexican market. Women prepare them sitting on the bare ground next to a small market stall on which they have set out bowls with dough and cooked stuffings— tortilla sauce, minced peppers, and sometimes mixtures of vegetables. They brown the tortillas on small stoves, little more than simple sheets of metal propped over a fire on three rocks. They are often eaten with grilled pig skin and the corn beer *chicha*.

Here is one suggestion for tortilla sauce:

Tortilla Sauce

Epazote, also known as Jerusalem oak or wormseed, can be found fresh or as a seed in some Latin markets.

> 1–2 chopped onions
> 2 lbs. (1 kg.) tomatoes, chopped
> *Epazote* to taste
> 1–2 hot, fresh or dried, chili peppers
> Salt, pepper
> Lard or oil

Remove stems and seeds from chili peppers, and, if using dried ones, soak in a little hot water for 30 minutes. Chop.

Sauté the onions in lard or oil. Add tomatoes and chiles. Simmer 5 to 10 minutes. Season to taste. Since the sauce should be smooth, mash it in a mortar and pestle or a *molcajete*—the typical Mexican stone or baked earth mortar—or puree in a blender.

Tacos

These stuffed meat tortillas can be served as a main dish.

> 1½ lbs. (750 g.) lean chopped beef
> 2 chopped onions
> 2−3 tomatoes, cut up
> 2 cloves garlic
> Crushed chiles
> Seasonings to taste: coriander, oregano, cumin, basil, salt
> Prepared tortillas (see p. 62)
> Grated cheddar or crumbled cheddar

Sauté the meat. When it is pale all over, add the onions. When the onions soften, add tomato pieces, garlic, and chiles. Season to taste.

Cook the tortillas. Stuff them with the meat and sprinkle with grated cheese. Serve as is or heat 10 minutes in the oven at 400° F (204°C) to melt the cheese before serving.

Chilaquiles
Cheese Tortillas

> 1 dozen folded tortillas
> 1 cup crumbled fresh cheese (e.g. farmer's cheese)
> Seasoning (thyme, basil, oregano, chili)
> 1 beaten egg
> 2 cups (500 ml.) tortilla sauce (see p. 63)

Stuff the tortillas with cheese. Fold over on themselves and coat with egg. Fry in lard or shortening. Serve hot with tortilla sauce.

VARIANT   Alternate layers of tortilla sauce, fried tortillas, and cheese in a casserole. Top with cheese and bake 30 minutes at 350° F (175° C) until the cheese has melted.

Arab Unleavened Bread

An expedient when there isn't much time, this bread is quickly kneaded and cooked.

> 6 cups (750 g.) fine semolina
> ½ cup (125 ml.) oil
> 1½ cups (350 ml.) water
> Salt

Beat the oil with some of the water, and mix with the semolina and salt. Knead, moistening the dough as necessary to make it supple. Shape into a ball.

Roll out to about ½ inch thick. Cook in a heavy frying pan at medium heat about 15 minutes, or bake 20–30 minutes at 350° F (175°C).

This bread is best when served still warm.

Matzah
Jewish Unleavened Bread

Jews eat matzah on Passover in memory of their hasty departure from the Pharaoh in Egypt, when they did not have time to let the bread rise. Matzah became the wafer of Christian communion by way of the Last Supper which was a passover *seder* (ceremonial meal).

Matzah, made properly, must not rise at all. This is insured by a ritual procedure involving careful selection and storage of whole wheat flour to keep it dry. Wild yeasts are everywhere and begin to grow wherever they find nourishment, such as in damp flour. Once the flour is mixed with pure, cold spring water, the kneading and rolling must proceed continuously— the whole process, including baking, should take little more than 20 minutes.

> 3¼ cups (400 g.) whole wheat flour
> 1 cup (250 ml.) water

Mix the water and flour and knead thoroughly. This is best done by dividing the dough into hand-sized balls and kneading steadily for 1–2 minutes. Then roll thin on a clean, dry board—it is ritually improper to sprinkle the dough with flour. As a consequence, lifting the rolled dough from the board may be a delicate operation. Wrap the dough around a rolling pin and use the pin to lift the dough. Score the dough with parallel cuts, and perforate the cuts. Then slide dough into a 600−800° F (300°−400° C) brick oven and bake 2−3 minutes. Or bake on a baking sheet in a very high oven.

The matzah should be crisp and light.

Matzah Balls

    Water
    6 eggs
    Salt, pepper
    Approximately 1 cup (200 g.) matzah meal (finely crushed matzah,
        see above)

Beat 6 half-eggshellfuls of water with the eggs, salt, and pepper. Slowly mix in matzah meal until the batter is thick but still pours off a spoon. Chill and let sit at least 6 hours. It will thicken. Boil a large pot of salted water. Shape the batter into balls about the size of walnuts and poach 45 minutes. They will expand to about three times their original volume. Drain.

Serve in chicken soup (see p. 126). It is traditional to make jokes about matzah balls, such as "my mother's matzah balls were so heavy they were round but wouldn't roll." Good matzah balls are, of course, light and delicate.

Matzah Meal Popovers

These popovers provide a substitute for bread on the Jewish holiday of Passover, when leavening may not be used in cooking.

    2 eggs
    1 cup (200 g.) matzah meal (finely crushed matzah, see above)
    1 cup (250 ml.) water
    Salt, pepper
    1 tbs. (15 ml.) oil

Beat the eggs until foamy, then beat in the other ingredients. Fill muffin tins 1/3 full and bake in a preheated oven at 450° F (230° C) for 25 minutes, then reduce heat to 350° F (175° C) for 15 minutes more.

Blintzes
Pancakes Stuffed with Cheese

An important dish in Jewish dairy cooking, blintzes are very popular.

PANCAKES:
3−4 eggs
1 cup (250 ml.) milk
1 cup (125 g.) flour
Salt

FILLING:
1 lb. (500 g.) farmer's cheese or dry cottage cheese
1 egg
1 tbs. (15 g.) melted butter
1 tsp. (5 g.) grated lemon peel

To make the pancakes, beat the eggs with the milk and mix in the flour and salt. Pour a couple tablespoonfuls of the batter onto a medium hot buttered griddle and spread to make a very thin pancake. Cook until bubbles appear on the top. Remove from heat and stack, cooked side up.

To make the filling, mix the cheese, egg, butter, and lemon peel. If desired, add a tablespoon of sugar.

Place a few tablespoons of the filling in the center of the pancake, cooked side up. Fold sides in over the filling and roll to make a cylinder. Fry in butter on both sides, or bake 10−15 minutes at 350° F (175° C) to brown.

Serve hot with sour cream or dusted with sugar and cinnamon.

SWEET BLINTZES   Replace the filling with the following:

1 lb. (500 g.) apples, grated
2 tbs. (30 g.) sugar
1 egg
½ tsp. (3 g.) cinnamon

Mix together and fill pancakes. Cook as above.

Serve hot with sugar and cinnamon or sour cream.

Arab Leavened Bread

1 package (20 g.) dried yeast
1½ cups (400 ml.) warm water
Salt
6 cups (750 g.) fine semolina

Mix the yeast with the water. Add salt and semolina. Knead into a supple but firm dough.

Shape into 2 or 3 flat cakes. Dust with flour, cover with cloth, and let rise in a warm place.

Once the loaves have risen, cook them over medium heat in a *tadjin*, or grooved, heavy-bottomed pan (an ungrooved heavy pan will do, but won't produce the pattern typical of this bread), pressing the dough firmly so that it takes on the pattern of the pan bottom. Cook on both sides, approximately 20 minutes.

You may also bake in the oven 35−40 minutes at 350° F (175° C). When done, the bread will make a hollow sound if tapped on the bottom.

Yorkshire Pudding

This is a traditional accompaniment to roast beef in England. The pan drippings are poured from the roasting pan to make gravy, but 2−3 tablespoons of fat are skimmed from the drippings and returned to the pan. The pan is then heated to oven temperature before the pudding batter is poured into it. More modern cooks sometimes use a muffin tin, but nearly all use pan drippings rather than shortening or oil.

2 eggs
1 cup (250 ml.) milk
1 cup (125 g.) white flour
1 tsp. (5 g.) salt
2−3 tbs. (30—45 g.) drippings from a roast

Have all ingredients at room temperature, or make the batter an hour before baking and leave it at room temperature to warm up. Beat eggs and milk together until foamy, then gradually add flour and salt, beating out all lumps. Heat oven to 450° F (230° C), preheat greased pan, then pour batter into greased pan and return to the oven. Bake without opening the door for 20 minutes. It should be golden brown and firm, not doughy. If necessary, leave for an extra 5 or 10 minutes to get a nice crisp outside, then serve immediately.

This is usually eaten with gravy as part of the main course (or preceding it), but it can also be sprinkled with a little granulated sugar and eaten as a dessert.

Pizza

1 tbs. (15 g.) yeast
1 cup (250 ml.) lukewarm water
3 cups (375 g.) flour
¾ tsp. (4 g.) salt
¼ cup (65 ml.) olive oil
1 lb. (500 g.) chopped, peeled ripe tomatoes
Oregano, salt, pepper
If desired: chopped garlic, crushed dried red pepper
½ lb. (250 g.) mozzarella cheese

Mix the yeast with the lukewarm water and let sit 5 minutes. Then mix with the flour and salt. Knead 8 – 10 minutes. Let rise covered, away from drafts, for 2 – 3 hours until it triples in volume. Punch down and divide into 2 even balls. Let rise under a cloth for another 1 – 1½ hours.

Preheat the oven to 600° F (315° C), or as hot as it gets.

Stretch and press each ball to make a thin, rimmed disk 10 – 12 inches in diameter. Brush with olive oil to within ½ inch of the rim. Spread each crust with chopped tomatoes, sprinkle with oregano, salt, pepper and, if desired, chopped garlic and crushed dried red pepper. Grate or chop the mozzarella cheese and sprinkle generously over the sauce.

Pizzas should be baked on hot stone—if you have a good flat, heat-resistant stone, or a *comal* for a small pizza, preheat the stone along with the oven, dust it with corn meal, slide the pizza in, and bake at 600° F (315° C) for 20 – 25 minutes, until the crust is browned. If you have no flat stone, use a lightly-oiled baking tin and bake on the lowest shelf.

Proja
Yugoslavian Corn Bread

Traditionally, this is served with *kajmak* cheese (see p. 00).

3½ cups (500 g.) corn meal
1½ cups (375 ml.) milk
2–3 eggs
½ cup (150 g.) lard or shortening
Salt

Mix the corn meal with some of the milk and the eggs. Beat until smooth; add the softened lard and salt. Mix well, then add the rest of the milk. Pour into a greased square or rectangular baking tin and bake ½ hour at 350° F (175° C). Cut into squares and bake another ½ hour.
   Usually served hot, *proja* is also very good cold.

Hush Puppies

Hush puppies are one of Virginia colonists' adaptations of native American cuisine. They are considered especially good with fried fish.

2 cups (325 g.) whole grain cornmeal
1 tsp. (5 g.) baking powder
1 tsp. (5 g.) salt
2 eggs
½ cup (125 ml.) milk
Seasonings (optional): basil, scallions, parsley

Stir together cornmeal, baking powder, and salt, pressing out lumps. Beat together eggs and milk, then stir into dry ingredients, forming into balls about an inch around. Cook in deep fat, about 375° F (190° C) until golden brown. Drain on paper towels and serve hot (usually with fish).

Spoon Bread

This bread is another American creation.

> 1 cup (160 g.) whole grain cornmeal
> 3 cups (750 ml.) milk
> 1 tsp. (5 g.) salt
> 2 tbs. (30 g.) butter or margarine
> 4 eggs

Cook cornmeal in milk until thick—approximately 5–7 minutes after it comes to a boil. Add salt and butter and cool to lukewarm. Meanwhile, separate eggs. Beat whites until stiff, and beat yolks until creamy. Stir yolks into lukewarm mixture; fold in whites. Pour into greased 1½ quart baking dish and bake in 350° F (175° C) oven for 35 minutes, until firm and slightly brown. Serve hot.

Hominy Bread

Hominy is dried hulled corn kernels and was first introduced to Virginia colonists by Indian women who used ashes and water to remove the skins. Hominy grits—broken pieces of dried hominy—can be bought commercially or prepared at home by soaking dried whole corn kernels in baking soda or lye and boiling for 6 to 10 hours.

> 1½ cups (375 g.) cooked hominy grits
> 1 tbs. (15 g.) butter
> 2 eggs, beaten
> 2 cups (500 ml.) milk
> 1 cup (160 g.) cornmeal

While grits are still hot, stir in butter. Add eggs, stirring rapidly to prevent bits of cooked egg from forming. Gradually stir in milk and cornmeal. Place in a greased baking dish and bake at 375° F (175° C). This "bread" is really a savory pudding.

Boston Brown Bread

This classic steamed bread is usually served with baked beans.

     2 cups (500 ml.) buttermilk
     ¾ cup (180 ml.) molasses
     1 cup (200 g.) raisins
     2 cups (260 g.) rye flour
     1 cup (120 g.) whole wheat flour
     1 cup (160 g.) whole grain cornmeal
     2 tbs. (30 g.) baking soda
     1 tsp. (5 g.) salt
     2 tbs. (30 g.) brown sugar
     2 tbs. (30 g.) butter, softened

Beat together buttermilk and molasses. Add raisins. Stir together flours, baking soda, salt, and brown sugar and add to first mixture. Beat in softened butter. Pour into greased one-pound coffee cans, filling no more than 2/3 full. Cover with foil and tie with string. Steam for 2 hours in a large kettle; cool 10 minutes before removing from pans. Makes 2 loaves.

Sally Lunn
Old American Bread

This was a common bread in England and in early colonial American kitchens. It is coarse in texture, as it only rises once, but when eaten fresh it is tender and moist.

     4 cups (500 g.) white flour
     1 tbs. (15 g.) yeast
     4 eggs, well beaten
     ¼ cup (60 g.) butter or shortening
     2 cups (500 ml.) warm milk

Stir together flour and yeast (if using dry yeast; if using cake yeast, crumble it into the milk). Stir in eggs and butter and beat well; add milk gradually and beat out any lumps. Place it in the pan in which it will be baked and set it aside to rise for about an hour. Bake in a moderate oven (350° F or 175°C) for about 40 minutes, or until it is crusty and brown. Brush top with butter and serve warm.

Salt Risin' Bread

STARTER:
2 cups (500 ml.) milk
2 cups (250 g.) white flour
1 tbs. (15 g.) whole grain cornmeal
1 tsp. (5 g.) salt

Stir together these ingredients and leave them to rise for about 24 hours (covered with a towel and left in a warm place). The batter should be light and bubbly, with a light crust on the surface. Stir in:

1 tbs. (15 g.) shortening
1 tsp. (5 g.) sugar
4 cups (500 g.) flour

Knead remaining flour into the mixture; knead thoroughly until dough is smooth. Divide into 2 small loaves and let rise until almost double in bulk. Bake in a 375° F (175° C) oven for about 45 minutes, or until brown on the top.

Sally Lunn

Oatmeal Bread

Colonial American housewives believed that bread to which oatmeal had been added would keep longer and they might have been right.

> 2 cups (500 ml.) milk
> 2 cups (250 ml.) rolled or steel cut oats
> ¼ cup (60 ml.) honey
> 1 tbs. (15 g.) salt
> 2 tbs. (30 g.) butter or shortening
> 2 tbs. (30 g.) yeast
> ½ cup (125 ml.) warm water
> 6 cups (750 g.) white flour

Scald milk; stir in oats, honey, salt and butter. Remove from heat and cool to lukewarm. Dissolve yeast in warm water; place in large bowl. Add milk mixture and 2 cups flour to yeast. Beat vigorously with mixer or wooden spoon, scraping sides, until batter is smooth. Stir in as much flour as you can, then turn dough out on a floured board or cloth, and knead in remaining flour (adding as necessary); knead until dough is smooth and silky, about 10 minutes. Place in lightly greased bowl; turn dough over to grease top.

Let rise, covered, in a warm place until double in bulk, about 1 hour. Punch down and let rise again until nearly doubled, about ½ hour.

Divide dough into 2 parts, shape into loaves, and place on a baking sheet or into greased loaf pans. Let rise until almost doubled, about 1 hour. Bake in moderate oven (375° F or 175° C) for about 40 minutes. Cool slightly before removing from pans.

Austrian Sourdough Rye Bread

This is a firm bread with a crisp crust. It is a staple of the Tyrol.

> STARTER:
> 1 cup (250 ml.) milk
> 1 cup (125 ml.) white flour
> 1 tbs. (15 g.) yeast

Stir ingredients together in a crock or jar and leave, uncovered, at room temperature for 3–5 days: it should be frothy and taste sour. Cover and refrigerate until ready to use (within 10 days or it may degenerate). To replenish starter, do not wash the container which starter was kept in; simply add equal parts flour and milk and let stand at room temperature without a top while bread is first rising. Cover and refrigerate until ready to use again.

BREAD:
2 cups (260 g.) rye flour
2 cups (250 g.) white flour
1 cup (250 g.) starter
2 tsp. (10 g.) salt
2 cups (500 ml.) water

Stir these ingredients together in a large bowl. Cover with a cloth and let stand in a warm place overnight, or for about 8–12 hours. At the end of this time, add:

1 cup (130 g.) rye flour
1 cup (125 g.) white flour
1 tsp. (4 g.) baking soda

Knead together the original bread batter and the 3 new ingredients until the dough looks silky. Form a large round loaf and place on a baking sheet which has been sprinkled with cornmeal. Let rise uncovered until double in bulk, about 2–3 hours. Bake at 375° F (190° C) for about 45 minutes.

Yorkshire Oatcakes

Though Scotland is typically thought of as the land of oats, these cakes have long beeen a traditional staple in the north of England.

1 tsp. (5 g.) sugar
1 tbs. (15 g.) yeast
2 cups (500 ml.) milk or buttermilk
¼ cup (35 g.) oat flour
1 tsp. (5 g.) salt
1 cup (125 g.) quick-cooking oats

Dissolve sugar and yeast in lukewarm milk. Stir in flour, salt, and oats. Stir gently and let stand in a warm place for 30 minutes. Stir again and cook on a griddle or in a large heavy skillet as you would a large pancake. Cut into wedges, or *farls*, and eat buttered, while still warm.

Bannock
Scottish Oatcakes

In name and form, these Scottish cakes curiously resemble *banik*, Eskimo wheat cakes made with leavening and seal fat. *Bannocks*, however, are served crisp.

> 2 cups (250 g.) oat, barley, or pea flour
> 1 cup (250 ml.) soured milk (see p. 29) or buttermilk
> 1 tsp. (5 g.) baking soda
> Salt

Mix ingredients to make a loose dough. Shape by hand into thick (¼ inch) disks. Cook on both sides on a medium hot, buttered griddle, or bake on a greased baking sheet 10−15 minutes at 400° F (200° C).

Serve hot with butter or cheese.

To vary the texture, replace half the flour with rolled oats.

Millet Bread

This is good with vegetables, soups, and borscht.

> 1¼ cups (250 g.) millet
> 2 cups (500 ml.) milk
> Butter, salt, pepper
> 2−3 eggs

Simmer the millet in milk 10−15 minutes until it thickens. Season and add a chunk of butter for taste. Let cool.

Separate the eggs. Beat the whites until they peak. Mix the yolks and beaten whites with the millet, then pour into a buttered baking tin. Bake 20 minutes at 350° F (175° C) until cooked through.

Sorghum Bread

Although the staple grain in many parts of the world, sorghum is not marketed commercially in the Western world except as sorghum syrup, which is popular in the southern United States but is not made from grain sorghum. Nevertheless, it is available from many animal feed dealers, at less than a third of the cost of the lowest priced wheat. If you buy it from grain dealers, you must be sure that it is free from pesticide residue (if marketed as poultry feed it usually is). It is also a grain that is relatively easy to grow yourself.

To make flour use a grain or flour mill—many natural food stores will grind it for you.

2 cups (250 g.) finely ground sorghum grain
1 tsp. (5 g.) salt
2 cups (500 ml.) buttermilk
2 eggs
1 tsp. (5 g.) baking soda

Stir together sorghum flour, salt, and milk in a saucepan. Cook over low heat, stirring frequently, for 5–10 minutes, or until stiff. Remove from heat and cool to lukewarm. Beat eggs, stir into cooled mixture; sprinkle soda over this and fold in.

Preheat oven to 450° F (230° C). Place 10-inch oiled skillet or oiled muffin tin in oven for 5 minutes before baking. Pour sorghum mixture into pan; return to oven and bake for 20–25 minutes, or until cake tester or toothpick inserted in center comes out clean. Bake muffins for 10–15 minutes. Split and spread with butter, or use as a base for a creamed entrée.

Tunisian Droo
Buckwheat Bread

2 cups (250 g.) buckwheat flour
½ cup (125 ml.) water
½ cup (125 ml.) oil
Salt
1 tbs. (30 g.) sugar

Mix the flour, water, and oil. Add salt and sugar and mix well. Let sit for several hours.

Turn into a greased heavy frying pan or mold. Bake 20 minutes at 350° F (175° C).

Bread Couscous

    1 lb. (500 g.) dry bread or 4 cups (500 g.) bread crumbs
    Water
    3 tbs. (50 ml.) oil

Grate dry bread into small crumbs the size of couscous or cracked wheat. Moisten with cold water. Toss with two forks. Moisten more if necessary, but do not soak. Mix in the oil.

    Put into a steamer and cook like couscous (see p. 89).

    This is a very common dish in North Africa, often served with *tchak-chuka* (see p. 211).

Aragon Migas
Bread and Sausage Fry

This Spanish dish is often served for breakfast and also with other meals.

    7 cups (650 g.) dry cubed bread
    2 cloves garlic, whole
    ½ lb. (200 g.) diced bacon
    ½ lb. (200 g.) diced ham
    ½ lb. (250 g.) diced *chorizo* (Spanish sausage)
    Olive oil
    2 tomatoes, chopped
    Salt, cayenne

On the night before, moisten the bread lightly with water. Cover with a cloth and let sit overnight.

    Brown the garlic cloves, bacon, ham, and sausage in oil. Remove the garlic and add the bread. Stir, then add the chopped tomatoes. Salt and season. Simmer a few more minutes, then serve.

GRAIN
DISHES

Bulgur

This is a very common (and practical) way to prepare wheat in the Middle East. (You can also buy ready-made bulgur in most natural food and Middle Eastern food stores.)

>Whole grain wheat
>Salt

Wash and pick over the wheat. Boil in abundant, lightly salted water. When the grains begin to burst, drain and let sit for at least 1 hour. Dry in a very low oven. The grains will harden.

When the dried wheat cools, grind it coarsely. Store sealed in a tight box. It will keep for many months.

Bulgur, also known as *burghul*, can be prepared hot or cold.

Hot Bulgur

>2 cups (500 g.) bulgur
>1¼ cups (300 ml.) water

Mix the bulgur with water, bring to a boil, cover, and simmer over a low flame, like rice, for about 10 minutes. The liquid should be completely absorbed. Serve with strong grated cheese.

Bulgur can also be used as a stuffing: add herbs and crushed cooked or fresh vegetables, maybe some minced lamb or mutton, and bind with an egg.

There are many other uses for bulgur:

Cooked in water and served with milk, honey, or raisins, it makes a good breakfast.

Browned in oil, then cooked with water (or stock) as above, it can replace rice pilaf or kasha.

It is often served with vegetables or meat, or added to stews. Milled very fine, bulgur can be used in place of flour in crêpes, brioches, and other delicacies, or for thickening sauces and soups.

Bulgur Salad

2 cups (500 g.) bulgur
1¼ cups (300 ml.) hot water
4 tbs. (60 ml.) olive oil
Black olives
Spices and herbs: fresh mint and/or basil, cumin, anise

Pour the hot water over the bulgur and sprinkle with oil. Mix well. Let soak and cool. All the liquid should be absorbed.

Add olives, herbs, and spices and serve cool. This is a refreshing dish in hot weather.

Tabooleh
Grain Salad

This cold North African dish is made from bulgur or uncooked couscous.

1½ cups (250 g.) bulgur or couscous (semolina)
2 minced sweet onions or scallions
Fresh parsley and mint
1 lb. (500 g.) ripe tomatoes
Juice of 2 lemons
6−7 tbs. (100 ml.) olive oil
Salt
Grape leaves or lettuce

Mix the grain, onions, parsley, mint, tomatoes, lemon juice, and oil in a salad bowl. Salt. Let steep and soak several hours. Cool.

Serve the *tabooleh* accompanied by a plate of supple grape or lettuce leaves. Each person can then roll some of the preparation on a grape leaf and eat it whole.

Tibetan tsampa
Barley Porridge

This dish is the Tibetan favorite. The Tibetans serve it with strong, rancid yak butter which has been stored in sheep stomachs. It is considered good hospitality to serve butter so strong that the guest gags. Real Tibetan *tsampa* is strong and smelly, but other than that, the dish is not unlike oatmeal porridge.

> 2/3 cup (100 g.) barley or whole wheat grains
> 2 cups (500 ml.) hot tea
> Butter

Grill the barley or wheat, then grind to a more or less fine flour. Mix with hot tea. Add butter.

Turkish Barley

> ½ cup (100 g.) prunes
> 1 cup (250 g.) hulled barley
> 2 cups (500 ml.) water
> Saffron (3−4 pistils dissolved in 1 tbs. hot water)
> Salt, pepper
> 2−3 sliced sweet peppers
> Oil (olive oil is best)
> Chopped fresh parsley
> ¾ cup (150 g.) sliced almonds

Soak the prunes, simmer 10−15 minutes. Pit, and chop coarsely. Soak the barley 1 hour, drain. Add water and cook 15−20 minutes until all the water is absorbed. Add saffron, salt, and pepper. Sauté the peppers in oil.

Mix all the ingredients together including almonds and parsley. Serve hot or cold.

Millet Porridge

This is the staff of life for many of the peoples of central Asia, central and West Africa, and much of Eastern Europe. Boris Pasternak in *Dr. Zhivago* credits it with keeping millions of Russians alive during the famine that followed the Revolution. In Sudan millet or manioc porridge is practically all there ever is to eat. On good days the porridge may be served with a bit of scrawny chicken fried in palm oil. The northern Chinese eat millet in place of rice. The poor make a whole meal of it with a little cabbage. As with rice, cooked millet grains should remain whole and not stick.

   1 cup (200 g.) millet
   2 cups (500 ml.) water
   Salt

Bring millet and salted water to a boil. Cover and simmer 15–20 minutes until all liquid is absorbed.

Asink
Crushed Millet Porridge

This is the staple of the Tuareg people of the Sahara.

   1 cup (250 g.) crushed or ground millet
   3 cups (750 ml.) water
   1 cup (250 g.) fine millet flour

Boil the crushed millet for 2 hours to make a thick soup. Gradually stir in the flour with a wooden paddle or spoon. (The Tuareg use an *esseroui*, a wooden paddle special to this dish.) Simmer 20 minutes until firm. Serve hot with milk or butter.

Tibik
Roasted Millet

This is the principal food of *meharists*, desert camel drivers. It is always made from millet.

>   Millet
>   Dried dates

To cook the millet in the desert, *meharists* pour the crushed, winnowed, and washed grain into a large wooden plate, the *tarahout*, and bury heated stones in the grain to grill it lightly. A more convenient Western method is to shake the millet in a heavy frying pan over a low heat until lightly cooked.

   Add dried, pitted dates and grind the mixture to a powder. The powder is eaten as is.

Millet with Pumpkin

This is a common dish in Slavic countries. Pumpkin is served with grain in most cereal-eating countries. The poor in corn countries, such as Spain, Italy and France prepare recipes similar to this with corn instead of millet.

>   1 lb. (500 g.) pumpkin flesh
>   2 cups (500 ml.) milk
>   5 tbs. (65 g.) millet or corn meal
>   2 tbs. (30 g.) sugar
>   Salt
>   2 tbs. (30 g.) butter

Mince the pumpkin and simmer 20 minutes in the milk along with the millet, salt, and sugar. Mash or put through a strainer and serve with butter.

VARIANT   Use proportionately more milk to make a soup.

Indian Millet

Although we associate rice with Indian cooking, millet is an equally important staple in India.

> 1 onion, chopped
> Butter or *ghee* (see p. 31)
> 1 cup (200 g.) millet
> 2 cups (500 ml.) vegetable stock (see p. 47) or hot water
> Cheese

Brown the onion in *ghee* (see p. 31) if possible. Add 1 cup millet. Sauté 3 – 5
minutes. Add the stock and simmer for 20 minutes.
  Serve with sautéed vegetables or onions, and sprinkle with cheese.

VARIANT   Add a cup of diced vegetables, such as cauliflower, okra, or
zucchini, or a mixture of these, to brown with the onion. Finish as above.

Millet with Dried Mushrooms

Dried mushrooms are a common feature of Slavic cooking.

> ½ oz. (15 g.) dried mushrooms
> 2 cups (500 ml.) water
> 1 cup (200 g.) millet
> Butter or vegetable oil
> 1 onion, minced

Soak dried mushrooms overnight. Drain, saving the water to cook the
millet.
  When the millet is cooked, brown a minced onion and add the mushrooms.
  Mix the millet and mushroom-onion preparation and serve with seasoning and gravy.

Kasha

Buckwheat groats, known as kasha, are popular among the peoples of
Eastern Europe. Kasha is traditionally served with borscht, shchi (see p.
123), pork or goose. Plain kasha:

1 cup (200 g.) kasha (buckwheat groats)
2 cups (500 ml.) water
Salt
Butter

Pour kasha into salted, boiling water. Add butter for taste. Cover and simmer. After 20 minutes the liquid should be completely absorbed. Cooked kasha should be dry and unclumped, like good rice.

VARIANT   First grill the kasha in a dry heavy frying pan over low heat. Beat an egg in quickly and continue to grill, making sure that each grain is separate and coated with egg. Add to boiling water as above. The kasha grains, when cooked, should be firm and separate.

SAUTÉED KASHA   Prepare plain kasha as above. Spread into a buttered pan and smooth over. Let cool. Cut into squares and sauté, browning both sides.

ROAST KASHA   Use the same ingredients as for plain kasha. Grill the groats in a dry heavy frying pan, stirring constantly. Pour kasha into a buttered baking tin and add boiling water, salt, and butter to taste. Cover and bake at 350° F (175° C) for ¾ hour.

Kasha with Marrow

½ oz. (15 g.) dried mushrooms
2½ cups (325 ml.) water
Butter
1¼ cups (250 g.) kasha (buckwheat groats)
¼ lb. (125 g.) marrow from beef bones

Soak mushrooms in the water at least 1 hour (overnight if possible). Drain, saving the water. Sauté the mushrooms in butter. Cook kasha in the water used to soak the mushrooms. When the kasha is almost done, spread it in layers in a baking tin, alternating with layers of marrow and mushrooms. Top off with marrow.
    Cover and bake 20 minutes at 350° F (175° C).

Fettucine al burro
Italian Noodles with Butter

> 2 eggs
> ½ tsp. (3 g.) salt
> 1 tbs. (15 ml.) water
> 1½ cups (200 g.) flour
> 2 qts. (2 l.) lightly salted water
> ¼ lb. (100 g.) melted butter
> ½ cup (80 g.) grated Parmesan cheese

Beat the egg, salt, and water lightly. Gradually mix into the flour. Knead 10 minutes. Add more flour, if necessary, for a firm dough. Let sit at least 1 hour. Divide into 2 pieces. Roll each as thin as possible on a floured board, stretching the dough over the rolling pin. Let dry hanging on a line for 20 minutes or so, then roll up into a cylinder and slice diagonally into strips ¼–½ inch wide. Shake loose.

Bring to a boil at least 2 quarts of lightly salted water. Add the fettucine. These fresh noodles cook almost instantaneously—they are done only 30 seconds to a minute after the water returns to a boil (and they have floated to the water's surface). Of course this depends on how thick they are as well. But be careful not to overcook. Drain and rinse quickly with cold water. Mix thoroughly with melted butter and about half the cheese. Serve immediately with the rest of the cheese alongside.

Serves 2–3.

Reshta
North African Noodles

These semolina noodles take little time to prepare. They are served with *tchakchuka* (see p. 211), and sometimes with chicken or mutton in chickpea soup.

> 2 cups (250 g.) fine semolina
> ½ cup (125 ml.) water
> Salt

Work ingredients together gradually to make noodle dough. Split up into balls and roll out as fine as possible. Dust the roller with flour from time to time. Slice into fine noodles.

Steam and serve with melted butter.

Couscous with Meat

This is a feast version of the classic North African dish. For a simpler meal the meatballs can be eliminated, and of course a vegetable sauce can be substituted for the soupy meat sauce given here. Cracked millet or wheat may be substituted for store-bought couscous, which is usually semolina. The *harissa* powder called for is usually available in Middle Eastern stores, but in a pinch you could substitute chile pepper or cayenne.

COUSCOUS:
2 cups (350 g.) couscous (semolina)
salted water
1½ quarts (1½ l.) water or soaking liquid from chickpeas (see below)
Olive oil

MEAT SAUCE:
2 lbs. (1 kg.) lamb shoulder cut into cubes, or 1 cut-up chicken
Oil
1½ lbs. (750 g.) stew vegetables (carrots, celery, turnip, etc.)
1 cup (175 g.) dry chickpeas, soaked overnight
Seasoning: garlic, basil, cumin, parsley, cayenne
2−3 lbs. (1−1.5 kg.) zucchini, peppers, tomatoes, or other fresh
   vegetables
Water

MEATBALLS:
1 lb. (500 g.) chopped beef or hamburger
3−4 cloves garlic, crushed
1 egg
Flour
Oil

GARNISH:
1½ lbs. (700 g.) sweet onions
½ cup (100 g.) raisins
1 tsp. (5 g.) *harissa* powder

THE COUSCOUS   One-half hour before cooking, put couscous into a big bowl and sprinkle with salted water. Aerate by tossing with two forks. Pour into the couscous maker—the real one is called *keskes* or *couscoussière*; but a simple strainer, steamer, or colander lined with cheesecloth and which fits closely into a large pot will do. Steam the couscous over boiling water or chickpea stock 10 to 15 minutes, until the grains swell considerably.

Turn out of steamer onto a big working plate with a flat bottom—this is called a kesra in North Africa. Aerate again by hand, breaking up any clumps. Sprinkle with salted water and a little oil. Return to the collander or couscoussière and steam another ½ hour maximum. Fifteen minutes should suffice.

To serve, put the couscous in a big serving plate and aerate once more by hand. Add butter to taste.

MEAT SAUCE   Cut up the lamb or chicken and brown in oil. Drain and season. Put in a large pot with stew vegetables and soaked chickpeas. Cover with cold water, bring to a boil, then simmer 2½ hours. Skim the foam and excess fat during the cooking process. Add the zucchini, peppers, tomatoes, or other fresh vegetables 20 minutes before serving.

MEATBALLS   Mix the ground beef with the crushed garlic. Season and bind with an egg. Divide and powder with flour. Brown in oil and drain.

GARNISH   Slice the onions. Sauté and season. Soak the raisins at least 1 hour, then simmer in a small amount of the meat stock for 15 minutes. Dissolve harissa powder into a ladle of stock. Prudence is a virtue.

TO SERVE   Shape the couscous into a mound in the middle of a large plate and surround with the raisins and onions. Serve the meat and vegetables, in their sauce, in a separate bowl, surrounded by the meatballs. Serve the harissa in a separate sauce bowl.

Serves 6-8

Mamaliga
Corn Porridge

Mamaliga, also called malaï, is the principal dish of poor Rumanians. This solid porridge takes the place of European-style bread, which is eaten only as a dessert or on Saint's days.

Mamaliga can be eaten hot or cold, usually cut into slices with a wire.

The poorest often make a whole meal of it, with perhaps an onion and some wine. If there is a guest or momentary affluence, they may enrich the dish with some grated cheese known as *brunza alba*.

> 2 cups (300 g.) corn meal
> 5 cups (1,300 ml.) boiling water
> Salt

Stir corn meal and salt into the boiling water. Simmer at least 20 minutes until it thickens. Press into a bowl with a round, moistened bottom. Turn out of the bowl onto a plate immediately.

Fancy *mamaliga*: Press cooked *mamaliga* into a greased baking tin. Spread with sliced onions, browned first in lard or vegetable shortening. Cover with a few soft poached eggs. Bake no more than 5 minutes at 350°F (175°C)—do not overcook the eggs.

Polenta

This solid corn porridge, similar to *mamaliga*, replaces bread and pasta in parts of northern Italy. The basic recipe can be enriched by adding butter, cheese, onions or whatever.

> 2 cups (300 g.) coarse corn meal
> 1 qt. (1 l.) boiling water
> Salt

Stir the corn flour gradually into boiling, salted water. Simmer and continue to stir until *polenta* is dry enough to come away smoothly from the sides of the pot. Shape into a mound on a serving plate.

Serve hot with Bolognese or Milanese (meat or tomato) sauce, or serve cold.

> VARIANT
> Cooked *polenta*
> 5 tbs. (80 g.) butter
> 5 tbs. (80 g.) grated Parmesan or Romano cheese

Remove polenta from heat and add butter and cheese. Pour into a square or round deep dish, to a depth of about an inch. Smooth over and let cool.

Cut in squares and sauté in butter.

Another possibility is to lay the squares in a greased baking tin, sprinkle with additional cheese, and bake approximately 10 minutes at 400°F (200° C) until brown.

Cooked Hominy Grits

Hominy is treated, soaked, de-skinned corn kernels, and hominy grits are broken pieces of dried hominy. "Grits" are a classic dish of poor Southerners, white and black.

>   4 cups (1 l.) water
>   1 tsp. (5 g.) salt
>   1 cup (250 g.) dried hominy grits

Bring salted water to a boil. Sprinkle in grits, stirring constantly, then cover pan and lower heat to a simmer. Cook for 10 to 20 minutes, or until all water is absorbed (check quickly and replace lid so that not too much steam escapes). If grain is not tender at the end of that time, allow pan to sit, covered, for 10 more minutes to complete cooking.

Tamales
Corn Husks Stuffed with Corn Dough and Meat

The poorest of the poor in Mexico, such as the Tarasques, live almost exclusively on corn, sometimes cooked as tortillas, sometimes as *atole*—a simple porridge occasionally mixed with cocoa. Atole without the cocoa is similar to *polenta*. The Tarahumaras also eat *pinole*: corn simply grilled and milled. The Otomis, like the Tarasques and Tarahumaras, cannot often afford the luxury of pork in their *choclo pastel* (see p. 95). They supplement their diets with lizards, doves, and agave worms.

Tamales, like *tacos* (see p. 64), are good with a wide variety of fillings, depending on what is available: pork (*cuche*), chicken, and so on. This Mexican dish is common all over Latin America. The corn husks (or banana leaves) can be found in some Hispanic markets, or you can save fresh ones, cutting off pointed tips and thick rounded bottoms before use.

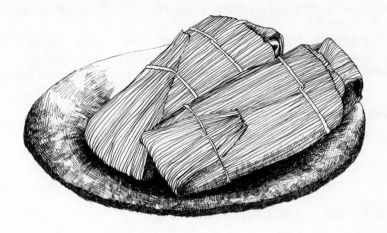

DOUGH:
3½ cups (450 g.) corn meal
1 qt. (1 l.) water
1/3 lb. (200 g.) lard
2 tbs. (30 g.) baking powder
Salt

FILLING:
1 lb. (500 g.) ground or minced pork
1–2 hot green fresh chiles, chopped or
  1 tsp. chili powder and a pinch of cayenne
1 tsp. (5 g.) allspice
3–4 pistils saffron dissolved in water
1 tsp. (5 g.) cumin powder
Lard
1 dozen corn husks or banana leaves
Meat or vegetable stock

Begin the filling by browning pork and chiles, allspice, saffron, and cumin in lard. Set to one side.

To prepare the corn dough, mix the corn meal with boiling water to make a thick porridge. Let cool. Knead with lard and baking powder. Add salt, and roll out with a rolling pin.

Blanch the corn husks, drain, and dry. Cut the dough and lay a piece on each corn husk. Fill with 1 tbs. of the pork filling, and fold to make a little packet, being sure the dough covers the meat filling. (Remember that the corn husks are easier to fold closed if you cut off the thick bottom edge and trim the tip.)

Lay tamales in a pot and cover with stock. Cover and cook as a casserole in a 350° F (195° C) oven or simmer over a low flame for approximately 45 minutes. When done, the *tamale* dough should peel easily from the husks which are not edible.

TAMALES CHIAPANECOS   Add chopped prunes to the pork stuffing, and prepare tamales as above.

Humitas or Choclotanda
Stuffed Corn Husks

These are found all over Latin America. The corn, called *choclo* by the Indians, must be fresh.

> 12 ears of fresh corn, with husks
> 4 chopped onions
> Lard
> 1−2 fresh chopped chiles or 1−2 dried, soaked chiles or 1 tsp. (5 g.) chili powder
> Suggested seasonings: thyme, coriander, salt, pepper
> 2 cups (500 ml.) tomato sauce (see p. 45)
> 1 cup (250 ml.) boiling milk

Husk the corn and grate it. Wash the husks and soak in hot water.

Sauté the onions in lard, add the grated corn, herbs and seasonings. Add the tomato sauce and boiling milk. Simmer, stirring constantly, until it thickens to a stiff paste.

Drain and dry the corn husks. Put one or two tablespoons of the paste on each husk and roll closed. Tie, if necessary, with thread or husk fiber.

Steam or poach ½ hour. Drain, pat dry, and serve hot. As with tamales, you do not eat the husks.

VARIANT   Add grated cheese to the stuffing.

Cheese Humitas

12 ears fresh corn, with husks
1 egg
2 tbs. (30 g.) lard
Pinch of baking powder
½ lb. (250 g.) farmer's cheese
Salt and suggested seasonings: *epazote, chiles, oregano, thyme*

Wash and soak the corn husks. Grate the corn. Separate the egg, save the yolk, and beat the white until it peaks.

Mix the corn with the softened lard, the yolk, the beaten egg white and baking powder. Add the cheese and season to taste.

Put some of the paste on each husk. Fold the husk to envelop the stuffing. It is easier to fold the husk leaves if you first trim the thick bottoms and dry tops of the leaves.

Steam in a strainer or colander ½ hour. As with tamales, you eat the stuffing off the corn husks not the corn husks themselves.

Choclo pastel
Corn and Meat Pie

CORN:
1 minced onion
8 ears fresh corn, with corn cut from the cob
1 cup (250 ml.) milk
Salt, pepper
Pinch of chili powder
Suggested seasoning: thyme, coriander, basil, oregano
1 egg
Sugar

STUFFING:
3 minced onions
½ lb. (250 g.) chopped pork
¼ lb. (100 g.) black olives
½ cup (80 g.) raisins
2 hard-boiled eggs, sliced
Salt, pepper

To prepare the stuffing, brown the onions and add the meat. Cook over low heat 15 minutes, then mix in the other stuffing ingredients. Spread out in a greased baking tin.

To prepare the corn, brown the onions, add the cut corn, then add milk. Season and simmer, stirring steadily. Separate the egg and beat the white until stiff. Remove corn mixture from heat, mix in the yolk and beaten white. Pour the mixture evenly over the stuffing and sprinkle with sugar. Bake 15 minutes at 450° F (230° C) until browned.

Creole Corn with Giblets

    1 lb. (500 g.) giblets
    Oil
    1 cup (250 ml.) tomato sauce
    1 cup (150 g.) corn meal
    Water or stock

Brown the giblets in oil. Wet with tomato sauce, adding water or stock if necessary to cover. Simmer 10 minutes. Remove the giblets from the sauce and drain. Stir corn meal into the sauce, adding more stock if desired. Simmer 15–20 minutes to thicken. Return the giblets to the corn mush and cook, stirring, another 5 minutes.

Add sautéed onions if desired.

Afghan Kitchiri
Rice and Corn Porridge

Along with *palao* or *polo*, a variation of *pulao*, this is a staple of Afghanistan, where it is served with strong Afghani *kuruti* cheese (made from dried sheep or goat curds) and chopped or boiled local herbs.

    ½ cup (125 g.) rice
    ½ cup (125 g.) dried corn
    3½ cups (875 ml.) water
    Fresh coriander, parsley, mint
    ¼ lb. (100 g.) dry sheep or goat cheese (e.g. Greek *kefalotiri* or
       pecorino)

Boil the rice and corn 1–1½ hours, until they soften to a thick porridge. Mash, mix in chopped fresh spices. Serve with the grated or crumbled cheese.

Rice

Rice feeds a vast part of Asia and much of the rest of the world. Its preparation varies almost as much as do the people over this vast and diverse terrain. When Indians boil rice they use a full pot of boiling water, then drain and dry it in a low oven. The popular Chinese method is to cook the rice in water that will be completely absorbed by the time the rice is cooked. Differences in the availability of fuel, perhaps. But the result is the same: each grain remains separate and firm. We must add to these simple boiled rices the various methods of frying rice before boiling it: the *pilafs*, *pulao*, *palaos* and other recipes common in the Middle East, India, and central Asia.

Indians say rice must be aged at least 5 years before it is good. They like to enrich it with almonds, fried onions, or raisins. For festivals they color it red, green, yellow, or brown. The rich sometimes decorate it with gold and silver. When means permit, meat or fish is added to the rice as it is cooked.

In India rice is usually fried first, then boiled and served with meat and vegetables. In China it is boiled first, then fried with meat and vegetables.

Indian Rice

> 1 cup (200 g.) rice
> 1½ qts. (1½ l.) water
> Salt

Add the rice to the boiling, salted water. Simmer 15 minutes until the rice is cooked but still firm. Drain. Rinse with cold water, then drain thoroughly. Spread the rice on a baking sheet and dry slightly in a low oven, turning the rice from time to time.

Chinese Rice

2 cups (400 g.) rice
3 cups (750 ml.) water
Salt

Put the rice in the water, add salt, and bring to a boil. Cover and simmer 12–15 minutes until all water is absorbed. Let dry 10 minutes over a very low heat.

On the subject of Chinese rice: the pigeons of Peking were famous carriers of rice stolen from the Imperial granaries. After their careful training, they were justly called "bearers of life." The pigeons flew to the granaries, gorged themselves on rice, and upon their return were given a mild emetic so that they would spit up the rice. After washing, the rice was sold. One good pigeon could pilfer a good half-pound of rice a day.

Rice and Fish

These comprise the daily meal for many in Asia, from China to Indonesia.

1½ cups (375 ml.) water
1 lb. (500 g.) fish—cleaned, whole fish or fillets
2/3 cup (150 g.) rice
Suggested seasonings: cardamom, saffron, pepper, garlic

Boil the water. Add fish then throw in the rice and seasonings. Simmer 15 minutes. Mix together and serve.

VARIANT   Add one more cup water for a rice and fish soup.

Tibetan Dresi
Sweet Rice

The Tibetans use yak butter in this recipe. Stored Mongol-style in yak bellies it has a strong taste and often has yak hairs in it. Use plain rice or sweet rice, a glutinous variety sold in oriental markets.

    ½ cup (100 g.) raisins
    1 cup (250 g.) rice
    1 ⅔ cups (450 ml.) water
    2–3 tbs. (45 g.) butter
    1–2 tbs. (30 g.) sugar

Soak raisins. Boil the rice with the water, then cover and simmer 12–15 minutes until very dry. Put on a serving plate and add butter. Add the sugar and raisins.

Serve with momos, large meat-stuffed ravioli not unlike Chinese chiao-tzu (see p. 221)

Indian Yellow Rice

    2 minced onions
    Ghee (see p. 31) or vegetable oil
    1 tsp. (5 g.) turmeric
    1 pinch cumin
    Salt
    1 cup (250 g.) rice
    2 cups (500 ml.) water

Brown the onions in ghee or vegetable oil. Add the spices and fry a few minutes. Add washed and drained rice. Salt. Let brown a few minutes before adding hot water, covering the rice not much more than an inch deep. Cover and simmer 12–15 minutes until all the liquid is absorbed.

Indian Kichri
Rice with Peas

This dish can also be made with fresh peas or diced vegetables.

> 2 minced onions
> *Ghee* (see p. 31) or vegetable oil
> Suggested spices: cardamom, cloves, cumin, saffron, cinnamon
> 1 cup (250 g.) rice
> 2 cups (500 ml.) hot water
> 1 cup (250 g.) soaked *dhal* (see p. 55) or lentils
> Salt

This dish lent its name to a different dish—Anglo-Indian kedgeree (see p. 245). It appears that since *kichri* often accompanies fish, the English thought it was a mixture of rice and fish. Actually, *kichri,* which means hodgepodge, is rice cooked with *dhal* (see p. 55), not fish.

Brown onions in *ghee* or vegetable oil and add spices. Fry. Add rice and brown it before adding the water. Mix in the *dhal.* Cover and simmer 30–45 minutes until the *dhal* is cooked.

Pulao
Indian Fried Rice

> 1–2 minced onions
> *Ghee* (see p. 31) or vegetable oil
> Suggested spices: curry or cumin, cardamom, turmeric, saffron,
>   cloves, cinnamon
> 1 cup (250 g.) rice
> 2 cups (500 ml.) hot water
> Optional: 1/3 cup (70 g.) raisins, soaked,
>   1/3 cup (50 g.) almonds
> Salt

Brown the onions in *ghee* or vegetable oil. Add spices, fry, then add rice. Brown the rice then add the water. Cover and simmer 12–15 minutes, until all liquid is absorbed. If desired, sauté almonds and raisins separately in *ghee*, and add them to the cooked rice before serving.

Burmese Rice

1 coconut, or ½ cup (70 g.) dried, grated coconut
2 cups (500 ml.) water
2 minced onions
Ghee (see p. 31) or vegetable oil
1 cup (250 g.) rice

Crack open the coconut, grate the coconut meat, and cover with half the water. Strain in linen or cheesecloth to press out coconut milk. Mix the rest of the water with the coconut pulp and press again. The final squeezes yield the richest milk. You can also make coconut milk in a blender (see p. 00).

Brown the onions in ghee or vegetable oil. Add the rice and brown that too. Add the coconut milk.

Bring the rice and coconut milk to a boil, cover, and simmer 12–15 minutes. When all the liquid is absorbed, the rice is ready to serve.

Chow farn
Chinese Fried Rice

5–6 tbs. (75 ml.) peanut oil
1 tbs. (15 ml.) sesame oil
Salt
2 eggs
4 cups (700 g.) cold, cooked rice
1 bunch of scallions, minced
1 tbs. (15 ml.) soy sauce

Heat the two oils together and pour in salted beaten eggs, stirring briskly until cooked. Add the rice. Stir quickly. Heat, adding scallions and soy sauce just before serving.

VARIANT   Fry bits of ham, bacon, or shrimp with the eggs.

Chinese Fried Rice II

A version of the preceding recipe, this was used by more prosperous Chinese.

4–5 tbs. (60 ml.) peanut oil or pork fat
1–2 tsp. (10 ml.) sesame oil
2 eggs
3 cups (550 g.) cold, cooked rice
Salt
¼ lb. (100 g.) cooked, minced pork
½ cup (60 g.) dried shrimp, soaked and drained (see p. 116)
1 tsp. (5 ml.) soy sauce
1 bunch scallions, minced

Heat oil in a wok or frying pan and stir in beaten eggs. Before the eggs are completely cooked, add the rice and salt. Mix in pork and shrimp. Add soy sauce and scallions just before serving.

If desired, chicken or beef may be substituted for pork.

Nasi goreng
Malaysian Fried Rice

Like the Chinese, the Malaysians often use cold, cooked rice.

Malaysians who are Moslem never eat pork, so their recipe uses chicken. The Chinese in Malaysia, on the other hand, who love pork, use chopped ham and bacon along with the traditional dried mushrooms.

½ lb. (250 g.) fresh shrimp
5–6 tbs. (75 ml.) peanut oil
3 minced onions
3 sweet red peppers, sliced
Salt
4 cups (700 g.) cold, cooked rice
½ lb. (250 g.) diced chicken
4 chicken livers
1 tsp. (5 ml.) soy sauce
2 eggs

Boil shrimp 5 minutes. Drain and save the liquid. Shell the shrimp, brown in oil and set aside.

Sauté one minced onion with the sliced peppers. Salt. Add the rice and then the shrimp, chicken, and livers. Stir well. Add the soy sauce and some of the water used to boil the shrimp. Stir and simmer 5 minutes. Stir in one egg. Cook 3–4 more minutes. The rice should be firm and dry.

Scramble the remaining egg. Press flat and cut into narrow strips. Fry the remaining onions.

Put the rice on a plate and garnish with strips of egg and onions. If desired, garnish further with sliced cucumber or minced raw scallions.

Indonesian Rice

2 minced onions
Suggested spices: coriander, cardamom, turmeric
3 cups (500 g.) cold, cooked rice
2–3 slightly green bananas or plantains
3–4 eggs

Brown the onions, then add spices as desired, and the rice.

Meanwhile slice the bananas lengthwise and fry in one pan. In another pan cook the beaten eggs as an omelet (it should be quite dry). Cut into strips.

Serve the rice piled on a plate, surrounded by the bananas and egg strips.

Mexican Rice with Frijoles
Rice and Beans

This is the daily food of poor people.

1 cup (250 g.) red, black, or pinto beans
1–2 minced onions
1 cup (250 g.) rice
Salt
Bits of dried meat (e.g. *carne seca*, see p. 238) or a bone
3 cups (750 ml.) water
1–2 dried or fresh chiles, or powdered chili

Soak the beans (the *frijoles*) overnight; then simmer 2–2½ hours. Drain. Brown minced onions. Add rice and beans. Salt. Remove seeds and stems from chiles. If using dried chiles, soak 20 minutes in warm water. Chop and add with the meat to the rice and beans. Add water, bring to a boil, cover and simmer 12–15 minutes. There should be enough water so that there will be some gravy after cooking, naturally thickened with starch from the beans.

Rice and Tomato

This is another of the daily foods of Mexico.

> 1 cup (250 g.) rice
> Oil, lard, or butter
> Suggested spices: chili, saffron, cumin, garlic
> Salt
> 2 chopped onions
> 1 lb. (500 g.) tomatoes, chopped

Fry the rice. Mexicans use lard for frying because oil and butter are too expensive. Add salt and spices. Add onions and chopped tomatoes. Pour in water to cover. Cover and simmer 15 minutes, as with any pilaf.

This rice can be enriched with some cubed dried or salted meat, bacon or ham, with fresh cooked corn in season or sautéed chicken livers.

Moors and Christians
Rice and Beans

This is the name the Cubans give their daily meal: rice and beans.

> 1 cup (250 g.) black beans
> 2 chopped onions
> 1–2 hot dried or fresh chiles, or powdered chili
> 1 cup (250 g.) rice
> ¼ lb. (100 g.) diced ham
> Garlic, salt
> 1 lb. (500 g.) chopped tomatoes

Soak the beans overnight, then simmer 1½–2 hours. Drain.

Brown the onions. Remove stem and seeds from the chiles. If using dried chiles, soak for 20 minutes. Chop and add to the onions. Add the other ingredients, including the beans, and water to cover. Bring to a boil, cover, and simmer 12−15 minutes. Add more water, if necessary, so that some liquid is left as gravy when cooking is finished.

In Haiti this dish is served, whenever possible, with fish or meat sauce.

Spanish Spring Rice

> 1 lb. (500 g.) fresh spring vegetables, e.g. cauliflower, peas, artichoke hearts
> 3 cups (750 ml.) water
> ¼ lb. (125 g.) diced ham
> 1 cup (250 g.) rice
> Suggested seasonings: garlic, salt, pepper, saffron
> Vegetable oil or lard

Gently boil the vegetables in water 7 minutes. Drain, saving the water. Brown diced ham in lard or oil, add rice. Season (remember, however, that spices are not generally used heavily in Spanish cooking).

Add the water saved from cooking the vegetables. Bring to a boil, then add the vegetables. Simmer 15 minutes until the liquid evaporates or is absorbed. Finish drying in the oven at 200°F (95° C).

If desired, serve with butter.

Arroz à la Cubana
Rice with Garlic

Despite the name, this is a Spanish dish.

> 1 cup (250 g.) rice
> 2 cloves garlic, whole
> 2 cloves garlic, minced
> Olive oil
> Salt
> Suggested seasonings: laurel, saffron

Gently cook the rice with the whole garlic cloves and an abundance of water in a covered pot for 12–15 minutes. Drain and rinse in cold water.

Fry the minced garlic gently in oil. Add the rice. Cook, stirring, for a few minutes. Season.

Serve with: fried eggs, fried tomato slices, and sliced *chorizo* (Spanish sausage).

Turkish Pilaf

Rice is the staple of Middle Eastern countries. They cook it in large hemispheric copper pots, called *djindjeres*. The rice is often soaked a short time in heavily salted water before being cooked with lots of butter or mutton fat.

The poor often eat no more than rice with perhaps some olives and raw onions.

> 1–2 onions, chopped
> Oil, butter, or lamb fat
> Suggested spices: saffron, cumin, cinnamon, dill
> Salt
> 1 cup (250 g.) rice
> 2 cups (500 ml.) boiling water
> 1 cup (100 g.) sliced almonds
> 1 cup (150 g.) prunes, soaked and pitted

Brown the onions in oil, butter, or lamb fat. Add the spices and rice. Brown, then add the water. Cover and simmer 12 minutes. Fry the almonds and prunes separately and mix in with the rice.

Serve garnished with hard-boiled eggs cut in half.

Greek Pilaf

With bread, rice is the staple of poor Greeks. Like bread, it is often served with fat black olives and feta or goat cheese—the delicious foods of poor people.

> 3 tbs. (50 g.) butter, lamb fat, or olive oil
> 5 cups (1,250 ml.) boiling water
> Salt
> 2 cups (500 g.) rice, preferably long grain

Melt the butter. Add the boiling water. Salt. Add washed and drained rice, carefully turned to remove clumps.

Cook on a high flame 5–10 minutes until most of the liquid boils off, then cover the pot tightly and simmer gently 8–10 minutes.

Press the rice into a salad bowl then quickly turn it out onto a plate. Serve sprinkled with melted butter.

This pilaf is often served with one of the following sauces:

> GLAZED TOMATOES
> 1 lb (500 g.) plum tomatoes
> 1 tbs. (15 g.) sugar
> Butter

Peel the tomatoes and boil gently in a little water. Add butter and sugar to taste. Simmer gently to reduce, occasionally basting the tomatoes.

> PEAS AND HAM
> ¼ lb. (100 g.) ham
> ¼ lb. (100 g.) fresh peas
> Olive oil or butter

Cube the ham and sauté with fresh peas in olive oil or butter. Serve mixed with the pilaf.

Risotto
Italian Pilaf

Rice is to the northern provinces of Italy what pasta is to the south. It is prepared in a different way from the Asian, American, and Middle Eastern methods. It is almost never served alone.

> 1 minced onion
> 1 tbs. (15 g.) butter
> 1 cup (250 g.) short-grained (Piedmontese) rice
> ¾ cup (375 ml.) white wine and 3½ cups (875 ml.)
>   water, or 4 cups (1 l.) stock
> Salt, pepper

Brown the minced onion in butter in a heavy frying pan. Stir in the rice. Add the wine and simmer, stirring until the wine is completely absorbed. Then add water gradually. (If using stock, add bit by bit, stirring constantly.) Add spices. Simmer, stirring, another 15–25 minutes.

Risotto in Salto
Italian Rice Pancakes

> 3 cups (500 g.) leftover *risotto*
> 1–2 beaten eggs
> Bread crumbs

Shape leftover *risotto* into thick pancakes, dip in egg and bread crumbs. Fry on both sides until golden, taking care when turning. Use a moderate flame. Serve with butter and cheese.

Suppli
Rice and Cheese

This is another excellent use for leftover *risotto*.

    3 cups (500 g.) leftover *risotto*
    2 eggs
    ¾ lb. (350 g.) mozzarella cheese

Mix the eggs into the rice. Put a large spoonful of rice in your hand and shape it into a ball around a small piece of mozzarella. Be sure the rice envelops the stuffing. Dip in bread crumbs and fry in oil.

    The melted cheese stretches into long strings as the ball is bitten into—which is why the dish is called *suppli al telefono*.

    If desired, replace the mozzarella with mortadella or ham.

Risi e bisi
Venetian Rice and Peas

    1 chopped onion
    Butter
    ¼ lb. (100 g.) ham
    1 lb. (500 g.) fresh peas
    1 qt. (1 l.) stock or water
    2 cups (500 g.) rice
    Salt, pepper
    Grated Parmesan cheese

Brown the onion in butter. Add diced ham, then peas. Brown. Add water or stock to cover. Pour in the rice, seasoning, and the rest of the liquid. Cover and simmer 15 minutes. Do not stir.

    Serve with butter and grated Parmesan cheese to taste.

SOUPS

Soup is a less widespread way of preparing food than many a Westerner might think, having grown up thinking good health depended on how many bowls of soup he could swallow without flinching. The greater part of the world's population lives in tropical climates where our familiar kinds of soup are perhaps too hot and take too much cooking. China, however, knows soup well, if without the same Western psychological savor. The Chinese serve soups throughout a meal whenever the meal has more than one course.

Mulligatawny
Indian Lentil Soup

This is a soup from southern India. Its name means "pepper water" in Tamil. The name applies to a soup made from black pepper and tamarind, taken as a remedy for indigestion. The following version is more filling.

> 1 cup (250 g.) lentils, soaked split peas, or *dhal* (see p. 55)
> 2 cups (500 ml.) water
> 3 minced onions
> 2−3 cloves garlic, chopped
> Bay leaves, salt
> *Ghee* (see p. 31)
> 1−2 tbs. (15 g.) curry spices, e.g. turmeric, fenugreek, cayenne, cumin, clove
> 1 qt. (1 l.) meat stock
> ¾ cup (200 ml.) thick coconut milk (see p. 47)

Cook the lentils (or peas or *dhal*) 30 minutes in the water with one minced onion, the bay leaves, and salt. Put through a strainer or food mill.

Brown minced onions and chopped garlic in *ghee*. Add curry spices and fry a few minutes. Add the lentils and stock, season, and simmer 5−10 minutes. Add the coconut milk at the last minute, and serve with a side dish of Indian rice (see p. 97)

Mulligatawny with Meat

> 2−3 tbs. (40 g.) curry spices, e.g. turmeric, fenugreek, cayenne, cumin, clove
> *Ghee* (see p. 31)
> 2 lbs. (1 kg.) cubed lamb
> 6−8 cups (1½ l.) water
> 1½ lbs. (700 g.) stew vegetables, e.g. celery, carrot, cauliflower
> 1 cup (250 g.) lentils, soaked split peas, or *dhal* (see p. 55)
> 1 cup (125 g.) crushed almonds or walnuts
> 3 minced onions
> 2−3 cloves garlic
> Bay leaves, salt
> 1−2 lemons
> 1 cup (250 ml.) thick coconut milk (see p. 47)

Fry half the curry spices in ghee, add the meat. Add water and stew vegetables and simmer 2–2½ hours. Add lentils, dhal or peas, and almonds. Brown onions with the rest of the spices, and add to the meat.

Simmer 20–30 minutes until the lentils are cooked. Add coconut milk and serve with lemon slices.

Serves 6–8.

Indian Fish Soup

2 lbs. (1 kg.) non-oily fish, e.g. haddock
Oil, preferably ghee (see p. 31) or mustard oil
1½ lbs. (750 g.) vegetables, e.g. okra, cauliflower, celery, carrot
2 tbs. (25 g.) curry spices
Salt

Bone the fish and cut into chunks; fry in oil. Add minced vegetables and curry spices. Salt. Add water to cover, simmer 5–10 minutes.

Malaysian Soup

1 lb. (500 g.) boned fish
1 lb. (500 g.) shrimp, shelled and deveined
Vegetable oil
2 minced onions
2 tbs. (25 g.) curry spices, e.g. fenugreek, cayenne, lemongrass,
   turmeric, cumin
Water
Salt
1 cup (250 ml.) coconut milk (see p. 47)
Lemon

Cut fish and shrimp in pieces and sauté in oil. Add minced onions and curry spices. Add water to cover. Salt. Simmer 10–15 minutes. Add the coconut milk shortly before serving.

Serve with lemon.

Burmese Soup

1 lb. (500 g.) fish trimmings, i.e. skin, head, and bones
1 qt. (1 l.) water
2 minced onions
2 cloves garlic
Oil or *ghee* (see p. 31)
2 chopped carrots
½ lb. (250 g.) chopped cabbage
Salt
Coriander

Bring the fish trimmings and water to a boil. Add one onion. Reduce heat and simmer ½ hour. Reduce to thicken. Put through a strainer or food mill.

Chop the garlic, brown it in a little oil or *ghee*, and add the strained fish stock. Add the other ingredients and simmer 5–10 minutes.

Thai Shrimp and Squash Soup

Dried shrimp can be bought at oriental markets.

1 cup (80 g.) dried shrimp
1 tbs. (10 g.) star anise or Szechuan pepper
3–4 shallots or scallions
.1 small, fresh hot chili, chopped, or ½ tsp. crushed chiles
Salt
1 lb. (500 g.) zucchini
4–6 cups (1 l.) water

Grind shrimp and star anise or Szechuan pepper very finely in a mortar and pestle. Put some of the shrimp powder in each person's bowl, along with finely chopped shallots and chili, and approximately ¼ tsp. salt.

Pare the zucchini and cut into ¼ inch slices. Bring the water to a boil; add the zucchini. As soon as the water boils again, pour it into the serving bowls. Stir up the seasonings and serve.

If desired, replace the zucchini with yam bean or bitter melon.

Mango Soup

1 tbs. (12 g.) curry spices, e.g. tumeric, cardomom, clove, fenugreek, cayenne
Ghee (see p. 31) or vegetable oil
3 chopped mangoes
1 qt. (1 l.) water
Salt
1 tbs. (15 g.) grated fresh ginger

Fry the curry spices in ghee or vegetable oil. Add 3 chopped mangoes, sauté briefly then add the water, salt, and ginger.
Let simmer 40–50 minutes. Strain, if desired.

Wakame no suimono
Japanese Clear Soup with Seaweed

Japanese soups both clear and flavored with miso, (see p. 118), are based on a stock made from dried bonito (katsuobushi) or sardines and kelp (kombu seaweed). The clear soups in particular are some of the most delicious and original of all the world's soups. In making stock for suimono you must be careful not to leave the seaweed too long in the boiling water or the broth will turn bitter. The briefly boiled kelp can be reused to make the coarser stock used for miso soup.

Japanese specialty shops stock katsuobushi, miso and varieties of seaweeds, including kombu and wakame. Health food stores stock miso and seaweeds.

1 sheet (approximately 1/3 oz. or 10 g.) dried kombu (kelp) seaweed
1 qt. (1 l.) water
½ cup (1/3 oz. or 10 g.) dried flaked bonito (katsuobushi)
½ oz. (15 g.) dried wakame seaweed
Soy sauce
Salt
1 bean curd pad, cut into ½ inch cubes

Rinse the kombu seaweed. To prepare a soup stock bring the water to a boil, add the seaweed, and stir it in the water for 30–60 seconds. Then remove the seaweed (save it for miso soup stock) and add the dried flaked bonito. Remove pan from heat and let stand for 1–2 minutes. Strain the broth and reserve the bonito for miso soup.

Soak *wakame* seaweed in cold water for 10 minutes. Drain and cut into ½ inch pieces. Season the clear stock with soy sauce and salt. Add seaweed and beancurd and bring to a boil. Lower the heat and simmer 3−4 minutes before serving.

Miso Soup

Miso is a fermented soybean product which is salty, flavorful, and high in protein. It is used in soups and stews and makes even a vegetarian meal taste meaty. *Miso* soups may be drunk at any meal in Japan, including breakfast.

>3−4 cups (750 ml.) water
>Leftover or unused *kombu* and dried bonito (see preceding recipe)
>1−2 carrots, thinly sliced
>½ cup (100 g.) thinly sliced *daikon* (see p. 158) or radishes
>1 scallion, chopped
>1 cup (170 g.) finely shredded Chinese celery cabbage
>4−5 tbs. (60 g.) red *miso* paste

Prepare a stock by boiling leftover *kombu* and bonito in the water for 10 minutes. Strain the broth through cheesecloth. Place the carrots, radish, chopped scallion, and cabbage in a kettle with the stock; cover and simmer until vegetables are just tender. Dilute *miso* with a little of the soup stock, stir until all lumps are removed, and then add to the soup pot. Keep the soup hot but do not boil again after adding *miso*.

Bitter melon

Bitter Melon Soup

Bitter melon is a green, wrinkled, and warty vegetable, resembling a cucumber in both size and shape. It is sold in Chinese markets, and should be firm and unblemished. Bitter melon has an unusual bitter taste, highly prized by the Cantonese.

    1–2 bitter melons
    4–6 cups (1 l.) water, salted
    ½ lb. (250 g.) chicken or pork
    1–2 tbs. (30 ml.) soy sauce
    1 tbs. (15 ml.) dry sherry

Wash the bitter melon and slice lengthwise. Do not peel. Scoop out the seeds and discard. Cut the shells in half and slice into strips. Blanch in salted boiling water for 2–3 minutes and drain. This reduces the bitterness.
    Shred the chicken or pork finely.
    Bring the water to a boil. Reduce to a medium heat. Add the melon. Return to a boil. Add the meat. Return to a low boil, add the soy sauce and sherry. Simmer 1–2 minutes until the meat is done, and serve hot.
    If desired, soak Chinese dried mushrooms 15–30 minutes, slice, and add with the water in which they soaked to the soup with the melon. Or add garlic shoots or scallions and cubed bean curd. For a richer soup, use stock (any variety) instead of water, or add crushed dried fish or shrimp.

Soup with Chinese Meatballs

    ½ lb. (250 g.) minced pork
    1 egg
    1 tbs. (15 ml.) soy sauce
    1 minced white leek
    1 tbs. (12 g.) cornstarch
    Pinch of MSG
    Dash of dry white wine or dry sherry
    Salt
    1–2 tsp. (10 g.) fresh ginger
    1 qt. (1 l.) meat stock

Mix together minced pork, soy sauce, ginger, leak, MSG, cornstarch, egg and wine. Shape into small meatballs.
    Poach in lightly boiling stock 10 minutes. Season and serve.

Chinese Cabbage Soup

This soup can be made with any kind of cabbage but is especially good when made with Chinese celery cabbage.

    ½ lb. (250. g.) pork or chicken
    Peanut oil
    ½ lb. (250 g.) chopped cabbage
    4 dried mushrooms, soaked (see p. 35)
    1 qt. (1 l.) meat stock
    Dry white wine or dry sherry
    Salt, MSG
    Suggested seasonings: garlic, Szechuan pepper, sesame oil, ginger

Mince the meat and sauté in peanut oil. Add the cabbage and mushrooms, chopped evenly. Cook several minutes.

Add hot stock, wine, or sherry, and seasonings. Simmer 5 minutes until the cabbage is tender but firm.

Soy Soup

Soy, well appreciated in China, is served in many forms (see p.00) but most often as bean curd—cubes of curdled white soy milk.

    ½ lb. (250 g.) minced pork
    ¼ lb. bean curd (see p. 00)
    5 dried mushrooms, soaked (see p. 00)
    1 qt. (1 l.) meat or fish stock
    2 tbs. (30 ml.) soy sauce
    2 tbs. (30 ml.) vinegar
    Salt, pepper
    1 tbs. (12 g.) cornstarch

Slice the meat, bean curd, and mushrooms. Add boiling stock and simmer 5–10 minutes. Add soy sauce, vinegar, salt, pepper, and cornstarch premixed with a little cold water. Simmer until thick.

Goimontoi shulyu
Mongolian Lamb Soup

Mongols enjoy this robust soup sitting inside warm felt yurts, while blizzards sweep the steppe outside. The Mongols, like many other peoples of central Asia, live a primarily pastoral life, almost purely nomadic, following their herds to greener pastures. The Mongols' cooking reflects the fact that meat is more readily available—unlike most poor people, they eat more meat than vegetable or grain dishes. Their constant wandering accounts for the use of noodles made freshly before each meal, a practice common among all nomads. It is worth remembering that these nomads of north and central Asia are credited with the invention of ravioli, which apparently developed with Siberian Kirghiz *pelmenies*, which became Lithuanian *kolduny*, than *pieroshky* among the Poles, who transmitted the recipe to the Italians during a period of close relations between the two countries in the time of Queen Bona. In China, too, the popularity of ravioli stuffed with meat reveals the culinary influence of this simple but once powerful people. Their influence is also seen in Tibet where *momos* are served at every feast.

In Mongolia this soup is usually made with yak bones, yak meat, and yak bacon.

SOUP:
2 lbs. (1 kg.) lamb marrow bones
1 lb. (500 g.) roots and herbs, eg. parsnip, turnip, parsley, dill
Suggested spices: pepper, coriander seeds, dill seeds
8−10 cups (2½ l.) water
1 lb. (500 g.) lamb meat, cut in chunks
¼ lb. (125 g.) lamb or bacon fat

NOODLES:
1 cup (125 g.) flour
Water, salt

Boil the bones with the available roots, herbs, and spices 2½−3 hours to make approximately 2 qts. of good stock.

In the meantime, mix the flour with a little water and salt to make firm noodle dough. Let sit a few hours. Roll thin and slice into ribbons.

To the highly seasoned stock add pieces of meat and firm pieces of lamb or bacon fat. Simmer the meat 2½−3 hours.

Add the noodles and simmer 10−15 minutes more. Serve piping hot.

In Mongolia this dish is washed down with gulps of *airag*, a strong drink made from fermented mare's milk. Strong beer is an acceptable Western substitute.

Serves 6−8.

Lagman po Uyegursky
Lamb and Noodle Soup

This is a very savory soup from Uzbekistan in the Soviet Union.

NOODLES:
3 cups (375 g.) flour
Water
Salt
Butter

SOUP:
1 black radish, small *daikon* (see p. 158), or turnip
3−4 sweet peppers
3−4 tomatoes
Clarified butter (see p. 32)
1 lb. (400 g.) chopped lamb or beef
1 cup (250 ml.) tomato puree
3−4 cloves garlic
6−8 cups (1.5 l.) lamb or beef stock
Salt, pepper
4 potatoes
Parsley

NOODLES   Prepare firm noodle dough from flour, salt, and a little water. Roll it into sausage shape and smear with butter. Let sit, covered, several hours. Roll thin and fold over. Repeat the rolling and folding 3−4 times. Roll thin once more and cut into wide noodles.

SOUP   Chop the vegetables except for the potatoes, and sauté in butter. Add the meat, then the tomato puree and chopped garlic. Add the stock and season. Cut potatoes into chunks and add to the soup. Simmer 30−45 minutes.

To serve, cook the noodles in lightly boiling water 4−5 minutes and drain. Put some noodles onto each person's plate and cover with soup. Sprinkle with parsley and chopped herbs.
   Serves 6−8.

Shchi
Cabbage Soup

Served with heavy rye bread and salted cucumber, this soup is a whole meal for many in northern Russia.

 1 small white cabbage
 2 lbs. (1 kg.) stew vegetables, e.g. onion, carrot, leek, turnip, parsnip,
   rutabaga, and celery
 1–1½ lbs. (500 g.) potatoes
 1½ qts. (1.5 l.) beef stock
 Salt, pepper, bay leaf, parsley

Cut up the vegetables. Add to the stock and season. Simmer gently 20–30 minutes until cooked. Stir from time to time.

   Serve hot over spoonfuls of hot cooked kasha (see p. 86) or serve with a side dish of dried mushrooms cooked with potatoes or kasha.

Mushroom and Barley Soup

This is very common in Slavic countries.

 Handful dried mushrooms (Eastern European or Italian variety—see
   p. 35)
 1 qt. (1 l.) water
 4 tbs. (60 g.) pearled barley
 Salt, pepper
 2–3 cloves garlic
 2–3 shallots or small onions
 4–6 tbs. (70 ml.) heavy cream or sour cream

Soak the mushrooms in a small amount of the water for 1 hour. Soak the barley in the rest of the water at least 1 hour.

   Add the mushrooms and the water they soaked in to the barley. Bring to a boil. Add spices, ga.lic, and shallots. Simmer 30 minutes, until the barley is cooked. Serve with heavy cream or sour cream.

VARIANT   Use stock instead of water.

Russian Millet Soup

4 tbs. (50 g.) whole millet
1 qt. (1 l.) water or stock
2–3 cubed potatoes
2 minced onions
1 stalk fresh dill or fennel, chopped
1 tbs. (15 g.) butter
Salt

Mix the ingredients and bring to a boil. Simmer 20–30 minutes until the millet and potatoes are cooked. Serve with buttered bread.

Borscht
Beet Soup

Borscht, the greatest of Ukrainian soups, is a substantial main dish when served with kasha (see p. 86) or *pieroshky* (large ravioli stuffed with meat, cabbage, or practically anything else).

As is usual with such popular dishes, *borscht* has many versions. Besides this basic Ukrainian recipe, there are thin *borschts*, green *borschts*, cold and hot *borschts*, Muscovite *borschts*, clear *borschts*, etc.

1 white cabbage
1 lb. (400 g.) beets
2 lbs. (1 kg.) stew vegetables, e.g. carrot, onion, potato, turnip, celery, rutabaga, and leek
4 tomatoes, or 4 oz. (125 ml.) tomato paste
2–3 qts. (2 l.) beef stock
Salt, pepper, bay leaves, parsley
1–2 tbs. (30 g.) sugar
Juice of ½ lemon
2 cups (500 ml.) sour cream

Peel the beets and other vegetables. Grate some of the beets and set aside. Chop finely the remaining beets and all the vegetables except the tomatoes; add them to boiling stock. Simmer ½ hour. Add whole tomatoes, seasonings, sugar, lemon juice, and simmer 5–10 minutes. Ten minutes before serving, add the grated beets that were set aside; the soup will have a deep red color because of the fresh beets.

Serve with a big spoonful of sour cream in each dish.
Serves 6–8.

MEAT BORSCHT
All the above ingredients
2 lbs. (1 kg.) beef cup into ½ inch cubes

Proceed as above except use water instead of stock. Simmer the beef with the water for 2 hours before adding the vegetables. Proceed as above. For firmer, textured meat, brown the meat before adding water. In hard times, you can make do with a piece of salt pork or bacon.
  Serves 6−8.

Okrochka
Beer and Vegetable Soup

It is easy to understand the passion of sunny countries like Spain and Greece for cold soups, but we may be surprised at recipes of this sort from cold countries like Russia. The hot summers of so-called temperate climates go a long way to explain the apparent contradiction.

  The original of this cold summer soup called for *kvass*, a thin rye or barley beer that is practically the national beverage. It is often sold by the glass from kegs on the street corner. *Kvass's* natural companion is heavy rye bread. Note that this soup is *not* cooked.

  1 cucumber
  2−3 cold cooked potatoes
  1 bunch scallions
  2−3 hard-boiled eggs
  1 lb. (400 g.) cold cooked beets
  1 cup soaked dried fruits, e.g. prunes, apricots, apples, pears
  ½ cup (20 g.) dried mushrooms, soaked (see p. 35)
  Chopped fresh parsley or dill
  Salt
  1 qt. (1 l.) *kvass* or light Pilsner beer
  ¾ cup (200 ml.) sour cream

Peel the vegetables. Dice all the ingredients, mix, and season. Add the *kvass* or beer. Chill for at least 4 hours.
  Serve with an ice cube and a big spoonful of sour cream in each dish.

Chicken Soup

In Eastern Europe they used to say that the only time a poor man eats chicken is when he's sick or the chicken was. This soup can be made with just chicken feet and necks.

> 1 chicken, including feet and neck
> 1−2 lbs. (500 g.) short ribs of beef (*flanken*), if desired
> 2−3 lbs. (1 kg.) stew vegetables, e.g. onions, celery, carrots, parsnip
> Fresh dill
> 3−4 cloves garlic
> Salt, peppercorns, bay leaves
> Suggested spices: marjoram, thyme, mace, coriander

Cut up the chicken, meat, and vegetables. Put them in a large pot with the other ingredients and water to cover. Bring to a boil, skim, cover and simmer 1½ hours, making sure the water doesn't boil away. Skim the fat.

Serve as is or with boiled noodles. Or drain and serve the broth with matzah balls (see p. 66), potato dumplings (see p. 176), boiled potatoes or noodles. On a separate plate serve the boiled chicken and beef hot or cold, with ground horse radish.

Serves 6−8.

Hungarian Cucumber Soup

> 1 small white onion, coarsely chopped
> 4 leeks (white part only), sliced
> 3 tbs. (45 g.) parsley
> ¼ lb. (125 g.) butter
> 4 large cucumbers, peeled and chopped
> 4 medium potatoes, peeled and cubed
> 2 qts. (2 l.) chicken stock (see p. 46)
> 1 cup (250 ml.) plain yoghurt

Sauté onion, leeks, and parsley in butter only until onion is tender, not brown. Meanwhile, cook cucumbers and potatoes in stock until quite soft. Put both mixtures together and press through a food mill or puree in an electric blender. Return to the pan and simmer for 10 minutes. Refrigerate until thoroughly chilled (4−5 hours). Stir in yoghurt and serve in chilled bowls, topped with chopped chives or finely chopped raw cucumber.

Serves 6−8.

Bulgarian Yoghurt Soup

2½ cups (600 ml.) yoghurt
½ lb. (250 g.) chopped, cooked chicken or lamb
2 cloves garlic, chopped
Fresh mint, chopped
Salt, pepper
1 cup (200 g.) leftover cooked rice

Beat the yoghurt in a pot until smooth and light; add seasonings. Heat gently until almost boiling. Add the rice and meat. Simmer 5–10 minutes, then serve.

Austrian Leberreis
Liver Dumpling Soup

Meatballs, fishballs, *pelmenies* (Russian ravioli), and other dumplings enrich soups from one end of Europe to the other. This dumpling features liver.

2/3 cup (165 ml.) bread crumbs moistened with hot milk
1/3 lb. (150 g.) finely minced pork liver
2 chopped onions, browned in lard
1 clove garlic
Salt, pepper
Marjoram to taste
2 eggs
1 qt. (1 l.) meat stock

Mix the bread crumbs, liver, onions, crushed garlic, and seasonings. Bind with the eggs. Shape into balls the size of walnuts. Let sit at least 1 hour.

Poach in abundant lightly boiling salted water. They should be done in about 8–10 minutes. Drain.

Add carefully to a good stock and serve.

Mauve Soup
Flowers and Cream

The tradition of soups made from dried flowers originated in Germany and continues in countries where large numbers of Germans have settled, such as Argentina. Dried mallow (also called mauve and malva) or pumpkin flowers are available in some spice shops, notably Aphrodisia in New York (28 Carmine St., New York, N.Y. 10014) who will also supply by mail.

½ cup (10 g.) dried mallow (mauve or malva) or pumpkin flowers
1 minced onion
Butter
1 tbs. (12 g.) cornstarch
3 cups (750 ml.) milk
Salt, pepper
Cinnamon to taste
½ cup (125 ml.) heavy cream

Crush the flowers. Brown the onions in butter and add the flowers. Sauté briefly. Add milk. Season. Simmer 45 minutes.

Add cornstarch mixed with a little cold water or milk. Simmer 5 minutes more to thicken.

Serve with cream.

For a lighter soup, use skim milk and omit the cornstarch.

Arab Garlic and Tomato Soup

2 chopped onions
3–4 cloves garlic, chopped
Coriander seeds
4–5 tomatoes, chopped
Salt, pepper
1 cup (250 g.) semolina
1 qt. (1 l.) water or stock
Oil

Brown the onion and garlic in oil. Crush coriander in a mortar and pestle. Add coriander and chopped tomatoes, salt, pepper and semolina to the onions. Remove from heat and let sit for at least 15 minutes. Add the water or stock, bring to a boil, and simmer another 15 minutes.

Mast va khiar
Yoghurt, Cucumber and Egg Soup

This Persian cold soup can be prepared in advance, as it keeps well refrigerated.

3 cups (750 ml.) yoghurt
½ cup (125 ml.) heavy cream
1 large, peeled cucumber, finely sliced
4 minced scallions
2 chopped hard-boiled eggs
1 cup (150 g.) soaked, drained raisins
Salt, pepper
1 cup (250 ml.) ice water
Fresh dill or parsley

Mix all the ingredients together. Chill. Serve sprinkled with chopped fresh dill or parsley.

Chorba
Mutton and Bean Soup

1 lb. (500 g.) lamb cut into 1-inch cubes
Oil
2−3 onions
3−4 tomatoes
2−3 zucchini
1 cup (250 g.) dried beans, soaked overnight
1 cup (250 g.) chick-peas, soaked overnight
1 cup (180 g.) noodles
Fresh coriander
1/3 cup (75 g.) dried apricots

Brown the meat in oil. Add the onions and other vegetables, chopped evenly. Simmer ½ hour. Add the apricots, beans, chick-peas, and water to cover. Season, cover, and simmer 2−2½ hours.

Fifteen minutes before serving, add the noodles and coriander to the soup and simmer.

Molokheya Soup

This is the favorite soup of Egyptians. The poorest eat it with some coarse bread and vegetables, often as the whole meal.

Molokheya is an herb that looks like mint, and is available in some Middle Eastern stores.

> 4—5 large cloves garlic, chopped
> 1 onion, chopped
> Lard
> Coriander seeds, cayenne
> Salt
> 1 qt. (1 l.) meat or chicken stock
> 1 cup (10 g.) *molokheya*
> Juice from 1—2 lemons

Brown the garlic and onion in lard. Crush coriander in a mortar and pestle. Add coriander, cayenne, and salt to the onions. Pour in stock. Chop the *molokheya* finely and add to the soup. Simmer 5 more minutes.

Serve with lemon juice and rice pilaf.

Peanut Soup

Peanuts, a staple of Black Africa, find their way into many African recipes, from soup to dessert.

> 2 tbs. (25 g.) flour
> Mutton or lamb fat (or oil)
> 1 qt. (1 l.) chicken stock
> ¼ lb. (100 g.) roasted, unsalted peanuts
> ½ lb. (250 g.) white chicken meat, minced
> Suggested spices: cayenne, pepper, cumin, salt

Stir flour into hot fat to make a brown sauce. Add stock. Mash the peanuts with the chicken in a mortar and pestle. Mix with the soup and simmer 10—15 minutes. Spice well and serve.

Heavy cream is sometimes mixed with the chicken and peanuts.

Coconut Soup

Although not a common dish, soup in Black Africa is often surprising and exotic.

        2 cups (500 ml.) chicken stock
        2 cups (500 ml.) coconut milk (see p. 47)
        1 cup (250 ml.) heavy cream
        Suggested seasonings: cayenne, cumin, coriander
        Salt
        Roasted peanuts or cashews, chopped

Mix the stock with the coconut milk. Add cream and season. Simmer gently 5–10 minutes.
    Serve with bits of roasted nuts.

Avgholemono
Egg Lemon Soup

This soup is one of the basic recipes of poor Greeks.

        1/3 cup (85 g.) rice
        1 qt. (1 l.) chicken stock
        2 eggs
        Juice of 1 lemon
        Salt, pepper

Simmer the rice in the stock 12–15 minutes. Separate the eggs, beat the egg whites until stiff. Beat the yolks with lemon juice in a soup tureen and fold in the beaten egg whites.
    Slowly add the hot stock and rice, stirring constantly.
    Season. Serve hot.

Tzatziki
Cucumber Yoghurt Soup

This cold Greek soup is a favorite of the dog days. Yoghurt is a common base for many dishes throughout the Balkans and Middle East.

> 4 cups (1 l.) yoghurt
> 2 – 3 cloves garlic, chopped
> 1 large peeled cucumber, finely chopped or sliced
> Juice of ½ lemon
> Salt, pepper
> Fresh dill or mint, chopped

Mix the yoghurt, garlic, cucumber, and lemon juice. Add salt and pepper. Chill.

Serve sprinkled with dill or mint.

The soup tastes better if allowed to sit a few hours or even overnight before serving.

Andalusian Egg Soup

Quick to prepare, this egg soup is common fare in southern Spain.

> 2 – 3 cups (500 ml.) water
> 1 – 2 eggs, separated
> 2 – 3 tbs. (30 ml.) olive oil
> Salt, pepper
> Suggested spices: marjoram, thyme, basil, dill, mustard

Boil salted water. Beat in the egg whites. Remove from heat for as long as it takes to make a mayonnaise by beating together the egg yolks, oil, and seasoning until smooth. (To make mayonnaise, beat egg yolks with a wooden spoon; add oil a drop at a time at the beginning, beating all the time. Egg yolks should be at room temperature.)

Mix the egg bouillon slowly into the mayonnaise. Serve with fried croutons.

Almond Soup

The Spanish enjoy this soup as a Christmas eve specialty, although almonds are the base of many dishes the year round.

¼ lb. (85 g.) hulled almonds
3–4 cups (1 l.) water
1 tbs. (15 g.) sugar
Cinnamon to taste
Sliced bread

Crush the almonds in a mortar, adding water. Mix in sugar and cinnamon.
Toast slices of bread. Lay them out in a baking pan. Strain the soup and pour it over the bread. Bake 10 minutes at 450°F (230°C).

Cod Soup

This particular soup comes from Murcia province in Spain.

Flour
1 cup (250 g.) chickpeas, soaked and drained
2–3 cloves garlic
3–4 cups (1 l.) water
Salt
Olive Oil
1 lb. (400 g.) salt cod (bacalao) (see p. 36), soaked and drained
    overnight
Slice of bread
1 tbs. (15 ml.) vinegar
A few pistils saffron
Pepper to taste

Simmer the chickpeas 45 minutes with water, some garlic, salt, and a dash of oil.
Shortly before the chickpeas are done, dip the cod in flour and sauté in oil. Remove fish from the frying pan and replace with a slice of bread. Brown the bread on both sides, remove, sprinkle with vinegar, then mash with remaining garlic, saffron mixed in a little warm water, and pepper.
Add fish and spiced bread to the chickpeas and cook another 5 minutes.

Garlic Soup

Appreciated all over Spain, this soup has many regional variants.

> 3–4 cloves garlic, minced
> ¼ lb. (100 g.) diced ham
> 1–2 tbs. (30 ml.) olive oil
> 2/3 cup (60 g.) bread crumbs
> 4–5 tomatoes, chopped
> 3–4 cups (750 ml.) water
> Salt, pepper
> Tabasco sauce
> 1 egg, beaten

Brown the garlic in olive oil along with the ham. Add bread crumbs and chopped tomatoes. Add water to cover. Season and simmer 20–30 minutes. Shortly before serving mix in a beaten egg to thicken.

Cadiz Soup

> 3–4 cloves garlic, crushed
> ¼ lb. (100 g.) diced ham
> 1–2 tbs. (30 ml.) olive oil
> 1 cup (100 g.) diced fried bread or croutons
> Salt, pepper, chopped parsley
> 2 hard-boiled eggs, sliced
> 1 egg, beaten
> 1 qt. (1 l.) meat stock

Fry the garlic and ham in olive oil. Mix in a tureen with the bread, parsley, salt, pepper and sliced hard-boiled eggs. Add the beaten egg. Mix these ingredients well, then stir in hot stock and serve at once.

Gazpacho

This popular cold Spanish soup is called *gazpacho colorado* (red gazpacho) when served hot.

> 4 large ripe tomatoes, peeled
> 1 large cucumber, peeled
> 1 small onion, peeled
> 1 small green pepper, seeded
> ½ cup (125 ml.) red wine vinegar
> ½ cup (125 ml.) olive oil
> 1 tsp. (5 ml.) chili sauce (or tabasco)
> 1 tsp. (5 g.) salt
> ½ tsp. black pepper
> 2–3 cups (500 ml.) chopped, cooked tomatoes, or tomato juice
> 3–4 cloves garlic

Chop all vegetables finely. Add remaining ingredients and press through a food mill or blend in an electric blender. Serve chilled with cucumber and tomato chunks floating in the bowls.

Mint Soup

A flowery delicacy from Portugal.

> 1 small chicken, cut up into 8 pieces
> 1½ lbs. (750 g.) stew vegetables, e.g. onion, carrot, celery
> 4–6 cups (1½ l.) water
> ½ cup (100 g.) rice
> Salt, pepper
> 1–2 lemons
> Fresh or dried mint

Simmer the chicken and vegetables together in the water for 1½ hours to make stock. Skim the fat and discard. Drain the chicken and vegetables. Simmer the broth another 20–30 minutes in order to concentrate the flavor. Add rice to the broth and simmer approximately 12 minutes. Puree the vegetables and mix into the soup. Season. Add a dash of lemon juice.

To serve, pour over crumpled mint: 1 tbs. fresh or ½ tbs. dry for each serving. Garnish with lemon slices. Serve the boiled chicken separately.

Portuguese Garlic and Egg Soup

In Western as in Eastern Europe, soup is often the whole meal for a family. If there is bread or raw onion too, the family is eating well. In Portugal the bread is often *broa*, a heavy corn bread which, with slices of smoked ham and swallows of sharp green wine, makes for a fine country lunch.

    4 tbs. (60 g.) fresh herbs: coriander, rosemary, basil, parsley
    4 cloves garlic
    Salt, pepper
    1–2 tbs. (30 ml.) olive oil
    Slices of toasted bread
    4–6 eggs
    1 qt. (1 l.) water
    Black olives

Crush the herbs in a mortar with the garlic, salt, pepper, and oil.
   Spoon into a soup tureen. Cover with slices of toast.
   Poach eggs in the water, remove. Pour the hot water into the tureen. Stir up the seasoning. Lay the eggs on the bread floating on top of the soup. Serve with olives on the side.
   If desired, replace the eggs with shellfish, such as mussels.

Escarole Soup

A popular Italian recipe made from tender, strong-tasting lettuce, such as escarole, endive, or chicory.

    1 head of escarole, endive, or chicory
    1 small onion
    Optional: garlic clove
    Butter
    Lemon juice
    Salt, pepper, thyme
    3–4 cups (750 ml.) chicken stock (see p. 46)
    Grated Parmesan or Pecorino cheese

Wash the lettuce and discard the core. Chop. If desired, parboil 2–3 minutes in salted water to reduce bitterness.

Chop the onion (and, if desired, a small clove garlic) and sauté in butter in a soup pot. Add chopped lettuce and some lemon juice and sauté another 2–3 minutes. Add salt, pepper, and perhaps thyme. Add hot stock and simmer 20–30 minutes until tender.

Serve sprinkled with grated cheese.

Bulbura
Italian Pumpkin Soup

A light soup such as the poor typically eat in Italy. Originally from Ticino, the Italian-speaking canton of Switzerland.

1 lb. (500 g.) pumpkin or squash
1 minced onion
Optional: 1–2 tbs. (20 g.) sugar
1–2 cups (250 ml.) milk
Butter
1 cup (250 g.) cooked broad beans (fava beans)
Salt, pepper
Buttered Italian bread

Skin the pumpkin and chop the meat finely. Add the onion. Add just enough water to cover and sugar if desired. Bring to a boil and simmer 20–30 minutes. Strain or mill to make a creamy puree. Thin with milk, lace with butter and add cooked, drained beans. Simmer 5–10 minutes more. Season.

Serve with Italian bread and butter.

Bussega
Tripe Soup

This solid Lombard soup is a whole meal. Tripe can be bought from most butchers.

> 1 cup (250 g.) dried beans, soaked overnight
> ¼ lb. (100 g.) diced smoked bacon
> 2 minced onions
> 1½ lbs. (750 g.) cabbage, carrot, celery, onions, and turnip
> 3−4 tomatoes
> 1 lb. (500 g.) cooked tripe
> Suggested seasonings: 2−3 cloves garlic, sage, salt, pepper
> Hard-boiled eggs
> Grated Parmesan cheese

Simmer the beans for 40−60 minutes. Drain.

Brown the bacon. Add the onions, then the vegetables, cut up evenly. Sauté a few minutes, then add the beans. Add water to cover, then the tomatoes. Simmer 40−50 minutes.

Add the tripe, finely sliced. Season. Simmer 30 minutes more. Add more water if necessary.

Serve with quartered hard-boiled eggs and grated Parmesan.

Italian Egg Soup

> 1 qt. (1 l.) meat stock
> 2−3 eggs
> ½ cup (40 g.) bread crumbs
> Salt, pepper
> Grated Parmesan cheese

Heat the stock. Beat the eggs together with the bread crumbs. Season.

Stir the eggs into the stock. Simmer 5 minutes, then serve. Sprinkle with Parmesan.

Gul Artsoppa
Swedish Pork and Pea Soup

This thick split pea soup is served with crisp bread and cheese as a whole meal. At Christmas it is traditional to serve light pancakes after the soup.

        2 cups (450 g.) split peas
        3 qts. (3 l.) water
        1 lb. (500 g.) fresh pork, preferably shoulder
        Cooked hambone with some shreds of meat left on it
        2 chopped onions
        Salt, pepper, thyme
        Bread and strong hard cheese

Soak the peas overnight. Drain off the soaking water; add the 3 qts. water, boil. Skim. Simmer 1 hour.

Add meat, hambone, and onions. Simmer 2 hours. Remove the pork and hambone. Cut the cooked pork into cubes and scrape the shreds of ham from the bone. Return meats to the soup. Season well.

Serve with bread and strong cheese.

The hambone may be replaced with a salted pig's knuckle.

Serves 6–8.

Coconut Soup II

This is a common Latin American version of coconut soup.

        1 coconut
        1 qt. (1 l.) beef stock
        1 tbs. (12 g.) cornstarch
        2–3 tbs. (45 ml.) heavy cream
        Salt, pepper
        Suggested spices: coriander, cumin
        Nutmeg or mace

Break open the coconut shell, saving the sap. Grate the coconut meat as you would for making coconut milk (see p. 47). Add sap and grated coconut to beef stock, and simmer for 45 minutes.

Thicken with cornstarch and a little cream. Season. Sprinkle with nutmeg or mace.

Before serving beat the soup to make it light.

Colombian Almond and Onion Soup

        2 onions
        Lard or oil
        1 qt. (1 l.) meat stock
        1 cup (150 g.) almonds, sliced or chopped
        Salt, pepper
        Croutons
        Grated strong cheese

Brown the onions in lard or oil. Add stock and almonds. (If desired, brown the almonds with the onions first.) Season with salt and pepper.
    Serve with croutons and grated cheese.

Chupe

This thick soup is found in different versions in many Latin American countries. The best known, and supposedly the original, is Peruvian chupe. This basic recipe can be varied by mixing in different ingredients such as other meats, shellfish, and eggs.

        1–2 chopped onions
        1–2 cloves garlic
        1 cup (250 ml.) tomato sauce (see p. 45)
        1 cup (250 g.) rice or bread crumbs
        Salt
        Powdered chili
        1 lb. (500 g.) diced chicken or shelled and deveined shrimp
        4 cups (1 l.) water, stock, or milk or a mixture of these
        3–4 potatoes
        Goat cheese

Brown the onions. Add garlic and tomato sauce, then rice or bread crumbs, salt and powdered chili. Add 1 to 1½ cups water, stock, or milk. Cover and simmer 20–30 minutes. Mash to make a thick sauce. Add chicken or shrimp and simmer 3–5 minutes more. Strain, reserving the meat.
    Mix with water, stock, or milk. Add potatoes and simmer until potatoes are cooked, about 30 minutes.
    Serve, putting a piece of goat cheese and some of the meat or a fried egg on each plate. Cover with soup.
    Poor Indians make this soup with dried mutton and corn.

Aguada
Mexican Tomato Soup

Called *aguada* because it is very liquid.

> 1 lb. (500 g.) fresh noddles (or parboiled dried noodles)
> Lard
> 2 cups (500 ml.) tomato sauce (see p. 45)
> 1 qt. (1 l.) meat stock
> Suggested spices: pepper, cumin, coriander, powdered chili, basil, salt

Sauté the noodles in lard. Add tomato sauce. Let simmer a few minutes before adding the stock. Season. Cook for 4-8 minutes until noodles swell.

Mexican Vegetable Soup

Another popular Mexican dish.

> 2 lbs. (1 kg.) vegetables in season, e.g. peas, squash, broccoli, green beans
> 1 qt. (1 l.) meat stock
> 2 onions, chopped
> Oil
> 3−4 tomatoes, chopped
> Salt, pepper
> Suggested spices: bay leaf, basil, powered chili

Chop the vegetables and simmer in the stock until tender, about 15 minutes. Brown the onions in some oil, add the tomatoes and spices. Simmer 10−15 minutes to make a sauce, then add it to the soup.

Mexican Pumpkin Soup

This soup is good served hot in the winter and cool in the summer.

>   2 chopped onions
>   Lard or vegetable shortening
>   1 qt. (1 l.) chicken stock
>   Salt, mace, coriander, pepper
>   1 lb. (500 g.) cooked pumpkin puree (see p. 267)
>   ½ cup (125 ml.) cream or milk
>   4 tomatoes, peeled and chopped
>   1 bunch scallions, chopped

Brown the onions in lard or shortening. Add stock, salt, pepper, spices, and pumpkin. Simmer 10–15 minutes. Add cream or milk when the soup is mostly cooked.

Immediately before serving, mix in tomatoes and scallions. Reheat gently and serve.

Callaloo

The leaves of several varieties of tropical roots—especially taro, manioc, and malanga—are used in this popular Caribbean soup. American Indians boiled skunk cabbage, a related plant, to make a similar soup.

>   6–8 cups (1.5 l.) water or stock
>   1 onion, chopped
>   2 cloves garlic
>   ¼ lb. (125 g.) diced ham, bacon, or salt pork
>   1 lb. (500 g.) taro greens, Chinese spinach, or Swiss chard
>   ½ lb. (250 g.) okra
>   Tabasco sauce

Bring water or stock to a boil, add onion, garlic, and ham, bacon or salt pork. Simmer 5 minutes, then add greens. Simmer 10 minutes, then add okra. Simmer 10–15 minutes, strain to make a smooth puree. Return bits of pork that remain in the strainer to the soup. Add tabasco to taste and serve hot.

Indonesian Tripe Soup

Tripe is prepared in similar ways all over the world, perhaps because tripe varies less in character and taste than do people. In Indonesia the variation includes coconut milk. Parboiled tripe can be bought at many butchers.

1 lb. (500 g.) cooked tripe, cut up finely
Oil or clarified butter (see p. 32)
Suggested spices: coriander, cardamom, lemongrass
Salt, pepper
1 tsp. (5 g.) grated fresh ginger
2–3 minced leek whites
1 minced onion
1 cup (250 ml.) coconut milk (see p. 47)
Lemon

Brown the pieces of cooked tripe in oil or clarified butter. Add spices, crushed finely. Add all other ingredients except the coconut milk and lemon. Add water to cover. Simmer 15–20 minutes.

Add the coconut milk and lemon just before serving. Season well.

Mayeritsa
Innards Soup

Traditional Greek Easter soup. When the fortnight of fasting preceding the Holy Saturday is energetically broken after midnight Mass, *mayeritsa*, made from the innards of the Pascal lamb, is served, and greeted with general joy.

Liver, lungs, heart, and intestines of a lamb
Salt
Butter
1 bunch of scallions
Dill or fennel
Mint
Salt, pepper
½ cup (100 g.) rice
3 eggs
Juice of 2 lemons

Wash the innards. Cover with water and cook ½ hour. Salt. Drain, reserving the stock. Cut the meats into small pieces and brown in butter with scallions and herbs. Return to the stock. Season and simmer 1 hour, adding the rice 20 minutes before serving.

To serve, beat the eggs with lemon juice and mix gradually into the soup. Do not boil again.

Chinese Lung Soup

2 lbs. (1 kg.) veal lung
Salted boiling water
1½ lbs. (750 g.) stew vegetables, e.g. celery, turnip
1 lb. (500 g.) cabbage
Salt, pepper
2−3 tbs. (30 ml.) soy sauce

Blanch the lung in salted, boiling water for 3−4 minutes. Drain and cut into 1-inch cubes.

Cover the lungs and vegetables with water; simmer 45 minutes. Season with salt, pepper and soy sauce, and serve hot.

VARIANT   Blanch the lung, then brown in oil before adding vegetable and stock to make the soup.

Serves 6−8.

NOTE   Lungs have been withdrawn from the commercial retail meat market in the United States in recent years, under orders from the Federal government, ostensibly because they are not "wholesome" enough for human consumption—though many people both in and outside the United States have consumed these organs for hundreds of years. An Italian butcher in New York City believes the restrictive law was passed due to pressure from the American dog food industry, in order to keep down the commercial value of lungs. Until lungs are once again commercially available, the only source of them in America will be home-grown livestock.

Oxtail Soup

> 3 lbs. (1.5 kg.) cut up oxtails (or about 3 whole, skinned tails)
> Flour for dredging
> ¼ lb. (125 g.) butter
> 3 carrots
> 3−4 large onions
> 3−4 stalks celery with tops
> 1 turnip
> 5−6 cloves
> 1 tbs. (15 g.) salt
> Several whole peppercorns

Dredge tails in flour and sauté in butter until nicely browned. Chop carrots, onions, celery, and turnip and add them to the pot; cover with boiling water and throw in spices. Simmer until meat is very tender, about 3 hours. Serve right away, or lift meat from soup (remove meat from bones if whole tails were used), and strain stock from vegetables. Store vegetables and meat in refrigerator overnight; keep stock in covered container also in refrigerator. Before serving, lift fat from stock and discard; heat meat, vegetables, and stock together until boiling and serve with a sprinkling of cayenne.

Serves 6−8.

Lentil Soup

> 1 cup (250 g.) lentils
> 4 cups (1 l.) water or stock
> 1 medium onion, chopped
> 1 tsp. (5 g.) salt
> ¼ tsp. pepper

Soak lentils in water or stock overnight. The next day bring lentils and onion to a boil, add seasonings, cover, and cook slowly until tender, about 1½ hours. If you want the soup to be very smooth you can put it in a blender or through a food mill. Lentil soup is also good with the addition of bits of ham or pork.

Mock Turtle Soup

Turtle soup has been considered a delicacy in America ever since it left its Creole origins to become a fixture in the cuisine of nineteenth-century Philadelphia salons—but mock turtle soup has found its way into many a plain kitchen. Named because it is seasoned much like terrapin stew, it bears no other resemblance to a seafood dish.

2–3 lbs. (1 kg.) cooked stewing beef
1 cup (250 ml.) milk
½ cup (125 ml.) red wine
1 tbs. (15 g.) butter
1 tbs. (10 g.) flour
1 tsp. (5 g.) cloves
1 tsp. (5 g.) allspice
Salt, pepper, and cayenne to taste

Cut meat into small pieces; put in a bowl and let sit with milk and wine for ½ hour. Melt butter; stir in flour, cloves, and allspice. Thin with liquid drained from the marinating meat. Stir until smooth. Add meat to mixture, season to taste, and simmer 10 to 15 minutes. Thin the soup to your liking.
   Serves 6–8.

Oklahoma Nettle Soup

Nettles, when picked young and tender, are a wholesome and tasty green. They can be easily gathered wild in the spring and summer, and are available dried in herb and spice stores. They must be cooked to take away the sting, either steamed like spinach and served with butter, or parboiled, drained, and mixed with bits of bacon and baked *au gratin* (see p. 174). Here is an appetizing nettle soup:

1 lb. (500 g.) fresh nettles
¼ lb. (125 g.) bacon or sowbelly
3–4 cups (1 l.) water or stock

Wash the nettles. Cut up and simmer with diced bacon for 20–30 minutes. Serve hot.

VEGETABLES

Vegetable Cutlets

2 lbs. (1 kg.) vegetables, e.g. carrots, turnips, potatoes, celery
Curry spices: coriander, cumin, turmeric, clove, cinnamon,
   fenugreek
1–2 minced onions
¼ lb. (100 g.) grated almonds or coconut
2 eggs
Bread crumbs

Boil or steam vegetables. Drain and mash.

Brown minced onions and curry, grated almonds or coconut. Add vegetables. Sauté briefly. Mix in an egg to bind. Shape into balls or patties, dip in beaten egg and bread crumbs.

Fry in oil or without shortening, like *chapatis* (see p. 53). Serve crisp. If the only vegetable used is potato, add some chopped fresh mint.

Indian Stuffed Vegetables

Meat is a luxury for most in India, so vegetables that are to be stuffed, such as squash, peppers, eggplant, and tomatoes, are often stuffed with the following:

2 chopped onions
Curry spices: turmeric, clove, cumin, cayenne
2 mashed potatoes
4 tbs. (25 g.) grated coconut
1 lb. (500 g.) minced vegetables, e.g. peppers, carrots, peas

Brown the onions and curry. Add the other ingredients, mix, and simmer 5–10 minutes.

Indian Greens

Not solely a vegetable dish, as it often includes ground mutton. Made with the tender leaves of almost any vegetable, even leaves we would ordinarily throw away: radish, turnip, cauliflower, carrots, beets, squash, pumpkin.

> Ghee (see p. 31) or vegetable oil
> 1–2 minced onions
> Curry spices: cumin, cardamon, clove, turmeric, anise, fenugreek
> 2–3 cloves garlic
> 1–2 tsp. (5 g.) fresh grated ginger
> 1–2 hot fresh chiles, or cayenne
> 1 lb. (500 g.) ground lamb
> 3 lbs. (1.5 kg.) greens, shredded
> Salt, pepper

Brown the onions in the oil. Add curry, garlic, ginger, and chiles. Add the meat, cook until brown, then add greens. Add a little water. Add salt and pepper and simmer 20–30 minutes until the meat is cooked.

Indian Banana Foogath

A vegetable curry made with banana peels.

> 1 lb. (500 g.) banana peels (peels from 6–8 bananas)
> Curry spices: turmeric, fenugreek, cardamom, cloves, cumin, anise
> Ghee (see p. 31) or vegetable oil
> 1 minced onion
> 2 cloves garlic
> 2 hot fresh chiles, or cayenne

Cut up banana peels into medium-sized pieces, wash, and soak in water 1 hour.

Fry curry spices in ghee with onion, garlic, and chiles. Add drained pieces of banana peel and cook 15–20 minutes.

This can be made equally well with green bananas.

If desired, add grated coconut, tamarind paste (mix 1 tsp. paste with 1–2 tsps. water) or sliced fresh ginger.

Gado-gado
Indonesian Vegetable Salad with Peanut and Coconut Sauce

This Indonesian salad, made with a mixture of raw and cooked vegetables, varies greatly from region to region.

DRESSING:
2–3 onions, chopped
2–3 cloves garlic, crushed
Ghee (see p. 31) or vegetable oil
2–6 fresh or soaked dried chiles with seeds and stems removed, chopped or 2–5 tsp. (10 g.) powdered chiles
3 cups (750 ml.) coconut milk (see p. 47)
3 cups (500 g.) freshly crushed or ground roasted peanuts or 12 oz. (375 g.) natural peanut butter
2–4 tsp. (15 g.) grated fresh ginger
2 tbs. (30 g.) brown sugar
Salt
Juice from one lemon

SALAD:
2 large bean curd cakes (see p. 161), cut into cubes and fried in peanut oil
½ lb. (250 g.) boiled new potatoes, sliced
1 lb. (500 g.) green beans, lightly cooked
½ lb. (250 g.) carrots, sliced lengthwise and lightly cooked
2 cucumbers, partially peeled, cut in half and sliced lengthwise
1 lb. (500 g.) bean sprouts, blanched
1 Chinese cabbage, finely shredded and blanched
2 hard-boiled eggs, sliced

Prepare the dressing first by lightly sautéing the onions and garlic in the ghee or oil for a few minutes, then adding the chopped chiles. Sauté a few more minutes, mashing the chiles as well as you can. Now add the coconut milk, crushed roasted peanuts (or peanut butter), ginger, brown sugar, and salt. (You can also grind the roasted peanuts together with the coconut milk, fried onions, chiles, and other ingredients using a blender, returning the mixture to the heat only to thicken it.) Simmer, stirring, for approximately 10 minutes until the sauce is fairly thick but will still pour without difficulty. You may need to add as much as 1–1½ cups water to get the proper thickness. When the sauce is done, remove from heat, add lemon juice, and let cool to room temperature.

SALAD   Layer the salad ingredients in a large bowl (or place side by side on a platter), topping with bean sprouts, cabbage, and sliced hard-boiled eggs. Pour the sauce over the salad and serve.
Serves 8 — 10.

Vegetable Curry

Curry spices: cardamom, turmeric, fenugreek, coriander, cumin
Ghee (see p. 31) or butter
2 chopped onions
2 — 3 cloves garlic
1 — 2 tsp. (5 g.) grated fresh ginger
2 lbs. (1 kg.) diced vegetables, e.g. cauliflower, okra, celery, eggplant
½ cup (125 ml.) coconut milk (see p. 47)
1 cup (250 ml.) yoghurt or curds (see p. 29)
1 — 2 hot fresh chiles, or cayenne

Fry curry spices in *ghee* with onions, garlic, chiles, and ginger. Add blanched vegetables. Add a little water, coconut milk, and yoghurt or curds. Cover and simmer 30 minutes.

Pe t'sai
Celery Cabbage

Do not confuse *pe t'sai* with *bok choy* (Chinese chard), even though both are often sold as "Chinese cabbage" and are often interchangeable—in fact, this dish could be easily made with *bok choy.*

1 lb. (500 g.) chopped celery cabbage
Pinch of bicarbonate of soda
5 dried mushrooms, soaked at least ½ hour
1 tbs. (12 g.) cornstarch
1 cup (250 ml.) chicken stock
2 tbs. (30 ml.) milk
MSG and pepper
¼ lb. (100 g.) diced cooked ham

Blanch the cabbage by simmering 2 — 3 minutes with a pinch of bicarbonate of soda added to the water. Drain.

Drain and mince the mushrooms. Stir the cornstarch into the stock, add milk and seasonings.

Heat a little oil in the wok and pour in the liquid. Simmer sauce a few minutes to thicken before adding the cabbage and mushrooms. Cook 3 minutes. Serve sprinkled with diced ham.

Very poor Chinese rarely eat anything more than rice and cabbage or rice and soy beans.

Chinese Sweet and Sour Cabbage

1 cabbage (celery cabbage or Chinese chard), chopped
1–2 tsp. (10 g.) sliced fresh ginger
Peanut oil
1 tbs. (12 g.) cornstarch
2 tbs. (30 ml.) soy sauce
2 tbs. (30 g.) sugar
Dash of vinegar
Salt

Soak the cabbage in cold water 20 minutes. Drain. Sauté with the ginger in oil in a wok. Mix the cornstarch with the soy sauce, and add this mixture along with the other ingredients.

Finish cooking quickly as the cabbage must remain firm, as always in Chinese cooking.

Bok choy

An important Chinese variety of cabbage, bok choy has thick, crisp white stems with dark green leaves. Remove the leaves, which are good for soups, and slice the stems evenly. The slices can be steamed and served plain, with a little soy sauce, but are best in soups or stir-fried. Heat peanut oil or lard very hot in a wok then stir in finely sliced meats or vegetables. Bok choy retains its crispness well but should be added not long before cooking is done.

Mix bok choy with shredded beef, chicken or pork, scallions, Chinese mushrooms, etc., and season with soy sauce, sesame oil, garlic and ginger, as desired.

Kimchi
Korean Pickled Cabbage

> 1 lb. (500 g.) chopped Chinese cabbage and/or coarsely grated black
>   radish
> 2−3 fresh or dried hot chili peppers
> 1 clove garlic
> 1−2 tsp. (5 g.) grated fresh ginger
> 2 scallions, chopped
> 6 tbs. (90 g.) salt

Salt the cabbage heavily, add water to cover, and let soak at least 2 hours. Rinse and drain.

Chop the seasonings together and mix with the cabbage. Add the salt. Put in a glass or porcelain container and add just enough water to cover. Keep covered and marinate in a cool place for at least 3 days.

Serve with Chinese-style rice or millet porridge (see p. 84).

Kimchi can also be bought prepared in Japanese or Chinese markets.

Water Chestnuts

Water chestnuts are eaten daily in many countries, but they have passed out of most Western cooking, though they grow wild in many marshes and ponds and can be gathered on a pleasant summer outing. They are the same color as chestnuts but smaller and covered by a soft shell ending in four crossed horns. The meat also resembles that of chestnuts but is crisper. Stored under water, they can keep through the winter. Cultivating them is easy: simply throw some water chestnuts in shallow water and they will take root.

Water chestnuts can be eaten raw, boiled, or baked in coals, just like chestnuts. They must be peeled. (Once peeled, they will discolor unless placed in water to cover.)

China cultivates the plant seriously, as it is very nourishing and easy to produce. Its crisp texture, unaffected by cooking, is highly prized in many dishes. Much of the harvest comes from Chekiang, a region of very pure lakes with especially fertile bottoms. These water chestnuts are smooth, tender, and succulent, with fine skins, and rich in sugar, starch, vitamins, and minerals. They can be eaten fresh but are often dried in the open air for storage. The Chinese also use them to make sugar, vinegar, and many liqueurs.

Canned water chestnuts do not have the sweetness of fresh water chestnuts, which can be bought at many Chinese groceries.

Rumaki
Chicken Livers and Water Chestnuts

Despite the apparently Japanese name, this is originally a Chinese dish. Most of the ingredients, except for the water chestnuts which define the recipe, can be replaced by what is available.

½ lb. (250 g.) water chestnuts
1 cup (250 ml.) chicken stock
2 cups (500 ml.) soy sauce
1–2 tbs. (15 g.) sugar
Cinnamon, bay leaves
1–2 tsp. (5 g.) grated fresh ginger
2 cloves garlic
Star anise or Szechuan pepper
1 lb. (500 g.) chicken livers
1 lb. (500 g.) sliced bacon

Peel fresh water chestnuts and steam or parboil 5–10 minutes. Drain. (Canned water chestnuts need no parboiling.)

Mix the stock, soy sauce, and spices. Bring to a boil and simmer 5 minutes. Add the livers and simmer 15 minutes. Drain the livers and let cool. The marinade can be set aside and saved for future use.

Cut each water chestnut in halves or thirds. Wrap a piece of liver and water chestnut in a strip of bacon and tie with thread.

Put a tiny bit of oil in a frying pan, and fry the *rumaki* so that the bacon is crisp. Drain and serve hot.

Water Chestnuts with Giblets

A common dish in southern China.

> ¾ lb. (350 g.) fresh (or handful dried) water chestnuts
> 3 cups (750 ml.) water
> 1 lb. (500 g.) chicken giblets
> 2 tbs. (30 ml.) soy sauce
> 1–2 tsp. (8 g.) sugar

Canned water chestnuts should not be used in this recipe.

Pare and slice the water chestnuts. Simmer them gently in the water along with the giblets 10–15 minutes. Add soy sauce and sugar.

If desired, add some chopped onions or scallions and fresh ginger when serving.

Chinese Meat Roll

> DOUGH:
> 2 cups (250 g.) flour
> ¼ lb. (125 g.) lard or shortening
> 1 egg

> STUFFING:
> ½ lb. (250 g.) minced pork
> ¼ lb. (125 g.) flaked crab meat or minced shrimp
> ½ lb. (250 g.) cooked water chestnuts, chopped
> 1 bunch scallions, minced
> 2 tbs. (30 ml.) soy sauce
> Salt
> 2 pinches powdered ginger
> 2–3 cloves garlic, minced
> 1 egg
> Bread crumbs

DOUGH   Knead the flour, lard, and egg together to make a supple dough. Add a little water if necessary.

STUFFING   Sauté the pork briefly in a wok or skillet. (The wok makes it possible to cook with very little grease or water, which accounts for the crispness of Chinese cooking.) Add the other ingredients, except the dough. Let cool.

Roll the dough and divide into 4 rectangles. Lay some of the stuffing on each piece of dough and roll up into long cylinders. Seal the edges and lay out on a cookie tin. Bake ½ hour at 350°F (175°C) Cut in slices and serve.

Good cold as well as hot.

Dried Vegetables

In China, especially in the north where the severe winter prevents year-round cultivation of any vegetables, the need to preserve vegetables has led to the development of strange techniques. For instance, vegetables gathered at the onset of winter are piled in the courtyard and covered with earth. The pile is drenched with water, which quickly freezes. The vegetables thus stored will keep fresh until spring. When a cook needs a cabbage, a well-aimed pick can knock one out, protected by a shell of dirt and ice. This method, which works well for green vegetables, is varied for roots, which are buried 15 feet deep and dug up when needed.

A more useful technique for modern kitchens is drying vegetables; until recently it was one of the talents expected of a Chinese girl aspiring to marriage.

Vegetables sliced delicately, washed and salted, are strung on cotton thread and set to dry in the sun for a day. The needle used for stringing is always bamboo, and the method is used mainly in the south.

Dried Chinese vegetables are commonly available in oriental markets and can be used to substitute for fresh vegetables in soups and some other dishes, though the flavor is often quite different. Dried water chestnuts and dried bitter melon strips are particularly recommended.

Daikon
Oriental Radish

A long, thick white radish, often weighing 2 or 3 pounds, *daikon* is one of the most commonly used vegetables in China and Japan.

> 1 small daikon
> 2–3 tbs. (30 g.) sesame seeds
> 1–2 tbs. (15 ml.) soy sauce
> 1 tbs. (15 ml.) vinegar

Scrub the *daikon* and grate or slice finely. Toast the sesame seeds in a dry pan. Mix the ingredients together and serve.

If desired, replace sesame seeds with 1–2 tbs. sesame oil.

Daikon can also be sliced and stir-fried with shredded chicken or bean curd, like water chestnuts or *bok choy* (see p. 153).

Sautéed Pancake Strips and Vegetables

> 1 cup (125 g.) flour
> Salt
> Approximately 1 cup (250 ml.) water
> 2 lbs. (1 kg.) fresh vegetables, e.g. broccoli, onions, peas, snow peas, cabbage
> Peanut oil
> 2–3 tbs. (30 ml.) soy sauce
> Fresh coriander, watercress, parsley, sesame oil, hot peppers

Make a batter from the flour, salt, and water and cook as pancakes. Roll and cool, then slice into ribbons. In a wok or skillet, sauté the mixed vegetables quickly in a very little peanut oil. Add the pancake ribbons. Season with soy sauce, sesame oil, spices, and herbs.

Soy

This common Asian bean is practically unknown in Europe and until recently was known in America only as a health or exotic food and a commodity future, although Americans have awakened to the value of soy beans as a substitute for meat.

The daily food of the Chinese peasant, soy balances an otherwise protein- and vitamin-deficient diet. Soy lends itself for use in many recipes in many different forms, from flour to bean curd. Its hardiness as a plant is no small advantage: it is not attacked by insects and grows even in arid lands. Cultivated in China for at least 6,000 years, it did not reach Japan until the sixth century A.D. Europe never heard the name until the seventeenth century. Now, although the human consumption of soy products is relatively low there, the United States is the leading producer of soy beans in the world.

There are many varieties of soy beans: yellow and red for salads, black—almost sweet—for soups, green for soups too. Sprouted soy beans, if less economical, are prized as green vegetables. Ground to a fine flour in the family mill, soy can be kneaded into noodles that keep through the winter. The simplest use of the flour is to boil it into porridge, often all there is to eat through lean periods. Serve soy porridge with bowls of hot water, without even a tea leaf for flavor, and hunger and thirst are officially relieved. Northern Chinese peasants make two kinds of "butter," called *chiang*, from soy—one red, one black. Bean curd, bought from a grocer when means permit though it is also prepared at home, has a firm, smooth texture and can be fried or boiled in soups for simple meals or used in more elaborate recipes.

Although similar to other beans in appearance, soy's composition is different. Its proteins have the same balance of nutrients as animal proteins. Soy is also very digestible, due to low starch content and the presence in its oil of enzymes that break down proteins, sugars, and fats.

Soy flour can be used anywhere in place of wheat flour; for instance, in soy noodles. It also is used to make *shoyu* (soy sauce) and *miso. Shoyu* is a brown liquid obtained by the fermentation of soy mash mixed with barley and sea salt. The fermentation proceeds for 2 years before the mash is pressed to yield *shoyu*, the oriental seasoning *par excellence*.

Soy sauce is used carefully in soups and sauces, generally when the cooking is almost done.

Soy Salad

    1 cup (250 g.) soy beans
    2 cups (500 ml.) water
    1–2 tbs. (15 ml.) soy sauce
    2 tbs. (30 ml.) oil
    2 tbs. (30 ml.) vinegar
    1½ lbs. (700 g.) diced or sliced fresh vegetables, e.g. cucumber,
       radish, cabbage

Bring soy beans and water to a boil. Cover and simmer 30–40 minutes. The beans will keep their texture no matter how long you cook them. Drain. Season the beans with soy sauce, oil, and vinegar. Mix in the vegetables.

Soup with Soy

    2 onions
    2 lbs. (1 kg.) celery, cabbage, carrot, *bok choy* (see p. 153)
    Oil
    1 qt. (1 l.) water or stock
    2 tbs. (25 g.) soy flour
    1–2 tbs. (30 ml.) soy sauce
    3–4 tomatoes, diced

Chop coarsely onions and vegetables, then brown in oil. Add water or stock. Simmer 5–10 minutes. Thicken with soy flour, previously mixed with a little cold water. Simmer 5 minutes. Add soy sauce. Serve with diced tomatoes.

Soy Milk

Thirty percent sugars, thirty-five per cent proteins and fourteen percent fat, soy beans can be made into a wonderfully rich vegetable milk, which can be used by itself or further processed to make bean curd.

    1 cup (250 g.) soy beans
    6 cups (1.5 l.) water

Soak the soy beans at least 10 hours. Puree in a food mill or blender and return to the water in which they soaked. Let the pureed soy soak for 24 hours, then squeeze out the milk by pressing through a cotton sack. Or boil the mixture gently for 5–10 minutes, squeeze out the milk in a cotton sack, return the remaining pulp to heat with a little more water, boil and press again, then mix the two filtrations. The milk has a fine aroma of malt and resembles condensed milk in texture. 3.13 percent vegetable casein, 9.81 percent fat, soy milk can be used to enrich soups and sauces, and in place of milk in baked goods.

The dry pulp left over, known as okara, can be used like bran in baked goods.

Tofu
Soy Bean Curd

> 2 cups (500 g.) soy beans
> 10 cups (2.5 l.) water
> Curdling agent: 1¼ tsp. (6 g.) nigari (Japanese sea salt)
>   or 2½ tbs. (35 ml.) lemon or lime juice
>   or 1¼ tsp. (6 g.) epsom salts

Soak beans. Mill, boil, and press to make soy milk (see above). Boil the soy milk over a medium heat for 5—7 minutes. Mix curdling agent in a cup of water. Stir one-third of the curdling solution thoroughly into the soy milk. Sprinkle another one-third of the solution over the surface and let sit 3 minutes. Sprinkle the last third of the solution over the soy milk and stir gently, barely dipping the stirrer below the surface. Wait 4–6 minutes, then again stir gently on the surface for 20–30 seconds. Try to avoid breaking up the curds.

The curds should by now be suspended in almost clear whey. Gently ladle curds, breaking them up as little as possible, into a fine strainer lined with cheesecloth and dampened with whey. Fold the cloth over the curds and cover with a fitted lid that can sit directly on the curds. Put a weight on the lid and let drain. After 10–15 minutes, there should be no more whey dripping.

Carefully lift the curds in the cheesecloth out of the strainer and place in a bowl of cold water. Remove the cheesecloth.

Keep bean curd cool under water until you are ready to use it.

The whole operation takes less than an hour if you have the utensils at hand.

Bean Curd with Mushrooms

½ lb. (400 g.) mushrooms
Peanut oil
1 large bean curd pad
2 tbs. (30 ml.) soy sauce
Salt
1 tbs. (12 g.) cornstarch

Sauté mushrooms in peanut oil. Add fine slices of bean curd, soy sauce, and salt. Sauté 2 minutes more, then thicken with cornstarch previously mixed with a little cold water. If desired, add sesame oil, grated fresh ginger or scallions for taste.
  Serves 2.

Fried Bean Curd

1 lb. (500 g.) bean curd
½ cup (60 g.) flour
1 egg
1/3 cup (100 ml.) milk or beer
Peanut oil

Cut bean curd into cubes or slices. Mix flour, egg, and milk to make a thick frying batter. If desired, separate the egg first and beat the white before mixing into the batter. Dip the bean curd in the batter and deep fry in peanut oil. Serve with sautéed onion rings and shrimp.

Sautéed Bean Curd

1 large bean curd pad
Peanut oil
2 tbs. (30 ml.) soy sauce
1 tbs. (12 g.) cornstarch
2 cloves garlic
2 shallots

Cut the bean curd into ½ inch cubes. Sauté quickly in a little peanut oil in a wok or skillet, stirring constantly. Add soy sauce, cornstarch (mixed first with a little water), minced garlic, and shallots. Salt, serve.

Hiya Yakko
Japanese Bean Curd with Shrimp

1 handful dried shrimp or tuna
1 large bean curd pad
1 small onion, chopped
1 tbs. (15 ml.) soy sauce
1 pinch MSG
Optional: fresh ginger

Soak the shrimp or tuna in a little warm water 15 minutes. Cut the bean curd in thick slices and lay out on a serving plate. Cover with shrimp and raw onion. Sprinkle with soy sauce and MSG. Add grated fresh ginger if desired.

Serve cool, as is.

Soup with Bean Curd and Water Chestnuts

½ lb. (250 g.) water chestnuts
1 qt. (1 l.) stock
½ lb. (250 g.) finely minced pork
½ lb. (250 g.) chopped celery cabbage
1 lb. (500 g.) bean curd, cut into ½ inch cubes
2 tbs. (30 ml.) soy sauce

Pare and slice the water chestnuts. Heat the stock. Add pork. Simmer 3 minutes before adding cabbage, water chestnuts, and bean curd. Simmer 5 minutes more, add soy sauce, and serve.

Sautéed Soy Beans

2 cups (500 g.) soy beans
½ lb. (250 g.) pork or fish
1 tbs. (15 ml.) oil
1 minced leek
1–2 tsp. (10 g.) grated or sliced fresh ginger
2 tbs. (30 ml.) dry white wine or dry sherry
3 tbs. (45 ml.) soy sauce
1 tbs. (15 g.) sugar

Soak soy beans 2 hours. Drain.

Sauté ½ inch cubes of pork or slices of fish in 1 tbs. oil. Add leek, ginger, wine, soy sauce, and sugar. Mix in the beans and cover tightly. Simmer gently ½ hour.

Serve hot or cold. Soy beans remain firm no matter how long they are cooked, unlike ordinary beans.

Ful medames
Arab Beans

This is the staple of the *fellahin*, the Arab peasants, who buy it from the local grocer—the man who supplies the poor on shaky credit in many lands. For a few cents an Egyptian, like a Mexican or an Indian, can buy beans to match his purse and fill his belly.

Ful is eaten with flat, braided Egyptian bread.

2 cups (500 g.) dry red beans
¾ cup (200 g.) red lentils
8 cups (2 l.) water
Salt
2/3 cup (160 ml.) olive oil
Juice of 2 lemons

Put beans and lentils into an earthen or copper pot. Add water. If not soaked first, the beans should take 3–5 hours to cook. If the beans are soaked overnight, you need cook them only 2–2½ hours. Make sure to keep the water level up. Avoid lifting the pot cover often or the beans will blacken.

When cooked, salt and sprinkle with olive oil and lemon juice.

Serve with hard-boiled eggs, onions or fresh herbs, such as mint, parsley or coriander.

Ta'amia
Bean Croquettes

These Arab croquettes are very good with aperitifs.

> 1 cup (250 g.) dried beans
> Chopped fresh parsley
> 1 cup (150 g.) moistened bread crumbs
> Salt
> Coriander
> 2 chopped onions
> Pinch of bicarbonate of soda
> Oil
> 1–2 cloves garlic
> Optional: ½ cup chopped almonds or walnuts

Soak the beans overnight. Drain. Put through a food grinder and mash together with the other ingredients (except oil) in a mortar and pestle. Let sit about 2 hours. Shape into croquettes and fry in oil.

If desired, grind in ½ cup chopped almonds or walnuts.

Ethiopian Wot
Bean Stew

This very spicy concoction complements *indjera* (see p. 62), wide gray pancakes made from millet flour. *Wot* is cooked in a clay pot over a fire of dried cow dung. It is served to a circle of gathered guests, who convivially dip *indjera* in the common pot to soak up the sauce. The Ethiopians wash it down with gulps of *talla*, a tart barley beer. Women eat after the men have finished. The meal is rounded off with some dental hygiene—chewing on a twig—then some spiced coffee sweetened with honey.

> 2 chopped onions
> Butter
> 1 cup (250 g.) dried beans, soaked overnight, or 2 cups (500 g.) fresh
>   beans in season
> Cayenne
> Salt

Brown onions in butter. Add beans and lots of cayenne. This dish should be hot. Add water to cover and simmer 1½–2 hours. Salt.

On flush days, add a chicken or pieces of lamb or beef to stew with the beans. Otherwise, serve with hard-boiled eggs.

Boston Baked Beans

The New England classic.

> 2 cups (500 g.) small white (pea) beans, washed and soaked over-
> night in water 3 to 4 times their volume
> 1 small onion
> 1 clove garlic
> ½ cup (125 ml.) molasses
> ¼ cup (60 ml.) beer or bean water
> 1 tbs. (5 g.) dry mustard
> ¼ cup (60 ml.) catsup
> 1 tbs (5 g.) salt

Stir together all ingredients except the beans and allow to sit. Cook beans in soaking water until tender, about 1 hour. Drain beans, reserving liquid. Stir sauce and drained beans and turn into a well-greased baking dish (or bean pot). Bake covered for 8-10 hours at 250°F (120°C). Stir once an hour for the first 3 hours; add reserved liquid as needed to keep them from drying out. Remove cover for the last ½ hour of cooking.

Bruna bonor
Brown Beans

These Swedish brown beans are special to that country but can be replaced by dried fava beans or large dried yellow peas.

> 1 lb. (500 g.) brown beans
> 1 qt. (1 l.) water
> Bay leaf, mace
> 1/3 cup (170 ml.) molasses or honey
> 1/3 cup (170 ml.) vinegar

Soak the beans overnight. Drain. Add the water and cook with bay leaf and mace for 1 hour. Add molasses and vinegar. Let simmer another ½–1 hour. Keep an eye on the water level. Serve with meatballs.

Cassoulet

This simple French bean stew is best known in the following version from Toulouse, but there are many regional variations. Cassoulet owes its name to a kind of clay pot once used to cook the stew slowly through the day as it sat near the warm hearth. The dish is still best prepared in an earthenware dish in a low oven.

> 1 lb. (500 g.) dried white beans (great northern or navy beans)
> 1½ qts. (1.5 l.) cold water
> Bay leaves, sage, rosemary, parsley
> 1 onion stuck with 3 or 4 cloves
> 1–1½ lbs. (600 g.) chopped bacon, rind, ham and salt pork, mixed
> 3–4 lbs. (1.5 kg.) lamb, whole or cut up coarsely
> 1 lb. (500 g.) smoked garlic sausage, such as *cervelas*
> 1 cup (80 g.) bread crumbs

Pick over the beans carefully and rinse twice. Add 1½ qts. cold water. Soak overnight or bring to a boil, remove from heat and let soak for 40 minutes. Drain.

Tie the herbs and spices up in a piece of cheesecloth and put into a large clay pot with the beans, the onion, the pork and enough water to cover the beans by at least ½ inch. Bring to a boil slowly and simmer for 1 hour. Be sure to use very low heat or an asbestos pad to prevent cracking. During that hour cook the lamb partially by baking at 200°F (95°C).

Drain the beans, reserving the liquid. Discard herbs and onion. Return about 1/3 of the beans to the pot, cover with a layer of sliced sausage, then a layer of beans, then the lamb, then the rest of the beans. Cover with a thin layer of bread crumbs and sprinkle with about half the liquid. Bake in a low oven (250°F or 120°C) for 1 hour, checking to be sure the beans do not dry out. The bread crumbs should brown.

Stir the mixture, top with another layer of bread crumbs, then add the rest of the liquid. Add water or stock if the beans are too dry. Let cook another hour until the bread crumbs brown and form a crust.

Serve in earthenware bowls.

Serves 6–8.

Feijoada
Brazilian Black Bean Feast

Feijoada is the Brazilian national dish, made with black beans and as many different kinds of meat as possible. The various parts of the pig—ears, snout, knuckles, trotters, tongue, jowls, organs, and rind—usually relegated to sausages in this country—in addition to the more familiar fatback and salt pork, are particularly important in giving a fine richness to the black beans. It is curious to note that Brazil's "economic miracle," its fast industrial growth and entry into the world market, included neglect of its black bean crop in favor of dramatic increases in export cash crops such as soy beans and coffee. As a result this popular staple has had to be rationed.

    2−3 lbs. (1 kg.) salt pork, ears, tail, skin, knuckles, snout, etc.
    2 lbs. (1 kg.) black beans
    1 large fresh or smoked beef tongue, or a large joint of meat such as
        lamb shoulder
    Bay leaves, mace
    2−3 onions
    1 lb. (500 g.) tomatoes
    2−3 cloves garlic
    Parsley
    Oranges
    ½ lb. (250 g.) bacon
    1 lb. (500 g.) *linguiça* (Brazilian sausage), *chorizo* or other sharp,
        smoked sausage

Soak the pork in cold water overnight, rinse, and drain.

Pick over the beans carefully—there are often stones among the beans even when they come in a plastic package. Rinse twice and let soak in 3 qts. water overnight. Or rinse twice, cover with cold water, bring to a boil, remove from heat and let sit 40−60 minutes. Drain.

Put drained beans, bacon, sausage, pork, and tongue in a big kettle. Add fresh water to cover. Add bay leaves and mace. Bring to a boil and simmer gently for 2 hours. If using a salted or pickled tongue, soak several hours, rinse, and drain before cooking. Also, if the tongue is over 5 pounds, simmer it 30−60 minutes before adding the beans and pork.

Sauté the chopped onions, tomatoes, garlic, and parsley in fat skimmed from the beans or in butter. Add a ladle or two of the cooked beans from the pot, sauté and mash to make a thick, smooth sauce. Use a blender, if desired.

Remove the tongue or joint from the pot. Mix the sauce in with the beans. Salt to taste. Skin the tongue and slice, or carve the joint. Serve on a platter alongside bowls of beans, rice, *farofa* (see below), and sliced oranges. If desired, take unwanted pieces of pork out of the beans before serving.

Serves 8–10.

Farofa
Manioc Garnish

Served with *feijoada*. The *mandioca* meal is available at Latin markets.

> 1 cup (150 g.) manioc (*mandioca*) meal
> 2–3 tbs. (30 g.) fat or butter

Brown the *mandioca* meal in the hot fat. It should be crisp. Sprinkle over the *feijoada*.

Frijoles
Mexican Beans

A Mexican favorite, also called refried beans.

> 1 lb. (500 g.) black beans, soaked
> 2–3 hot dried or fresh chiles, or 1 tsp. (5 g.) chili powder
> ¼ lb. (100 g.) diced ham
> Lard
> 2–3 minced onions
> 2–3 sliced sweet peppers
> 2–3 cloves garlic
> Salt, pepper

Cook the beans 1½ hours in the water they soaked in. Drain, saving the water. Remove seeds and stems from chiles. If using dried chilis, soak 20–30 minutes in warm water. Drain, saving liquid to add to the beans. Chop.

Sauté the ham in lard. Add onions, chiles, sweet peppers and garlic and sauté a few minutes longer.

Add beans, garlic and other seasoning. Cook, stirring and mashing, occasionally adding a little of the water saved from cooking the beans so that the sauce is a smooth cream.

Serve piping hot. Like tortillas, this is often a complete meal.

Dhal

1½ cups (375 g.) *moong dhal* (small yellow grains similar to split peas), or other *dhal* (see pgs. 55, 285)
4 cups (1 l.) water
2 cloves garlic, chopped
3–5 whole cardamoms
1 tbs. (15 g.) cumin seeds
Ghee (see p. 31) or oil
1 lime
Salt

Bring *dhal* and water to a boil, salt, cover and simmer 1 hour. The result should be a moist but thick porridge.

Fry garlic, cardamoms, and cumin 5 minutes in ghee. If you prefer not to have whole spices in this dish, grind them in a mortar and pestle before frying. Mix with the *dhal*. Sprinkle with the juice of the lime and serve with rice.

VARIANT Boil the *dhal* with whole cardamoms and cumin for 1 hour. Mix with lime juice and serve with rice.

Creole Lentils

3 cups (700 g.) lentils, soaked
3 sliced sweet peppers
3 minced onions
1 lb. (500 g.) tomatoes, chopped
Salt, pepper, sugar

Cook the lentils 30 minutes. Drain.

Brown onions and peppers, add the tomatoes. Season and add lentils. Simmer ½ hour or so.

Serve with rice.

Mexican Lentils

Also commonly made with black beans.

>   1 cup (250 g.) lentils
>   1 cup (250 ml.) tomato sauce (see p. 45) with chiles and *epazote* (see
>   p. 32)
>   2 minced onions
>   2 minced sweet potatoes

Simmer lentils in water 30 minutes. Drain. Add to thick, highly seasoned
tomato sauce and simmer 5–10 minutes.

Brown onions and sweet potatoes (called *camotes* in Mexico, often
available as *batatas*). Add to the lentils, simmer gently another few minutes, and serve.

Serves 2–3.

Black-eyed Peas

A standard vegetable from the American Deep South, black-eyed peas are
usually bought dried, and prepared like other dried legumes. Cooking time
is greatly reduced if they are soaked overnight before cooking.

>   1 cup (250 g.) black-eyed peas
>   3 cups (750 ml.) water
>   ½ lb. (250 g.) salt pork or 3 strips bacon
>   1 large onion
>   Salt, pepper, basil to taste

Soak black-eyed peas overnight, then bring to a boil in the soaking water,
reducing heat to simmer. Cook until tender, about 2 hours. Add onion and
salt pork at beginning of cooking time; season at the end.

Hoppin' John

This black-eyed pea and rice meal is traditionally served in the American South on New Year's Eve as assurance of good luck for the coming year. Southern food at its finest, Hoppin' John is especially good with stewed greens and corn bread.

1 cup (250 g.) dried black-eyed peas, soaked overnight
1 cup (250 g.) rice
4 cups (1 l.) water or stock
¼ lb. (125 g.) bacon or salt pork
1 large onion, chopped
¼ tsp. cayenne
Salt and pepper to taste

Combine black-eyed peas and rice in saucepan with water; bring to a boil, reduce heat, and simmer, covered, for ½ hour. Meanwhile, fry together bacon or salt pork with onion until onion is soft. Add to beans and rice and simmer for another hour, or until beans are tender. Remove from heat, add cayenne, and salt and pepper, to taste.

Green Tomatoes

Tomatoes are good to eat some time before they start to redden on the bush. Garden-grown tomatoes are delicious early in the season, and at the end of the season when the approach of the first frost prevents vine-ripening. The red tomatoes available in supermarkets are often less ripe despite their red color.

Green tomatoes have been staples in American cooking for centuries. They are used in pickles or relishes, or even pies, fried plain or in batter or barbecued. A simple sautéing sometimes brings out the best flavor: Wash and slice tomatoes. Sauté in oil with fresh basil, salt, and pepper. Mix with other common garden vegetables (also sautéed) that generally ripen at the same time the tomatoes are swelling.

VARIANT   Salt, pepper, and sugar the thickly-sliced tomatoes. Dip in batter made with egg, water, and cornmeal; then fry in butter or bacon drippings until golden brown.

Stewed Greens and Pot Likker

Greens are the most common element of all "soul food"—the typical food of black (or white) Americans from the rural South. They can be collard greens, mustard greens, turnip or beet tops, kale, dandelion, cress, or pokeweed, but they are all cooked in about the same manner. If meat is added to the dish, it can be served as the main course; if meat isn't added, try to put in a little bacon fat or salt pork for flavor.

3 lbs. (1.5 kg.) fresh greens
1 lb. (500 g.) ham or ½ lb. (250 g.) salt pork or bacon
6–8 cups (1.5 l.) water
¼ tsp. red pepper
Salt and black pepper to taste

Wash and drain greens; if they are old, place them in ice water to help draw away the bitterness. Chop coarsely. Chop meat into small chunks and cook in water for about an hour. Add greens, season and simmer another 30 minutes. Drain greens and ham, spoon over corn bread or potatoes, and spoon the cooking juice—pot likker—over all.

Creole Okra

1 medium onion, chopped
1 bell pepper, chopped
1 clove garlic, minced
2 tbs. (30 ml.) oil
4 cups (800 g.) okra
3 ripe tomatoes, finely chopped

Wash okra and trim ends. Drain. Sauté onion, pepper, and garlic in oil until tender, about ten minutes. Add tomatoes and okra, season to taste, and simmer slowly for ½ hour.

Baked Lettuce

Any of the soft lettuces with a strong taste—such as chicory, escarole, or endive—is good cooked as well as in salads. Iceberg lettuce, grown for its crispness, does not have enough taste to be used in cooking. Chicory, escarole, and endive (not to be mistaken for the expensive Belgian endive) can be washed and steamed for 5−10 minutes and served like spinach with lemon or butter.

A popular French way to serve wilted lettuce, and for that matter any greens (turnip, carrot, beet, nettles), is *au gratin*, that is, baked until it has a crust.

> 1 head escarole, endive, or chicory
> 1 thick slice bacon, chopped
> Optional: thyme and pepper

Wash the lettuce and discard the core. Parboil in salted water for 2−3 minutes to reduce the bitterness and drain. Dry thoroughly. Chop and mix with chopped bacon (and if desired some thyme and pepper) and put in a baking dish. Bake at 375°F (190°C) for 30−40 minutes until crisp on top. Serve hot.

If desired, sprinkle grated hard cheese, such as Gruyère, over the lettuce before baking.

Antilles Corn

> 6 ears fresh corn
> 2 minced onions
> 2 sliced peppers
> 1 cup (250 ml.) thick tomato sauce (see p. 45)
> Salt, pepper
> Suggested spices: cayenne, cumin
> Bread crumbs, grated cheese

Cut the grains of corn from the cob.

Brown onions and peppers. Add tomato sauce and seasoning. Simmer 2−3 minutes before adding the corn. Cover and simmer 5−8 minutes until tender.

Pour into a baking tin, sprinkle with bread crumbs and grated cheese. Bake 20 minutes at 350°F (175°C).

Succotash

This fresh corn and bean stew, adapted by American colonists from the American Indian dish *m'sick-quotash,* has innumerable "authentic" versions, not the least interesting of which is a Pennsylvania Dutch variant which adds potatoes and tomatoes.

> 4–5 rashers bacon, minced
> 2 onions, chopped
> 1 green pepper, cut into strips
> 2 cups (400 g.) cut corn
> 2 cups (400 g.) lima beans
> ¼ cup (65 ml.) water
> 1 tbs. chopped parsley
> 1 tbs. (15 g.) butter
> Salt, pepper

Render the bacon over medium heat, add onions and pepper, and sauté until onions are golden. Add corn, lima beans, and water; cover and simmer until vegetables are tender. Mix in finely chopped parsley, butter, pepper (be liberal with the pepper), and salt, and adjust seasoning to taste. Serve.

Turkish Carrots

> 1½ lbs. (750 g.) carrots
> 1 egg, beaten
> 1 cup (90 g.) bread crumbs
> Oil
> 1 cup (250 ml.) yoghurt
> 1–2 cloves crushed garlic
> Crumpled fresh mint to taste
> Salt

Cook the carrots in water 10–15 minutes. Do not overcook, as the carrots should be firm. Drain. Dip in egg, then breadcrumbs. Fry in oil.

Beat the yoghurt mix with the garlic, salt, and mint. Pour over the hot carrots and serve. Also good cold.

Central European Potatoes

Potatoes are central Europe's standard fare, and are used there in innumerable recipes, though simple boiled potatoes are still favorites from the Atlantic to the Urals, whether served plain, with soup or with sour cream.

For variety, potatoes are often made into dumplings or *gnocchi*, and poached. Recipes of that type are numerous, from *knödels* to *kluskis*. Stuffed dumplings akin to *pieroshki* and ravioli can be found in the meat chapter of this book—they are really ways to stretch a little meat to feed a lot of people.

Potato Dumplings

1—2 eggs
1 lb. (500 g.) cooked, mashed potatoes
1/3 cup (50 g.) flour
If desired, 6—8 tbs. (100 g.) butter or chicken fat

Beat eggs. Mix ingredients together to make a thick paste. Cool for 1 hour to solidify. Shape into balls and poach gently in lightly salted water 5—10 minutes. They should expand and float.

Serve in soup or with cream.

Potato Kugel
Potato Pudding

6—8 potatoes
3 carrots
2—3 onions, chopped
3—4 eggs, beaten
Salt, pepper
Oil

Grate the potatoes and carrots coarsely. Mix with the beaten eggs and onions; add salt and pepper. Put in a generously oiled pan and bake 1 hour at 350°F (175°C).

Serves 6—8.

Hutspot
Dutch Potatoes and Carrots

Eaten every October 3 in Leyden in honor of the raising of a year-long siege by the Spanish in 1573. The starving Dutch broke the siege so suddenly that the Spanish left their dinners cooking behind them. This may have been the first time the Dutch saw potatoes, only recently brought to Europe from Peru.

1½ lbs. (700 g.) potatoes
2 – 3 carrots
2 – 3 onions
2 – 3 cloves
Salt, pepper

Peel potatoes, carrots, and onions. Cover with water along with the cloves, salt, and pepper and boil for 30 minutes. Drain and mash. Serve with boiled beef (see p. 234).

Stimpstamp
Potatoes and Escarole

A Dutch treat.

1½ lbs. (700 g.) potatoes
1 lb. (500 g.) escarole (or spinach)
Vinegar, salt
¼ lb. (125 g.) bacon

Peel and boil potatoes. Shred escarole and mash with the hot potatoes. Add vinegar and salt for taste. Fry then chop the sliced bacon. Add the bacon and its grease to the potatoes.

Serve with Polish sausage.

Bubble and Squeek (Champ)
Refried Potatoes

Champ, known in Yorkshire as "bubble and squeek" on account of the sounds of boiling and frying, is leftover mashed potatoes fried with some leftover green vegetable, usually cabbage or brussels sprouts. Stir the cold vegetables together with the potatoes and fry them lightly in butter, stirring occasionally. They should be moist and hot but not particularly crisp on the bottom. Scoop the bubble and squeek onto plates, making a depression in the center for 1 tbs. butter.

Stuffed Cabbage

Throughout much of Eastern Europe Jews and Christians shared villages and a taste for stuffed cabbage. The Christians made theirs with pork an a spicy meat gravy. The Jews made theirs with beef and a sweet and sour sauce. This is a Jewish recipe:

>1 large head of green cabbage
>1 onion, chopped
>1 lb. (500 g.) ground beef (or lamb)
>½ cup (125 g.) rice
>1 carrot, grated
>¼ cup (40 g.) raisins
>Salt, pepper
>1–2 cups (250 ml.) tomato sauce (see p. 45)
>1/3 cup (80 ml.) honey or brown sugar
>Juice of 2 lemons or ¼ cup (60 ml.) vinegar

Simmer the cabbage in salted water for 10–15 minutes. Remove from water and carefully peel outer leaves. Repeat, simmering 5–10 minutes more and removing another few layers of leaves. Cut away any tough rib that will make it difficult to roll leaves.

Brown the onion in oil, mix in meat, rice, carrot, and some of the raisins. Let cook 2–3 minutes. Add salt and pepper. Put one or two spoonfuls of meat on each leaf, fold the edges over the stuffing, and roll closed. Set in a casserole with the seam down.

Mix tomato sauce with honey, lemon juice, and the rest of the raisins. Pour over the stuffed cabbage. Cover and bake 40–50 minutes at 350°F (175°C).

Serve hot.

Parsnip, Turnip, and Rutabaga

These are all good winter vegetables.

Turnips have a fine white flesh and a slightly sharp flavor. They can be peeled, cut up like potatoes, and steamed until tender (10–15 minutes), or baked whole in their skins (30 minutes to 1 hour, according to size), and served plain or with butter. Use in stews as well, or raw in salads.

Rutabagas resemble turnips and are, in fact, often sold as yellow turnips, but they are larger and have a short neck with leaf scars. The yellow flesh is a bit more mealy than turnip, and the taste is coarser. Peel, cut up and boil or steam (15–20 minutes), and serve with butter or gravy like potatoes. Rutabagas, boiled with chopped bacon and pureed, make a tasty, nourishing soup, one of the staples of French country people. They are also good added to stews in the last 20–30 minutes of cooking.

The parsnip, a relative of the carrot, is a long, tapering white root with crisp flesh. Its taste is stronger and sweeter than turnip. Storage at near freezing temperatures improves the taste. Parsnip has a strong influence in stews and a lot of character raw in salads. Or steam 10–15 minutes and serve with lemon or butter.

All these "northern" roots get mushy if overcooked. The greens are also edible, especially when young and tender.

Salsify (Oyster Plant)

Salsify, also known as oyster plant because it tastes something like oysters, is a long, tapering white or black root that can be used like potato. Because of its stronger taste, it is considered something of a delicacy on ordinary tables in Europe. This is a popular Italian recipe.

    2 lbs. (1 kg.) salsify
    2 ozs. (60 g.) canned anchovies (1 small can)
    2–3 tbs. (30 g.) butter or olive oil

Scrape and trim roots. Parboil in lightly salted water for 5 minutes. Cut into thick slices and spread out in a baking pan.

Melt and mash the anchovies in butter or olive oil over a low heat. Pour the sauce over the salsify and bake for 30–40 minutes at 350°F (175°C). Serve hot.

Celeriac

The knobby root of a scraggly variety of celery, celeriac has a stronger but perhaps more complex taste and a denser texture. It can be peeled and grated coarsely or sliced finely to be served raw as a salad with some lemon juice or mayonnaise. Or, scrub it, cover it with salted water and boil gently, whole, for 20–30 minutes. Drain, peel, and cut up. Serve hot with butter or lemon.

It is a good substitute for celery in stews and salads.

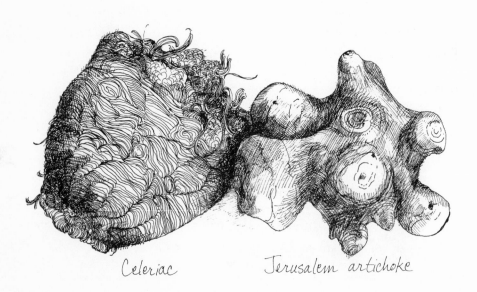

Celeriac   Jerusalem artichoke

Jerusalem Artichokes

The Jerusalem artichoke is the root of a common sunflower. Once a staple of the American Indians, it resembles a ginger root in appearance and has a fine delicate taste like artichoke. Although available in some markets here, it is not as popular as it is in France and Italy, where it is prized as a poor man's delicacy.

Peel and grate for a salad. Or, scrub and boil for 15 minutes and serve like celeriac (see above). Like celeriac, it gets mushy if overcooked, so check frequently while cooking to see if it is getting tender.
A popular way to prepare it is *au gratin*.

1 lb. (500 g.) Jerusalem artichokes
1−2 tbs. (30 g.) butter
Grated Parmesan or other hard cheese

Scrub the roots and put into lightly boiling salted water. Simmer 5−10 minutes until they begin to get tender. Drain and slice evenly. Lay out in a baking dish. Dot with butter and sprinkle with cheese. Bake 30−40 minutes at 375°F (190°C) until a crust forms. Serve hot.

Spinach with Sesame

A Japanese dish.

2 tbs. (30 g.) sesame seeds
2 tbs. (30 ml.) soy sauce
2 tbs. (30 ml.) rice vinegar
1 tbs. (15 g.) sugar
3−4 cups (800 g.) cooked, drained spinach

Grill the sesame seeds gently in a frying pan. Crush and mix with soy sauce and vinegar. Add sugar.
Mix with spinach and serve cold.

Spinach Cocas
Spinach Turnovers

From Majorca.

> BREAD DOUGH:
> 1 pkg. (20 g.) dry active yeast
> Approximately 1½ cups (375 ml.) water
> 4 cups (500 g.) flour
> ½ tsp. (3 g.) salt
>
> FILLING:
> Olive oil
> 2 cups (500 g.) cooked spinach
> 1–2 cloves garlic, minced
> Fresh, chopped parsley
> Salt, pepper, cayenne
> ½ lb. (250 g.) farmer's cheese
> Milk

Mix yeast with water. Add flour and salt gradually to make a firm dough. Knead 8–10 minutes on a floured board. Cover and let rise 1–2 hours in a warm place.

Reknead the dough, working in a little oil to make it softer. Let rise under a cloth 20–30 minutes.

Roll the dough and cut to saucer-size disks.

Stuff each disk with some spinach mixed with parsley, garlic, seasonings, and a piece of cheese. Fold over and seal the sides, like a turnover. Brush with milk and bake ½ hour at 350°F (175°C).

Kombu Seaweed Salad

A Japanese delicacy. Dried *kombu* or kelp is available at Japanese or health food stores.

> 3 cups (250 g.) dried *kombu*
> 3 tbs. (45 ml.) soy sauce
> Juice of 1 lemon

Soak *kombu* in water to cover for at least 30 minutes. Drain, reserving the liquid. Mix *kombu* with soy sauce, lemon juice, and about half the liquid. Marinate 20–30 minutes and serve.

Fresh Seaweed Salad

To find fresh seaweed you'll probably have to forage it yourself. If you live near the ocean you will discover that edible seaweed is easy to identify and pick. For detailed instructions you may want to consult *The Sea Vegetable Book* by Judith Madloner (Crown Publishers, New York, 1977).

> 1 lb. (500 g.) fresh seaweed (kelp, murlin, or laver)
> 1½ cups (400 ml.) coconut milk (see p. 47)
> Juice of 1 lemon
> ½−1 tsp. cayenne

Wash seaweed and marinate in coconut milk, lemon juice, and cayenne for at least 20 minutes.

Samphire or Glasswort

Often confused with seaweed, samphire (known in America as glasswort, chicken claws or beach asparagus, botanical name *Crithmum maritimum*) grows along the Atlantic and Pacific coasts in tidal flats and in cracks in the rocks. Samphire was once very popular along the shores of both France and England, usually preserved in vinegar, like gherkins. In France it is still commercially cultivated. Elsewhere you may have to gather it yourself—not such a difficult task if you live near the sea, since the plants are common and easily identifiable. Glasswort can also be served fresh in salad or cooked as a vegetable. Only the fleshy parts of the leaves are good to eat and only when very fresh.

> 3 lbs. (1.5 kg.) fresh samphire
> Butter

Wash well and trim, cutting away sticky and withered parts. Boil approximately 30 minutes. Drain carefully and serve with butter.

Eat by biting down on the stems and pulling out the edible pulp with your teeth.

Panisses
Chick-Pea Polenta

All around the Mediterranean chick-peas are not only used as a vegetable, indispensable in many recipes, but also ground for flour. The flour is used in this Provençale recipe for *panisses*, which are known as *panizze* in Portugal. Chick-pea flour can be milled at home in a blender or coffee grinder (see p. 27), if you can't find it in any stores.

>   2 cups (250 g.) chick-pea flour
>   1 qt. (1 l.) water
>   Olive oil
>   Bay leaves, salt

Mix the flour, with the water to make a smooth cream. Add bay leaves. Add a dash of oil and simmer the mixture in a pot, stirring steadily 20–30 minutes until it thickens. Remove bay leaves. Salt.

Pour into a wide rimmed plate or into saucers or molds. Cool, turn out of mold and fry.

NOTE   *Panisses* can also be made with corn flour.
Italian *farinada* is similar to *panisses* but is made with white pea flour.

Calentica
Chick-Pea Bread

Same ingredients as for *panisses*, except for the bay leaves.
Mix the chick-pea flour with the cold water. Add salt, pepper, and a dash of oil. Let sit for several hours.

Beat a short time, then pour into an oiled baking tin. Bake 20 minutes at 450°F (230°C). Serve hot.

Like *panisses*, often sold by street vendors.

Hummus
Chick-Pea Paste

> ½ cup (125 ml.) *tahina* (sesame paste or powder)
> 1 cup (250 g.) chick-peas, soaked
> ½ cup (125 ml.) olive oil
> Juice of 1 lemon
> Salt, pepper
> 3−4 cloves garlic, crushed

If you cannot locate prepared *tahina*, make it yourself by crushing sesame seeds in a mortar or mixing sesame powder with oil to the consistency of mayonnaise.

Simmer the chick-peas in water to cover for 1 hour. Drain, saving the liquid.

Mash the chick-peas in a mortar and pestle to make a thick, dry puree. Add *tahina*, oil, lemon juice, salt, pepper, garlic, and crushed mint. Or, mix chick-peas with other ingredients and puree in a blender, adding chick-pea liquid if the mixture is too dry.

Let cool in a serving plate or individual bowls. It should be firm.

Serve with salted cucumbers, raw vegetables, and the famous Arab round, flat bread, *pita*. Use pieces of *pita* or raw onion as scoops to eat the hummus. If desired, sprinkle with additional olive oil and chopped parsley, and serve together with *ful medames* (see p. 164).

Hummus may be prepared without *tahina* or oil.

Bollitos

> 1 cup (250 g.) chick-peas soaked
> 2 eggs
> 2−3 cloves garlic
> Salt, pepper
> Oil or fat

Simmer chick-peas 1 hour in water to cover. Drain. Crush with garlic in a mortar and pestle or a puree cone. Mix wth eggs and seasoning to make a thick paste. Let sit an hour or more. Drop spoonfuls into very hot fat. Fry on both sides. Drain. Serve burning hot.

Israeli Falafel

> 1 cup (250 g.) chick-pea puree
> 3–4 cloves garlic, crushed
> Salt, pepper
> 2 eggs
> Approximately 4 tbs. (60 ml.) water
> Flour

Mash ingredients together to make a stiff paste. Or puree in a blender. Place in the refrigerator for a few hours.

Shape into sausages or balls. Dip in flour.

Lay out on an oiled, floured cookie sheet. Bake 15–20 minutes at 400°F (200°C), until brown. May also be browned in a pan or deep fried.

Serve falafel hot, by itself, or with other dishes or salad. It is commonly served in round *pita* bread sandwiches, with salad, *tahina* (sesame paste) and *harif* (hot sauce).

If desired, add spices and herbs such as mint, basil, cumin, and fresh coriander to the paste.

Nahit
Roasted Chick-Peas

A traditional Israeli treat.

> 1 cup (250 g.) chick-peas, soaked overnight
> Salt

Simmer chick-peas 1 hour, drain. Spread on a large oiled baking tin. Sprinkle with salt.

Bake 20 minutes at 350°F (175°C).

Serve like salted nuts.

Tuoni e lampo
Chick-Peas with Pasta

The Italians call this *tuoni e lampo*, or "lightning and thunder." It is made from broken pasta, sold cheaply by the weight.

> 1 cup (250 g.) chick-peas, soaked overnight
> 2 cups (500 ml.) water
> Bay leaves
> 1 cup (200 g.) broken pasta
> 1 cup (250 ml.) tomato sauce (see p. 45)
> Salt, pepper
> Chopped fresh basil and parsley
> Oil or butter
> Grated Parmesan cheese

Cook the soaked chick-peas in the water with bay leaves 45–60 minutes. Cook the broken pasta separately in abundant salted water; drain. Drain the chick-peas, reserving the water in which they were cooked. Reduce this water to about ½ cup liquid and add to the tomato sauce. Mix sauce, seasonings, chick-peas, and pasta.

Serve sprinkled with oil and Parmesan.

Rumanian Chick-Peas

> 2 cups (500 g.) cooked chick-peas
> ½ cup (125 g.) rice
> 2 cups (500 ml.) water
> ¾ cup (180 ml.) honey
> Salt

Mix ingredients in a casserole and simmer 20 minutes. Add water as necessary.

Bake 15 minutes at 350°F (175°C) to brown the top.

Garbanzos and Rice
Spanish Chick-Peas

2 minced onions
Olive oil
2−3 lbs. (1.5 kg.) chicken or rabbit, cut up
¼ lb. (125 g.) ham
2−3 cloves garlic
Salt, pepper
2−3 cups (500 ml.) water
1 cup (250 g.) chick-peas, soaked overnight
1 cup (250 g.) rice
¼ lb. (125 g.) *chorizo* (Spanish sausage)
4 eggs, beaten

Brown the onions in oil. Add the chicken, ham, and garlic and brown. Season and add water to cover. Simmer 40 minutes.

Add chick-peas, rice, sliced *chorizo*, and water. Simmer 50 minutes. Pour over beaten eggs and bake 5−10 minutes at 350°F (175°C) until the eggs are just cooked.

Serve hot.

Bagna caôda
Raw Vegetables in Hot Anchovy Dip

This classic peasant dish from the Piedmont region of Italy is usually consumed with plenty of coarse red wine and bread. The sauce should be prepared in an earthenware pot and kept warm over very low heat while the dipping goes on. To finish off the meal (when you run out of vegetables and a little sauce is still left in the pot), break a couple of eggs into the pot, turn up the flame (or put on a very low flame over a gas burner), and scramble the mixture together.

4 tbs. (60 g.) butter
1 cup (250 ml.) olive oil
2−4 cloves garlic, chopped
2 oz. (60 g.) anchovies, chopped (1 small can)
Assorted raw vegetables, washed and peeled: sweet peppers, spinach, carrots, cardoons (if possible, or celery), zucchini, fennel, radishes, sliced cabbage, broccoli (especially the stalks)
Salt to taste

Melt the butter in the oil in a pot over low heat. Add the garlic and sauté for a minute or two; then add the chopped anchovies. The anchovies will gradually dissolve, and you can help the process by mashing with a wooden spoon as you stir. Simmer for about 10 minutes stirring occasionally. Transfer the pot to sit above a candle or spirit warmer on the table. Give the vegetables a good dip in the sauce, stirring up the anchovy paste from time to time to keep it mixed in with the oil. A chunk of bread held under the dipped vegetable will keep the dripping oil off the table.

Male blossom (on stem)

Female blossom (on young squash)

Fried Squash Flowers

Fried blossoms from all sorts of squash have long been favorites of both Mediterranean peoples and Indians of the American Southwest. They are readily available from any home garden that grows zucchini, pumpkin, or other squash, and sometimes, though rarely, can be found in markets. They must be fresh. If you are picking your own, try to pick male blossoms, but be sure not to pick all of them, otherwise you may never get any fruit. Squash flowers may be simply dusted with flour before frying. They are usually dipped in batter, as follows:

    ¼ cup (30 g.) flour
    Salt, pepper
    ½ cup (125 ml.) water or milk
    2–3 dozen zucchini or other squash flowers
    Olive oil or other high quality oil

Make a batter by sifting the flour, salt, and pepper slowly into the water or milk and stirring to make a paste. Dip flowers into the batter, then fry in hot oil until golden brown on both sides. Drain and serve.

Stuffed Squash Flowers

The Greek peasants who developed this recipe get their fresh-picked squash or pumpkin flowers from their own garden plots.

> 1–2 cloves garlic
> 1 bunch scallions
> Olive oil
> ¾ cup (200 g.) rice
> 4 oz. (60 ml.) tomato paste
> Fennel and mint
> Salt, sugar, cinnamon
> Fresh parsley
> 2 dozen squash flowers in full bloom
> 1 egg, beaten
> Lemon juice

Brown minced garlic and scallions in oil. Add rice, tomato paste, herbs, and spices.

Stuff each flower delicately and turn the petals in over the stuffing. Lay out in a frying pan and cover with water. Cook 25 minutes over a low flame. Thicken the gravy with a beaten egg, and add a dash of lemon juice.

VARIANTS   The water in which the stuffed flowers are cooked may be replaced with tomato sauce. Sometimes ground lamb is added to the stuffing, replacing some of the rice.

Radikya
Greek Dandelion Leaves

Young dandelion leaves or *radikya* are well appreciated in Greece, especially as a cooked salad.

> 2 lbs. (1 kg.) dandelion leaves
> Olive oil, lemon juice
> Salt, pepper

Wash dandelion leaves well and blanch (i.e. boil briefly) in salted water. Drain completely.

Serve sprinkled with oil, lemon, salt, and pepper. Radikya often accompanies fish and meat.

Bamias
Greek Okra and Tomatoes

These plump green vegetables are often found in Mediterranean cooking.

    2 lbs. (1 kg.) okra
    Salt
    2 minced onions
    Olive oil
    1 lb. (500 g.) chopped tomatoes
    Sugar, salt, pepper
    Dash of vinegar

Trim the ends of the okra. Salt and let them "sweat"—i.e. lose some of their moisture—preferably in the sun.

Brown the onions in oil and add the chopped tomatoes. Add rinsed and drained okra, then seasonings. Simmer approximately 1 hour.

Serve hot or cold, as in Greece.

Egyptian Bamias
Okra and Lamb

Dried bamias (dried okra) are available at some Middle Eastern stores.

    2 lbs. (1 kg.) fresh bamias or okra or
     2 cups (200 g.) dried bamias
    2–3 chopped onions
    2–3 cloves garlic, chopped
    Oil or lamb fat
    ⅔ lb. (300 g.) diced lamb
    ¾ cup (375 ml.) boiling water
    Salt, pepper
    Ground coriander, cumin

Soak fresh bamias ½ hour in salted water. Drain. (If using dried bamias, soak in fresh water at least 1 hour. Drain.)

Brown garlic and onions in oil or lamb fat, add the bamias and then the meat. Season. Add boiling water.

Simmer gently until the meat is tender, for about 1 hour. (If you use ground lamb, you only need cook 30–45 minutes.)

Dolmas
Stuffed Grape Leaves

Stuffed grape leaves are another of the dishes common all around the Mediterranean. The stuffing is not rich, being composed mainly of rice, but on flush days it may include some mutton, the local cheap meat. During the spring and summer in many parts of the country you can gather fresh young grape leaves off the vine; when grapes are out of season, use white and tender inner cabbage leaves, or pickled grape leaves.

        10−20 tender grape leaves
        2/3 cup (150 g.) rice
        1 bunch scallions
        Fennel and mint
        Salt and pepper
        Olive oil
        1 cup (250 ml.) water

Blanch the leaves delicately for 2 minutes and drain in cheesecloth.
    Mix rice, scallions, and herbs with a little oil. Brown, then cook 10−12 minutes in the water.
    Stuff each leaf with a spoonful of stuffing. Close by rolling the leaves and folding in the ends.
    Lay out in a frying pan and cover with water. Simmer 20−30 minutes.
    Serve hot or cold with whipped yoghurt or a sauce made by reducing the cooking juice, thickening it with egg, and adding a dash of lemon for flavor.

VARIANT   Use ground lamb and an equal volume of rice in the stuffing. Add some chopped lamb fat. Season and follow the above recipe.
    It is advisable to lay a flat plate over the *dolmas* as they are cooking to prevent them from bursting.

Marinated Eggplant

Keeps well. Accompanies meats and starches.

        2 lbs. (1 kg.) eggplant
        1 cup (250 ml.) vinegar
        2 cups (500 ml.) oil
        Fennel seeds, peppercorns

Cut eggplants in two; do not peel. Soak in heavily salted water. Drain and fry lightly.

Put in glass jars and cover with oil and vinegar. Add fennel seeds and peppercorns.

Fassolia
Beans in Tomato Sauce

> 1 cup (250 g.) beans, soaked overnight
> Olive oil
> Salt, pepper
> 2 cloves garlic
> Thyme, bay leaf
> ¼ cup (60 ml.) tomato paste

Dry the beans with a paper towel, then brown them in oil. Add garlic, tomato paste, and herbs. Add hot water to cover and season. Simmer 1½–2 hours, reducing the liquid to gravy.

Serve as in Greece with a dash of lemon and chopped onions. Hot or cold.

Zucchini Croquettes

This is another Mediterranean dish.

> 2 cups (500 ml.) cooked zucchini puree
> 2 cups (500 ml.) mashed potatoes
> 3–4 chopped onions
> 1 cup (125 g.) grated cheese
> Salt, pepper, parsley, mint
> 1 egg
> 1 cup (90 g.) bread crumbs

Mix all the ingredients except bread crumbs and egg. Bind with an egg. Shape into patties and bread with crumbs. Fry both sides and serve hot.

Sweet Acorns

From central Europe to Japan, from North America to the Mediterranean where Castille, Greek and *ballote* oaks thrive, and to southwest France where the holm-oak acorns prized by ancestors are now neglected, the poor have gratefully gathered nature's largesse of acorns. Acorns can be eaten boiled or roasted like chestnuts. They may also be roasted, ground, and brewed like coffee. In Portugal, North Africa, the Middle East, and Corsica, acorns still fill bellies that need to be filled.

The celebrated *racahout* of the Arabs is a sort of fine porridge, mainly for children, made from acorn flour, cocoa, sugar, starch and *salep*, a milky drink made from ground up orchid roots.

Here is how North American Indians made bread from acorns: first they broke the shells on a stone and crushed the meats into fine flour. The flour then had to be washed, mashed, dried, and precooked to extract the tannin before it was ready to be kneaded to make dough. (Acorns must always be soaked before use.) The dough was then worked down with a smooth rock roller on a flat rock to a thin flat cake that could be quickly cooked on hot hearth stones.

Chestnut Polenta

Chestnut flour, although almost unknown now in Europe where it more than once supported the people through famine, is still a staple for some. It lends itself to many savory preparations, giving even simple porridge an exciting flavor. Chestnut flour is available, irregularly, at Italian markets and can be made in the home by grinding dried chestnuts in a grain mill or blender.

>   2 cups (250 g.) chestnut flour
>   5 cups (1,250 ml.) water
>   Salt

Slowly stir chestnut flour into boiling, salted water. Simmer 20 minutes. Press into a bowl and turn out onto a plate while still hot. Slice and serve.

Cold chestnut *polenta* is good sliced and fried.

Acorn Squash

Easy to store through long winters, this small, round, dark green, hard-skinned squash is a favorite in traditional New England cooking.

    2 acorn squashes
    2 tbs. (30 g.) butter
    2 tbs. (30 g.) brown sugar
    Cinnamon or nutmeg

Wash squashes, cut lengthwise, and scoop out the seeds. Dot with butter and sprinkle with sugar and spice. Put in a pan with some water and bake 40–60 minutes at 400°F (200°C) until tender.
  Serve hot. Some enjoy eating the skin, others do not.

Indonesian Sweet Potatoes

    2 lbs. (1 kg.) sweet potatoes, cooked and sliced
    1 peeled orange, cubed
    1 tbs. (15 g.) sugar
    3 tbs. (45 g.) melted butter
    ½ cup (125 ml.) honey or brown sauce (flour cooked in oil or butter)
    ½ cup (50 g.) grated coconut
    1 cup (250 ml.) coconut milk (see p. 47)

Mix together sweet potato slices and orange cubes in a baking dish. Mix the other ingredients and pour over the mixture.
  Bake at 350°F (175°C) approximately ¾ hour.

Jicama or Yam Bean

This is a bulbous, smooth-skinned, off-white root found in Asian and Latin markets. It should be tender but not soft. Its crisp white flesh has a delicate fine taste like cucumber or water chestnut, and it can be used like cucumber or water chestnut in salads or to provide contrasting textures in soups or stir-fried dishes.

Peel and slice into thin julienne strips. Serve plain or sprinkled with lemon or lime juice, or vinegar. Or add to a soup shortly before serving.

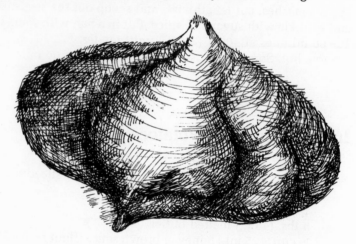

Stuffed Calabaza

The *calabaza*, a large squash or gourd like a pumpkin, is well appreciated in Latin America. It is a common vegetable in Latin markets.

> 1 larbe *calabaza*
> ½ lb. (250 g.) ground beef or pork
> ¼ lb. (100 g.) diced ham
> 2 chopped onions
> 2 sliced peppers
> 1−2 cloves garlic
> Salt, pepper, oregano
> 1 tbs. (15 ml.) vinegar
> ½ cup (80 g.) raisins
> ½ cup (80 g.) olives
> 1 cup (250 ml.) tomato sauce (see p. 45)
> 2 eggs

Cut off the top of the *calabaza* and set aside. Scoop out the pulp with a spoon. Steam pulp gently 10–15 minutes. Drain. (You can also leave the pulp in and gently cook the entire gourd, taking care not to break the skin. Once cooked you can cut off the top, remove the pulp, and stuff it.)

Brown the meat and ham separately. Add onions, peppers, garlic, salt, pepper, oregano, vinegar, raisins, olives, and tomato sauce.

Simmer 5 minutes or so, then thicken with the eggs. Mix in the *calabaza* pulp. Stuff the *calabaza* and put the top back on.

Bake 1 hour at 350°F (175°C). Let cool 15 minutes before cutting and serving.

If there is no beef or pork, use chicken; if no chicken, use simple mashed potatoes or corn porridge.

Serves 6.

Chayote

This smooth, clear green fruit, popular in the Caribbean and parts of Latin America and known as *xuxu* in Brazil, is shaped like a pear but eaten like zucchini. It has a mild, fresh taste, best when set off with lemon or cheese. Get young fruits, with firm unwrinkled skins. The skin and seed are tender enough to eat. Chayote is commonly found in markets, such as Latin markets, specializing in tropical foods.

    Chayote
    Lemon

Cut *chayote*—lengthwise through the seed—into quarters. Steam gently for 10–15 minutes. Serve hot, sprinkled with lemon juice.

STUFFED CHAYOTE
3–4 chayotes
1 small onion, chopped
Butter
1 cup (125 g.) grated hard cheese
Bread crumbs
Salt, pepper

Cut *chayotes* in half. Steam gently for 10 minutes. Let cool slightly. Scoop out some pulp and the seed, leaving a ½ inch thick shell.

Brown the chopped onion in butter. Mash with the *chayote* pulp and seed, mix with cheese and fill the *chayote* shells. Sprinkle with bread crumbs, and dot with butter, and season to taste. Set in a pan with about a half inch of water. Bake at 350°F (175°C) for 20–30 minutes, until the crust is browned.

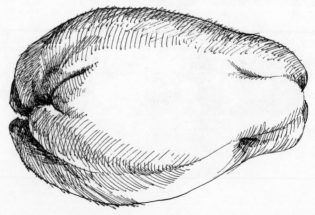

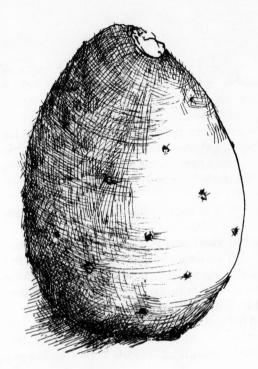

Cactus Salad

The young pads of the Opuntia cactus have long been appreciated by the American Indians and Mexicans. The Mexicans, who call these vegetables *nopales* or *nopalitos*, use the plant with great versatility. *Nopalitos*, also called prickly pears, are readily available in North American markets. The red, seedy insides vaguely resemble pomegranates. Everything but the skin is edible.

    2–4 prickly pears
    1–2 tomatoes, chopped
    1 white onion, chopped
    1 fresh or soaked dried hot chile, with seeds and stem removed
    Fresh coriander to taste (or substitute parsley)
    Oil and vinegar dressing
    Salt, pepper

Dig out the pointy black eyes of the prickly pears with the tip of a vegetable peeler; then peel and cut into ½ inch cubes. (It's often best to wear gloves while doing this, to avoid being pricked.) Cook in boiling salted water for about 5 minutes until tender. Rinse and dry. Mix together all the ingredients and let sit for a few minutes before serving.

Tropical Roots

Dasheen, yautia, malanga, ñame, yuca, and *batata* are names and varieties of tropical roots commonly available in Latin markets. They take the place of potatoes and even of bread in the Caribbean, Africa, South America, Southeast Asia, and Polynesia. There are cultivated versions of the roots that pre-agricultural and post-famine man turn to, along with berries, for sustenance in the last resort. They are almost pure starch, with little other food value. An important variety, bitter cassava (or bitter manioc) requires boiling to remove a poison, but the roots that can generally be bought fresh need only be boiled and served plain.

Dasheen and *yautia*, each of which is sometimes sold as *malanga*, are varieties of taro.

Dasheen, sold also in oriental markets and sometimes called Chinese potato, is a fat, regularly shaped ellipsoid root with rings of rootlets giving it a banded appearance. It should be thoroughly scrubbed. Bake it whole until tender all the way through—40–90 minutes depending on size—and serve it sliced; or cut it up and boil it for 10–15 minutes.

Yautia is an irregularly shaped hairy root, somewhat thinner, darker, and more pointed than potatoes. Peel, cut up, and boil for 10–15 minutes. It is usually served plain though without seasoning it tends to be very bland.

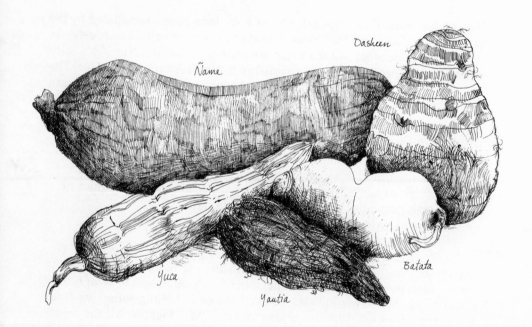

Ñame

Dasheen

Yuca

Yautia

Batata

Yuca—also known as sweet manioc, or cassava, or as *aipim* in Brazil where it is particularly popular—is a long, hairy, cylindrical root, tapering at one end, that can be boiled and eaten like potatoes. It is often reduced to a pulp and dried for meal, called manioc or *mandioca* meal, and used for *farofa* in Brazil (see p. 169) and *gari foto* in West Africa (see p. 212). Its close relative, bitter manioc or cassava, is poisonous until heated. It is most often used processed into manioc meal or tapioca. In its various forms manioc is one of the most important foods of Africa and Latin America.

Certain kinds of manioc have sweet and tender leaves. In Black Africa the leaves are cooked like spinach, with palm nut oil or karite butter (see p. 16) and liberally sprinkled with hot pepper. The dish is very savory and delicate when prepared by the Congolese, who are capable cooks.

Ñame is the most common kind of true yam, another important tropical staple. A brown, hairy, unpointed, cylindrical root, it can be prepared by peeling, washing, cutting up and boiling in salted water, for 10–15 minutes. Drain and serve plain or in any recipe in place of potatoes.

Batatas, known in Mexico as *camotes* (see p. 258), are a kind of sweet potato, generally pear-shaped, with a smooth, tender purplish flesh. Peeled and boiled, they become almost transparent and have a singularly fine and delicate sweetness, somewhat different from our familiar orange yams (not true yams like *ñame*) or sweet potatoes. They can also be baked or boiled whole.

Breadfruit

This fruit, although sometimes eaten when fully ripe, is at its best when harvested slightly green and its flesh is white and firm. This texture and appearance, together with a high starch content and a fresh taste with a hint of artichoke, are what earned this fruit its name. Breadfruit are occasionally available at Latin markets.

Peel, slice thickly, and roast breadfruit for 5–10 minutes. Or bake whole in the oven at 400°F (200°C) for 30–60 minutes, depending on size, until tender all the way through. Serve like potatoes.

Breadfruit may also be boiled or cut up and steamed.

Kaku
Breadfruit Mash

2 breadfruits
1 cup (250 ml.) coconut milk (see p. 47)

Bake whole breadfruit in a 400°F (200°C) oven for 30–45 minutes until tender all the way through. Peel, cut up, and mash in a mortar. Mix with coconut milk to make a thick creamy paste. Eat like *popoi* (see below), either plain or with fish or vegetables.

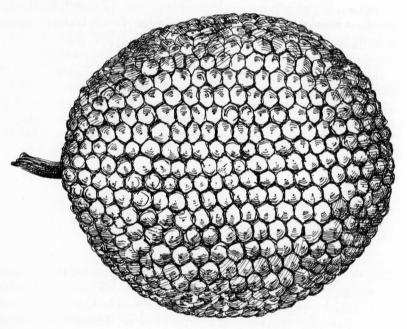

Popoi
Polynesian Breadfruit Paste

Popoi is one of the most common ways that Polynesians prepare breadfruit. *Popoi* is a thick, cool, yellowish cream eaten with cupped fingers. This staple dish has two virtues: coolness and a light acidity that makes it very digestible. The dish is also called *poi*, in Hawaii for instance, and can be made with taro.

Polynesians roast almost ripe breadfruits over coals, then peel them with a sharpened shell—metal knives may affect the taste. The pulp obtained—which is tender, white, and spongy with a faint taste of artichoke or chestnut—is put into wooden tubs, sprinkled with water, and mashed with stone pestles to reduce it to a fine smooth paste. The tubs are buried in trenches lined with large ti leaves and allowed to ferment. After a few days the fermented paste is watered and mashed again. The popoi is ready. They eat the popoi as is, or as a sauce for small, uncooked fish.

To prepare popoi or poi in the home, bake breadfruit or taro at 400°F (200°C) for 30–40 minutes until tender all the way through. Peel and mash in a nonmetallic bowl, sprinkling with water to make a thick paste. Cover and let sit in a cool place for 1–3 days. It will ferment naturally. Its taste will get pleasantly sour.

If possible, line the bowl and cover with ti leaves, which impart a faint musky flavor. Ti leaves are sometimes available through a florist.

Several other vegetables can be used to make popoi: taro and sweet potatoes. Bananas, almonds, and coconut are sometimes mashed with the breadfruit, taro, or sweet potatoes before fermentation, or more often served separately, alongside plain popoi.

Nursing infants begin to eat popoi shortly after birth. Popoi sweetened with mashed tropical fruits is known as keikai.

Plantains
Green Bananas

A fruit of the tropics, bananas are known there in many forms generally unknown in northern countries. For instance plantains: a hard, starchy variety of bananas which are an important part of tropical diet and which have become a familiar sight to Americans who frequent Latin markets.

Since plantains are tough, they should be pounded to prepare them for eating. They can be cooked with soup, chicken, or meat, or take the place of bread in the same way as yams. Different varieties, such as light *platanos* and dark *maduros* have different textures and tastes.

To prepare simply, pound with a wooden mallet or a rolling pin for a minute or two, peel and slice, then fry in lard, oil, or butter.

Bananas Baked in Sugar

This banana, or plantain, dish is served as a vegetable with chicken in Africa and India, as well as in Latin America. Bananas are an important source of protein.

     2 lbs. (1 kg.) bananas or plantains
     ½ cup (125 g.) sugar
     ½ cup (125 g.) butter
     Mace, pepper, cinnamon, salt

If using plantains, pound with a wooden mallet or rolling pin for a minute. Peel. Lay out in a baking pan, cover with a layer of sugar and pieces of butter. Sprinkle with spices. Bake 20–25 minutes at 350°F (175°C).

Poe
Polynesian Fruit Balls

     Taro or breadfruit
     Banana, pineapple, or papaya
     Palm leaves or banana leaves
     Sugar syrup or coconut milk (see p. 47)

Bake the taro or breadfruit 30–40 minutes at 400°F (200°C). Peel and mash with the fruit. Shape into balls. Wrap each ball in a palm leaf and bake 15–20 minutes at 400°F (200°C). Serve with sugar syrup or coconut milk.

   If you cannot find palm or banana leaves, you can substitute dried corn husks, available at many Latin markets. Soak dried leaves for at least 1 hour before using.

EGG AND CHEESE DISHES

Welsh Rarebit

This is often called Welsh Rabbit, supposedly because it often substituted for a meal of rabbit when no meat was to be had.

> 2 cups (½ lb. or 250 g.) aged sharp Cheddar cheese, grated
> 1 tbs. (15 g.) butter
> ½ cup (125 ml.) beer
> 1 egg, slightly beaten
> 1 tsp. Worcestershire sauce
> ½ tsp. salt
> ¼ tsp. dry mustard
> Pinch of cayenne pepper
> Slices of bread, sliced

Melt butter and cheese together over low heat; stir in beer and continue to stir until the mixture is well blended. Remove from heat and beat in egg and seasonings. Arrange several slices of freshly toasted bread in a shallow pan and pour rarebit over them. Brown briefly under a broiler and serve while still bubbling.

Serves 2, or 4 as an appetizer.

Saganaki
Greek Fried Cheese

One of the popular snacks served in local taverns, called *bouzoukias*. The Greek cheeses called for below are usually available in cheese shops.

> 1 lb. (500 g.) *kasseri* or *kefalotiri* cheese, or any hard, strong cheese
> Flour or fine bread crumbs
> Olive oil
> Lemon

Cut cheese in thick slices. Dip in flour. Fry in olive oil. Serve with a dash of lemon.

Kajmak
Yugoslavian Sheep Cheese

Accompanies corn bread in country meals. Raw sheep's milk is generally available only on farms. You can substitute raw milk of any kind—health food stores often carry raw cow's milk. Pasteurized, homogenized milk will not curdle naturally.

   Sheep's milk

Boil sheep's milk. Let cool in an earthen pot. The cream will rise. Skim and set aside in a wooden pot. Add salt. Repeat the same procedure with 2 or 3 fresh batches of milk, adding the cream to the wooden pot and salting each time. After a few days you get a real cheese, yellow, with a somewhat strong smell. Keep it in a cool place.

   When fresh this cheese is baked in delicious little cakes.

Yugoslavian Cheese and Corn Pie

   3 cups (700 g.) *mamaliga* (see p. 90)
   Lard
   Salt, pepper
   ½ lb. (250 g.) sheep cheese, e.g. *feta*, or *kasseri* or other strong cheese
   3 eggs

Press hot *mamaliga* into a greased baking tin. Cover with a layer of grated or crumbled cheese. Lightly scramble then season the eggs; pour over the cheese. Cover with another layer of cheese. Serve as is.

VARIANT   Save some of the *mamaliga* and spread it over the layer of eggs. Cover with cheese.

VARIANT   Bake 10 minutes at 400°F (200°C) to melt the cheese. For this version, beat the eggs but do not scramble them first.

Yugoslavian Paski
Fried Goat Cheese

> 1 lb. (500 g.) goat cheese, e.g. *kasseri* or other strong goat or
>   sheep cheese
> 1 egg
> Bread crumbs
> Corn or olive oil

Cube goat cheese. Dip in beaten egg, then in bread crumbs. Fry lightly in oil. Serve crisp.

Mozzarella in carrozza
Grilled Cheese with Anchovy Sauce

> 1 loaf of Italian bread
> ½ lb. (250 g.) mozzarella cheese
> ¼ cup (60 ml.) milk
> Oil, flour
> 1 egg
> 6 tbs. (90 g.) butter
> 2 oz. (60 g.) anchovy fillets

Slice the bread into 1½ inch chunks. Cut off the crust to make a rectangle. Hollow the bread and fill neatly with a piece of mozzarella. The result suggests a *carrozza*—a carriage with the cheese riding inside.

Sprinkle with milk, dip in flour, then beaten egg. Dredge in flour then deep fry in oil, starting with the cheese side up. Turn and fry quickly on the cheese side.

Meanwhile, melt the butter and mash in the anchovy fillets to make a smooth sauce.

Serve mozzarella in carrozza hot with the anchovy sauce.

Indian Cheese Curry

Curds are a basic ingredient of Indian cooking, used both in liquid form and drained and solidified.

    ½–1 lb. (250 g.) dry curds or farmer's cheese (see p. 29)
    1 lb. (500 g.) fresh peas
    Ghee (see p. 31) or vegetable shortening
    2 onions, chopped
    Salt
    ½ tbs. (8 g.) crushed coriander
    1–2 cloves garlic
    1–2 hot fresh chiles, or cayenne
    1 tsp. grated fresh ginger
    2 large tomatoes, chopped

Drain curds well in cheesecloth. Press flat and cut into cubes. Boil or steam fresh peas, set aside.

Fry the cheese in ghee. In a separate pan, brown the onions and spices. Add the chopped tomatoes and simmer 5–10 minutes (they should not be completely cooked). Add water to cover, and top with the fried cheese and peas. Bring to a boil, then serve.

Spanish Pisto

    2 minced onions
    2 minced peppers, without seeds
    4 minced zucchini
    6 tomatoes, chopped
    Olive oil
    1 lb. (500 g.) diced potatoes
    Salt, pepper
    4 beaten eggs
    Fried croutons

Sauté the vegetables, except the potatoes, in oil.

Sauté the potatoes separately 5–10 minutes. Add to the other vegetables, season to taste, and mix well. Add the beaten eggs and stir continuously until they take.

Serve immediately over fried croutons.

M'guena

African Omelet

2 potatoes, cooked and mashed
2 chopped onions
2–3 cloves garlic, minced
2 cups (500 g.) cooked carrots or peas
4–5 beaten eggs
Salt, pepper, tabasco
Nutmeg
2–3 chopped hard boiled eggs
Coconut oil or *ghee* (see p. 31), or palm nut oil if available

Mix all ingredients except the oil together. Pour into an oiled mold or pan. Bake 20 minutes at 350°F (175°C).

Serve hot or cold.

Tchakchuka

North African Eggs and Vegetables

2–3 onions, chopped
2–3 sweet peppers, sliced
3–4 tomatoes, chopped
Salt, pepper
Suggested spices: thyme, oregano, cumin
3–5 eggs

Brown onions and sliced peppers. Add tomatoes. Season. Simmer 15–20 minutes.

Break eggs into the pan with the vegetables, cover, and simmer another 5–10 minutes until the eggs are done. Serve.

VARIANT Add leftover ground meat to cook with the onions and peppers before adding the tomatoes.

Gari foto
West African Eggs and Manioc Meal

Manioc meal is generally available at Latin markets.

1 cup (125 g.) manioc meal
2 tbs. (30 ml.) water
3–4 tomatoes, chopped and peeled
1 tsp. powdered chiles
Salt, pepper
2–3 onions, chopped
½ cup (125 ml.) peanut oil
3–5 eggs, beaten

Place the manioc meal on a large plate and sprinkle with the water, stirring intermittently with two forks, so that the meal is evenly moistened. Let sit for ½ hour, then add tomatoes, powdered chiles, salt and pepper and stir again with the forks. Sauté the onions in the oil until they are soft but not brown. Pour in the beaten eggs gradually, stirring constantly. Once they have formed soft curds lower the heat and stir in the manioc meal/tomato mixture. Continue stirring and cooking for another 5 minutes or so, then serve.

Chu pa pa
Stuffed Egg Pancakes

The batter for these chu pa pa is halfway between omelet and crêpe batter. These egg pancakes are served with almost all meals in the parts of China where wheat and millet replace rice. They are also served rolled and cut into ribbons, sautéed with vegetables (see p. 158) or cooked in soup.

PANCAKES:
3 eggs
1 cup (125 g.) flour or 2/3 cup (80 g.) water chestnut powder
Water, approximately ½ cup (125 ml.)
Salt

STUFFING:
2 minced onions
2 sliced peppers
1 lb. (500 g.) chopped vegetables, e.g. cabbage, broccoli, celery
Peanut oil
2 tbs. (30 ml.) soy sauce

Mix eggs, flour, water, and salt to make a smooth, liquid batter. Cook as thin crêpes on one side only and pile on a cloth, cooked side up (same procedure as for blintzes).

Sauté the onions, peppers, and vegetables in peanut oil. Add soy sauce. Stuff the crêpes with the mixture, then roll up and fold closed, with the uncooked side of the crêpe outside. Brown in oil.

If desired, add a little sesame oil to the stuffing for taste.

Egg fu yung
Chinese Omelet

¼ lb. (125 g.) shredded chicken, beef, pork, or shrimp
2–3 scallions
1 small stalk celery or 4 sprigs watercress
2 tbs. (30 g.) lard or peanut oil
1 tbs. (15 ml.) soy sauce
t tsp. (5 ml.) sesame oil (optional)
4 eggs

Shred the meat, scallions, and celery finely. Stir fry (sauté quickly) the meat in 1 tbs. lard or oil for 1 minute in a hot wok. Add the scallions and celery and stir-fry another minute. Add soy sauce and sesame oil. Remove from wok and set aside.

Heat the rest of the lard or oil in the wok. Beat eggs lightly and pour into the wok, over medium heat. After about a minute, when the eggs are about half-cooked, add the meat and vegetables, reserving the juice. Fold over on itself and serve hot, using the juice as sauce.

To make more sauce, add some stock to the juice and thicken with corn starch.

Scotch Eggs

4 hard-boiled eggs
4 pork country sausages
2 beaten eggs or a thin batter
1–2 cups (125 g.) soft bread crumbs
Fat for deep frying

Cool the eggs and shell. Coat each with sausage meat, dip in beaten egg, and roll in bread crumbs. Fry in hot deep fat, drain on paper towels, then cut each egg lengthwise. Serve hot or cold.

MEAT
AND
FISH

Although it may seem strange to put meat and fish together in a cookbook they share the character of being occasional luxuries for most of the world's people. The exotic delicacies we associate with Third World cooking are rare delights. Peking duck, however delicious, never finds its way to a poor man's table, which is more likely to be graced with a garlic shoot wrapped in a pancake. That is not to say you will not find some true delicacies in the pages that follow, but remember that these are the feasts of the common man, not their usual daily fare.

Papuan Pork and Potatoes

Pork, like chicken, is important in the diets of all poor peoples. Pigs are so prized in some areas as to be treated almost like children. Papuan women in New Guinea do not hesitate to nurse a suckling pig deprived of its mother. The pig was brought to Papua by white men. Before, the Papuans raised dogs, resembling foxes, and fattened them like pigs. Papuans cook pork with sweet potatoes and sometimes fish from streams and rivers.

Sweet and Sour Pork

Poor Chinese usually buy pork from a butcher in infinitesimal portions—a tiny parcel wrapped in a dry lotus leaf.

    1 lb. (500 g.) pork, cut into ¼ – ½ inch cubes
    1 beaten egg
    Flour or cornstarch
    Peanut oil
    2 minced onions
    2 minced sweet peppers (with seeds removed)
    4 tbs. (60 g.) sugar
    3 tbs. (45 ml.) soy sauce
    3 tbs. (45 ml.) rice vinegar
    1 tbs. (15 ml.) dry white wine or dry sherry
    1 tbs. (12 g.) cornstarch

Coat the meat in egg, then in corn starch or flour. Fry in oil in a wok. Drain and set aside.

Sauté vegetables in the wok. Mix sugar, soy, vinegar, and wine, and pour over the vegetables. Mix the corn starch in a little water and add to the sauce. Bring to a boil, then add the meat. Mix completely before serving.

Roast Pork with Daikon

This feast dish employs the common oriental white radish.

>
> 3–4 *daikon*, oriental radishes
> 6–8 lbs. (3 kg.) pork roast
> Salt, pepper

Blanch the radishes, then arrange around the seasoned pork, ready to go into the oven. Bake at 325°F (160°C) for approximately 35 minutes per pound.
    Serves 8–10.

Mexican Pork

>
> 2 lbs. (1 kg.) pork shoulder, cut up
> Lard
> 4 minced onions
> Salt, pepper
> 1 tsp. powdered chiles
> Bay leaf, oregano
> 2 cups (500 ml.) water
> 1–2 tbs. (15 g.) corn meal

Brown the meat in lard. Add onions, let soften. Add seasonings. Add 2 cups water. Cover and simmer 1½ hours until the meat is tender.
    Skim off fat and add corn meal mixed with a little cold water. Simmer 15 minutes more.
    Serve in a wooden bowl.

Ameijoas na cataplana
Portuguese Clam Stew

This pork stew with clams or cockles is cooked in a primitive pressure cooker, called *cataplana*. Any pressure cooker will do the job.

    4 onions, chopped
    1½ lbs. (750 g.) pork, cut into ½ inch cubes
    ½ cup (125 ml.) tomato paste
    1 cup (250 ml.) dry white wine or meat stock
    Salt, pepper
    30 clams or 40 cockles

Brown the onions, add the meat. Mix in tomato paste, then add the wine. Season with salt, pepper. Seal in pressure cooker and simmer 20 minutes (or simmer 1½ hours in a covered pot). Wash the shellfish carefully to remove all sand and add to the stew. Simmer 15 minutes more.

Kari
Réunion Island Yams and Pork Chops

    4−6 pork chops
    Lard or fat
    3 onions, chopped
    2−3 cloves garlic
    4 tomatoes, chopped
    Salt, pepper
    1−2 lbs. (700 g.) yams

Sauté the chops in lard or oil. Add onions and garlic. Moisten with tomatoes. Add salt and pepper. Peel yams, known as *kari*, cut into thick slices, and add to the meat. Cover and simmer 25−30 minutes.

Serve, crushing some of the yam into the juice to thicken it.

Chiao-tzu
Chinese Ravioli

Poor relations of a culture of great culinary finesse, less-favored Chinese make artful dishes from meager resources. With art even simple dishes are very tasty, like these Chinese ravioli.

Chiao-tzu are a central feature of New Year's celebrations in the Gobi Desert. A peasant cook shapes them into little ears in the hope that by eating many of them, he will not lose his own ears to frost in the cold winter ahead. Tibetan *momos* are a close cousin.

    3 cups (375 g.) flour
    1 cup (250 ml.) hot water
    ½ lb. (250 g.) chopped celery cabbage
    ½ lb. (250 g.) minced fresh pork
    Minced white leek
    Soy sauce, salt
    1–2 tsp. (5 g.) fresh, grated ginger
    Dash of sesame oil
    Water or stock

Knead flour and water into a supple dough. Let sit several hours. Then roll dough on a floured board and using a cup, cut into disks.

While the dough is sitting, soak the cabbage in salted water to draw out some of the moisture. Drain and mix with the other ingredients.

Fill each disk of dough with a spoonful of stuffing. Fold over to form an ear-shaped ravioli. Seal the edges.

Poach gently in water or stock for about 20 minutes. Serve in stock, or plain.

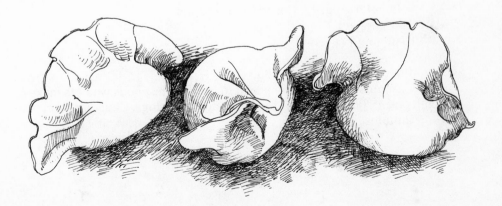

Steamed Chicken

Cheaper to raise than even the most economical pig, chicken is the most easily available meat all over the world. The Chinese have even mastered techniques of drying, salting and smoking it just as they have pork—they gut and stuff the chicken with salt and hang it to dry unplucked.

> 1 tender chicken
> 1 tbs. (15 g.) sugar
> Salt
> 1–2 tsp. (5 g.) fresh, grated ginger
> Fresh coriander, parsley, watercress
> 1 tbs. (15 ml.) dry wine
> 3 tbs. (45 ml.) soy sauce
> 1 tbs. (12 g.) cornstarch

Brown the chicken thoroughly by sautéing. Drain well. Place in a large pot with the herbs, seasonings, and a little water. Add wine and soy. Cover tightly and steam gently approximately ¾ hour. The skin should remain intact. The flesh should be tender enough to be eaten with chopsticks.

Thicken the sauce with a little cornstarch and pour over the chicken when serving.

Chicken with Peanuts

This is a Congolese feast dish.

> 1 chicken, cut up
> Coconut or peanut oil
> ¼ lb. (100 g.) grilled or roasted peanuts
> Salt, pepper
> 1 tsp. (5 g.) cayenne

Brown the chicken all over in oil.

Crush peanuts in a mortar then heat in a few tablespoons water to make a smooth cream. Pour over the chicken. Add seasonings. Cover and simmer 30–45 minutes.

Chicken and Coconut

This is a central African recipe, where chicken is the easiest meat to get but still generally too expensive to be used except on festive occasions.

    1 coconut
    1 chicken
    2 cups (500 ml.) chopped tomatoes
    Onion, garlic
    1 tsp. (5 g.) cayenne

Boil the coconut 20 minutes. Drain and remove shell. Mash in a mortar to make a pulp.

Roast the chicken. While chicken is roasting, prepare a tomato sauce by browning the onion and garlic, and simmering 30 minutes with the tomatoes. Add cayenne. Thicken the sauce with coconut pulp and simmer 10–15 minutes longer. Meanwhile remove chicken from oven and cut into pieces.

Chicken Paprikás

Chicken with paprika, as the name indicates. No feast among Gypsies or Hungarians is complete without hot paprika.

    1 large chicken (3½–4 lbs., 1.8 kg.), cut into pieces
    Flour
    Salt
    Oil
    2–3 onions, chopped
    3–4 cloves garlic, chopped
    1 cup (250 ml.) yoghurt or sour cream
    2–3 tsp. (10 g.) paprika

Dredge pieces of chicken in flour. Salt. Sauté in oil. Let brown deeply. Drain.

Put the onions and garlic in the pan used for the chicken while it is still hot. Add the chicken and yoghurt. Sprinkle with paprika and cover. Simmer approximately ½ hour.

(It is also common to cook the chicken in a tomato sauce, saving the yoghurt for the last minute.)

Serve sprinkled with herbs such as dill, mint, or parsley accompanied by noodles or knödels (potato dumplings–see p. 176).

Indian Chicken

This "chicken sausage" is wrapped in banana leaves, available dried in many Latin markets. Banana leaves can be replaced by corn husks or cheesecloth.

> 1 boiled chicken
> Juice of 1 lemon
> ½ coconut or ½ cup (60 g.) dried coconut, pureed
> 1–2 cloves garlic
> 1–2 tsp. (5 g.) fresh, grated ginger
> 2 tsp. (10 g.) ground coriander
> 1 tbs. (15 g.) sugar
> 3–4 tbs. (45 ml.) vinegar
> ½ tsp. (2 g.) cayenne
> Banana leaves

Bone the boiled chicken. Sprinkle with lemon juice. Pour pureed coconut pulp over the meat. Add seasonings; chop and mash the meat and seasonings together.

Wrap the chicken mixture in an oiled or buttered leaf and tie. Place the roll into a greased casserole and moisten with a little vinegar. Cook 15 minutes over a low flame, covered but turning often. When the vinegar is absorbed, remove the cover and let sit 2–3 minutes.

Unwrap the leaf and serve.

Chicken with Curds

Curds, a common ingredient in India, is used here as a marinade for chicken—as always the poor man's meat.

> 2 cloves garlic, minced
> 2 tsp. (10 g.) grated fresh ginger
> Salt
> 1 cup (250 ml.) curds (see p. 29) or yoghurt
> 1 chicken, cut up

Mix garlic, ginger, and salt with the curds or yoghurt. Marinate the chicken in the seasoned curds for a few hours, then bake at 450°F (230°C) or simmer 45 minutes.

Mole poblano
Chicken with Chili and Chocolate Sauce

This is a Mexican specialty.

> 1 large chicken, or 4−5 lbs. (2 kg.) turkey, cut up
> Salt
> 6−8 dried *ancho* chiles (mild, sweet chiles)
> 2−3 dried hot chiles (4−5 *pequins*)
> ¼ cup (50 g.) raisins
> ½ cup (80 g.) hulled almonds
> 2 sprigs fresh coriander
> 6−8 coriander seeds
> 1 tbs. (15 g.) sesame seeds
> 2 cloves garlic
> 1 onion
> 1 clove
> Pinch of anise
> 1 cup (250 g.) chopped tomatoes
> Lard, oil, or chicken fat for frying
> 1 oz. (30 g.) unsweetened chocolate
> Flour
> 1 toasted tortilla, crushed, or ½ cup (45 g.) bread crumbs

Put the chicken or turkey pieces in a pot or casserole, add salted water to cover, bring to a boil, and simmer 1 hour. Drain and reserve the broth.

Remove the stems, seeds, and membranes from the chiles and soak 20−30 minutes in hot water to cover. If using a *molcajete* or mortar and pestle: drain the chiles, reserving the liquid, and grind together with the raisins, almonds, fresh coriander, coriander seeds, sesame seeds, tortilla or bread crumbs, garlic, onion, clove, and anise. Mix with the chopped tomatoes, the liquid from soaking the chiles, and 1 cup of the broth to make a thick, smooth sauce. If using a blender: coarsely puree the soaked chiles in their water with the other seasonings, raisins, nuts, tomatoes and 1 cup of broth to make a thick, smooth sauce. Salt.

Fry the sauce in the lard, oil, or chicken fat in a heavy frying pan for 5 minutes, stirring often. Remove from the heat and stir in the chocolate, chopped or grated, to make it melt faster.

Dry the cooked, drained turkey or chicken pieces, dip in flour and brown in oil, lard, or chicken fat. Drain, put in a casserole and spread with the sauce. Cover and bake at 250°F (120°C) for 30 minutes.

Serve sprinkled with ground pepper, sesame seeds, and/or pignoli nuts. Serve with Mexican rice and beans (see p. 103).

Southern Fried Chicken

2 young chickens (about 3 lbs., 1.5 kg., each), cut up in serving
  pieces
Salt and pepper
2½ cups (300 g.) flour
2½ cups (625 ml.) buttermilk
About 1 cup (250 ml.) vegetable oil

Wipe chicken pieces with paper towels, sprinkle pieces with salt and
pepper. Coat each piece with flour, dip in buttermilk, then again in flour. In
deep skillet, heat vegetable oil to 350°F (175°C) (oil should be at least 2
inches deep). Lower heat to 325°F (160°C), then cook chicken, a few pieces
at a time, turning once or twice during frying, for about 10 minutes. Drain
well on paper towels. Keep warm until ready to serve.
   Serves 6–8.

Pulao
Lamb or Chicken with Rice

As is common in India, curds are used here as a sauce and flavoring.

2½ lbs. (1.2 kg.) chicken, cut up into small pieces, or lamb, cut into
  1-inch cubes
1 cup (250 g.) curds (see p. 29) or yoghurt
1 tbs. (15 g.) curry spices: turmeric, cumin, anise, fenugreek, cinnamon, clove, and coriander
3 minced onions
Ghee (see p. 31) or vegetable oil
1 cup (250 g.) rice
Approximately 1½ cups (400 ml.) water

Soak the meat in curds and curry spices for a few hours. Sauté onions in
ghee, add to meat, cover and cook gently for 1 hour. Add water and rice,
cover and simmer 20 minutes more. The juice should be completely absorbed.

Afghani Pancakes
Lamb Patties

In Afghanistan these patties are made with *dumba*, the fat from the tails of certain oriental species of sheep. Some tails can yield up to 7 pounds of fine fat. Use regular lamb fat cut from stew meat or chops.

>   1 lb. (500 g.) ground lamb
>   1/3 lb. (200 g.) minced fat
>   1–2 cloves garlic
>   Salt, pepper
>   2 onions, chopped
>   Juice of 1 lemon
>   2 eggs, separated

Simmer lamb in a little water until browned, about 10–15 minutes. Grind together with fat, garlic, and onions in a mortar. Season with salt and pepper. Moisten with lemon juice and bind with egg yolks. The mixture should be a thick paste. Shape into patties and roll in lightly beaten egg whites.

Fry on both sides until done, about 5 minutes a side.

Pakistani Lamb

>   1 lb. (500 g.) ground lamb
>   ½ cup (125 g.) lentils, soaked
>   2 cups (500 ml.) water
>   2 eggs
>   ½ cup (125 g.) curds (see p. 29) or yoghurt
>   1 onion, chopped
>   Salt
>   1–2 cloves garlic, minced
>   2 sprigs fresh coriander
>   1–2 tsp. (5 g.) fresh, grated ginger
>   ½ tsp. (2 g.) cayenne

Simmer meat and lentils in 2 cups of water for about 45 minutes. Mash and thicken with eggs and curds. Let cool.

Mix together the chopped onion, salt, garlic, fresh coriander, ginger, and cayenne. Take tablespoonfuls of this onion stuffing and shape meat/lentil patties around them. Fry in fat or oil, or grill on both sides.

Leben immou
Meat with Curds

Recipes based on curds and yoghurt are well known from North Africa to India, especially in countries formerly dominated by the Turks, such as Rumania, Bulgaria and Greece.

> 1 lb (500 g.) lamb, cut into 1-inch cubes
> Lamb fat cut from stew meat or chops
> 4 cups (1 l.) curds (see p. 29) or yoghurt
> Salt, ground coriander, cumin

Sauté the meat in lamb fat. Add water to cover. Simmer 1½−2 hours or until cooked. When done, add curds and seasonings. Simmer 5−10 minutes more. The sauce should be thick.
  Serve with rice.

Afghani Lamb

Afghanis use herbs such as madder, castor bean, and manna, that are not easily available in this country. They also use rhubarb, which is in season here in the spring. Fresh coriander can replace the exotic herbs.

> 1 lb. (500 g.) ground lamb
> 1 stalk rhubarb, sliced
> 1 cup (250 ml.) tomato sauce (see p. 45)
> 2−3 sprigs fresh coriander
> Crushed fresh mint
> Cayenne, black pepper
> 3−4 leeks
> 1 bunch of scallions
> 1 cup (250 ml.) yoghurt

Sauté the meat with the rhubarb until it turns pale. Add tomato sauce, coriander, mint, cayenne and pepper. Cook 5−10 minutes. Add minced leeks and scallions. Cook 3−5 more minutes. Add yoghurt.
  Serve with rice pilaf (see p. 106).

Kobbe
Lamb Loaf

A recipe from the Near East.

> 1 lb. (500 g.) chopped or ground lamb
> 2 onions, chopped
> Salt, pepper
> 2 cups (500 g.) *bulgur* (see p. 81)
> 2–3 oz. (70 g.) pine nuts or sliced almonds
> ½ cup (100 g.) chopped lamb fat cut from stew meat or chops

Mix the ground lamb together with one of the chopped onions, the salt and pepper. Mash together with the *bulgur* to make a smooth paste.

Brown the remaining chopped onion with the pine nuts in lamb fat.

Spread half the meat on a large greased plate. Spread the browned nuts and onions over the meat then cover with the rest of the meat. Press with your hands or a plate to make a firm loaf. Cut into squares and rectangles and sprinkle with melted lamb fat. Bake at 350°F (175°C) for 30–40 minutes or fry on both sides.

KOBBE SAMAK   Fish loaf.
Prepare as above, replacing the meat with fish, and the lamb fat with olive oil.

Brunswick Stew

There are countless variations of this American "soul food" dish, but purists insist on the squirrel meat.

> 2 chickens, 2 rabbits, or 4 squirrels
> 2 cups (500 g.) cooked butter beans
> 4 cups (1 kg.) stewed tomatoes
> 3–4 cups (800 g.) cut corn
> Salt, pepper, and red pepper to taste
> ¼ lb. (125 g.) butter

Boil meat in 3–4 qts. water until very tender—3 to 4 hours. Take out chicken, rabbit, or squirrels, cut into small pieces and put back into pot. Add beans, tomatoes, and corn; cook together for 30 minutes. Season to taste and stir in butter just before serving.

Serves 6–8.

Rabbit in Cider

Rabbit is both a poor man's meat and a luxury. It is not uncommon for a poor man in Europe or Latin America to raise a few rabbits behind his house as an additional source of protein. The firm but tender white flesh of rabbit has earned it a secure place in fine cookery.

> 1 4−5 lb. (2 kg.) rabbit (including head), cut up
> 1/3 cup (100 ml.) cider vinegar
> 1½ cups (450 ml.) hard cider or dry white wine
> 1−2 onions, chopped
> Bay leaves, sage, thyme, crushed peppercorns
> Flour
> Salt
> Lard or butter

Soak the rabbit 1 hour in salted water to clean out the blood. Rinse and drain. Marinate, preferably in a nonmetallic casserole, in the vinegar, cider, onions, and spices for at least 4 hours. Drain and pat dry, reserving the marinade. Set aside the kidneys, liver, and heart.

Dip the rabbit pieces in flour and fry quickly in lard or buttter in a large heavy frying pan or dutch oven, until brown. Add the marinade and salt. Cover and simmer 1 hour. Slice the organs, salt and pepper, and fry in butter or lard.

Serve the rabbit with the organs alongside, accompanied by boiled potatoes, drenched in cream or butter, and kale.

Serves 6.

Retfo
Ethiopian Beef Sauté

> 1 onion, chopped
> 1 sweet pepper with seeds removed, chopped
> Oil
> 1 lb. (500 g.) ground beef or lamb
> Salt, pepper
> ½ tsp. (2 g.) cayenne

Brown the vegetables in oil. Add the meat and seasoning. Simmer a few minutes.

To serve, mix with rice pilaf (see p. 106).

Gehakte leber
Chopped Liver

1 large onion, chopped
1 tbs. (15 ml.) chicken fat or corn oil
½ lb. (250 g.) liver, preferably chicken or turkey, but also calf or beef
Salt, pepper
1 carrot

Brown the onion in fat or oil. Add liver, salt and pepper, and simmer 5–10 minutes until cooked through. Chop in a wooden bowl with the raw carrot until it is all more or less finely minced, according to your preference for texture.

Serve on celery sticks or crackers, either warm or cold.

Serves 4 as an appetizer.

Mexican Meatballs

½ lb. (250 g.) ground beef
½ lb. (250 g.) ground pork
1 egg
1–2 sprigs fresh coriander
Oregano, salt
Bread crumbs
1–2 cloves garlic, chopped
Lard
2 cups (500 ml.) chopped, peeled tomatoes
Parsley, ground chiles, cumin, *epazote* (see p. 32) salt

Mix together beef and pork. Bind with an egg. Add chopped fresh coriander, oregano and salt, and thicken with bread crumbs. Shape into meatballs.

Brown garlic in lard, add tomatoes and other seasonings. Simmer 20–30 minutes.

Brown meatballs in lard, then cover with the hot and spicy tomato sauce. Add garlic. Simmer 45 minutes.

Chili

Real chili, so say the Texans, is made only with chunks of beef, not ground beef. Chili peppers come in many varieties, some hotter than others, so caution is advisable. (For fuller discussion of chiles see p. 33.) The different varieties of peppers have, of course, different tastes.

> 2 cups (500 g.) kidney beans
> 3 lbs. (1.5 kg.) beef, cut into ½ inch cubes
> Salt
> 6−8 large dried mild chiles (such as *ancho* chiles)
> 2−4 dried hot chiles (4−8 *pequín* chiles)
> 2 onions
> 4−6 cloves garlic
> Oregano, cumin, salt

Soak beans overnight. Drain, add water to cover, cover and simmer 2 hours. Add more water as necessary.

Simmer beef in water to cover for 1½−2 hours. Salt.

Remove stems and seed from the chili peppers. Soak the chiles 30 minutes in warm water. Grind the chiles, garlic, onion and spices together in a *molcajete* (stone mortar and pestle), adding the water in which the chiles soaked to make a liquid sauce. You can also puree the ingredients in a blender. Fry the sauce in a tablespoonful of oil or fat for about 5 minutes.

Add beans to the beef and broth, then the chili sauce. Let simmer gently 30 minutes. Serve hot.

Often tastes even better the next day.

Serves *6−8.*

Pigs in Blankets

> 1 lb. (500 g.) ground beef, or beef and pork
> 2 cups (400 g.) cooked rice
> Suggested seasoning: marjoram, oregano, mace, pepper
> 1 cooked head white cabbage, whole or quartered
> Tomato sauce (see p. 45)

Fry together ground beef, rice, and seasonings of your choice: chopped onion, peppers, or celery, may be added if desired. Place a tablespoonful of this mixture on a cabbage leaf and wrap into a snug package; tie with a piece of thin string. Place in a casserole. Repeat until the casserole is layered tightly with these "pigs." Cover with tomato sauce and bake for 30—40 minutes at 350°F (175°C) or until most of the liquid is absorbed. This dish is better the second or third day—just keep adding a little liquid and warming up.

Scrapple

This Pennsylvania Dutch creation has had a glorious history in mid-Atlantic American kitchens for over two centuries. It is generally served at breakfast.

> 1 lb. (500 g.) beef or pork liver
> 1 lb. (500 g.) pork or bacon scraps, lamb or beef pieces without bones
> 3—4 qts. (3—4 l.) water
> 1 tsp. (5 g.) thyme
> 1 tsp. (5 g.) sage
> 1 tsp. (5 g.) black pepper
> 3 cups (375 g.) cornmeal
> 2 cups (500 ml.) water

Cook meat slowly in 3—4 qts. water for about 2 hours until quite tender. Add water to cover if necessary. Cool, reserving broth, and chop meat finely or put through a meat grinder. Measure 6 cups of broth and add seasonings. Mix cornmeal with 2 cups of cold water. Add meat to broth and bring to a boil, then add cornmeal gradually, stirring constantly until the mixture is thick and bubbling. (Add more cornmeal if mixture doesn't thicken well.) Pour into a greased pan (or 2 bread tins) and chill overnight. To serve, slice scrapple ½ inch thick, dredge with flour, and brown quickly on both sides in a hot buttered skillet. Serve with maple syrup and pancakes.

Corned Beef

Corned beef, which can be quite expensive if bought prepared, is actually quite cheap if you prepare it yourself. The name has nothing to do with corn of course, but comes from the kernel-size salt originally used in curing the meat.

> 2 cups (500 g.) salt
> ¾ cup (170 g.) brown sugar
> 2 tsp. (10 g.) saltpeter
> 2 qts. (2 l.) boiling water
> 5–6 lbs. (2.5 kg.) boneless beef brisket

Dissolve salt, sugar, and saltpeter in boiling water; simmer for 10 minutes and skim any foam from the top. Cool to room temperature then pour over meat. Cover and keep cool for 4 weeks, turning each day and making sure that meat is completely immersed in brine. After the meat is cured, store it in the brine or cook it.

To cook, soak in cold water overnight, then bake slowly in a tightly closed pan with a small amount of water for 3–4 hours. (Another method is to boil in a pressure cooker for about 30 minutes with a quartered onion and a bay leaf.)

Serve with cabbage for a traditional meal: cook cabbage separately, then slice beef and place together in a shallow bowl with a little of the cooking juices dribbled over both.

To use leftovers, make a hash by frying diced meat and potatoes in browned onions, garlic, and peppers and season strongly.

Serves 8.

Meat and Grain Stew

> 1/3 cup (80 g.) whole wheat or cracked wheat
> 1/3 cup (80 g.) sorghum
> ¼ cup (60 g.) whole oats, rice, or barley
> 2 qts. (2 l.) water or meat stock
> 1 lb. (500 g.) cooked meat: beef, pork, lamb, and any available bones
> 4 cups (800 g.) coarsely chopped vegetables (onion, carrot, celery, turnip, rutabaga, beets, beans, corn)
> 1 cup (250 ml.) milk
> 1 tbs. (15 g.) salt
> 1 tsp. (5 g.) black pepper
> ¼ tsp. (1 g.) chili powder or cayenne, or crushed fresh chiles

Clean and soak grains overnight in water or stock. Boil grains in the liquid they were soaked in for about an hour. (If bones are to be used, add them to the liquid for this cooking.) Add cooked meat, vegetables, milk, and seasoning. Cook, covered, until tender, about 15–20 minutes.

Earth Cooking

Earth, or pit cooking, is a common way of preparing meat all over the world.

A Papuan oven is a hole about 3 feet deep, carpeted with live coals, then a layer of glowing hot stones, covered in turn by a thick layer of leaves. Meat and vegetables are laid on top, covered with leaves and then earth to seal the primitive oven. Meats are seasoned with salt before cooking. Snake cooked this way is exceptionally succulent, not unlike smoked eel. Fires must be kept burning night and day to feed these ovens.

In Madagascar, a fire is built in a hole lined with stones. When the fire burns down, pieces of meat wrapped in banana leaves are laid on the hot stones and embers. The hole is sealed with earth. Then the wait begins.

In Hawaii, a big hole is dug and lined with stones. The varied foods to be cooked are laid in concentric circles: suckling pigs in the center, then chickens and fish wrapped in banana leaves, and outside that, another circle of balls of vegetables and banana and papaya *poe* (see p. 204), also wrapped in banana leaves. All this is covered by thick mats of braided leaves and branches, and cooked at least 3 hours.

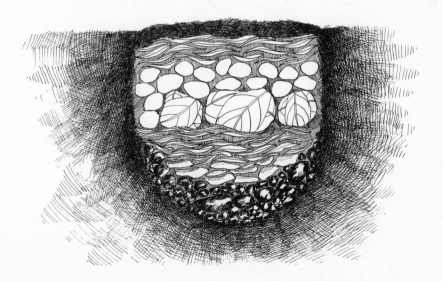

A Mexican *barbacoa* pit is dug 5 feet deep by 2 feet wide. The sides are daubed with mud and the bottom carpeted with *tezontles*, porous volcanic rocks that hold in heat. A fire built in the pit heats the rocks. Most of the live coals are dug out, and the bottom is covered with a layer of maguey leaves. A rack is then placed in the pit; on the rack is placed a pot filled with beans, rice, soup, etc., to be served with the meat. On top of that is placed a sheep quartered or cut to smaller pieces, with the shoulders, legs, shins and head on top; no salt. Maguey leaves are then laid over the meat. The pile is held down by a metal sheet covered with leaves, a mat, and then mud for a hermetic seal. On top, a fire is kept burning steadily for around 6 hours.

Pit cooking is readily adaptable to temperate climates, and particularly appropriate for outdoor expeditions. Be sure to line the pit well with big stones that hold heat, such as granite, and to make the pit large enough to hold the meat. Heat the pit well by keeping a big fire burning in it for several hours. The meat, a small pig or turkey, should be wrapped in burlap soaked in salad oil. When ready to cook, dig out the coals and ashes, leaving some covering the bottom of the pit. Put in the meat and fill in the pit with more live coals. Seal carefully with dirt—if there is any steam escaping, the oven will cool off rapidly. Allow 6 to 7 hours for a 10–12 pound turkey.

The major difficulty in cooking in earth ovens is knowing when the meal is cooked. Once the oven is opened, it cannot be sealed again.

Another variety of earth cooking, common in Africa, uses *pot-pot*, or laterite, a common component of central African soil. The *pot-pot* is thinned with water and used to coat an unplucked chicken. A termite hill, heated by burning a fire around it and partly filling it with hot stones, often serves as an oven. The chicken is placed in the termite hill and sealed shut; the fire continues roaring around it. After several hours the chicken is cooked; it is removed from the termite hill. Natives break away the clay shell with a machete, and serve the chicken with tomato sauce spiced with cayenne or wild peppers.

Meat Barbecued with Ground Peanuts

In Africa elephant, buffalo, or monkey is often cooked with ground up peanuts. Of course beef, pork, and chicken are also excellent this way.

½ lb. (250 g.) raw, shelled peanuts
1 lb. (500 g.) tomatoes, chopped
2 onions, chopped
3–4 cloves garlic, chopped
1–2 tsp. (5 g.) cayenne pepper
1 tbs. (15 g.) flour
1 tbs. (15 g.) butter
2 lbs. (1 kg.) meat, barbecued

Grill peanuts on a baking sheet at 400°F (200°C) for 20 minutes. Crush in a stone mortar to make a thick, smooth puree.

Sauté tomatoes with onions and garlic, adding a good dose of hot pepper. Mix together flour and butter over heat and add to the tomato sauce. Add barbecued meat. Simmer 10 minutes, thickening the sauce with the ground peanuts.

Pressed Tongue

A fresh beef or calf tongue, 2–3 lbs. (1 kg.)
1 small white onion, quartered
1 tsp. salt
¼ tsp. pepper (or 6 peppercorns)

Cover tongue with boiling water. Add other ingredients and simmer uncovered until it is fork-tender, 2½–3½ hours (or 30 minutes in a pressure cooker). Drain tongue, preserving cooking liquid, and soak it for 3–5 minutes in cold water so you can handle it. Using a fork to help you hold the tongue, skin it and remove any gristle and bones from the base (the skin is difficult to remove once tongue has cooled). Place tongue sideways in a small deep bowl, curled around itself. Pour cooking liquid around it to the level of the tongue and weight it with a plate. Refrigerate. When cold, tongue may be sliced and served with mustard or horseradish.

Jerky

Most types of muscle meat (as opposed to organ meats) can be used for jerky (venison, lamb, veal, mutton, beef are generally preferred), but the meat must be lean and without any fat, so trim carefully.

Slice meat into thin slices (about ¼ inch). Salt well on both sides (or marinade in lime juice). Hang the meat strips outdoors in full sun to dry, turning from side to side frequently. Bring the meat indoors to hang in a dry place when the sun begins to go down. Return outside daily during the full sun until jerky is totally dry—3 to 5 days if the weather is dry and hot, longer if not. Store in a dry place in a covered container.

In the United States jerky is usually consumed as a snack or on long hikes, but in Latin America it is often added to other dishes. Dried beef known as *carne seca* or *charqui* is sold in slabs or ground all over Latin America and is especially popular in Chile. *Charqui* soup is made from ground *charqui*, onions, and pumpkin and is served over poached eggs, as soups often are in South America. *Carne seca* or *charqui* may also be used to enrich other dishes, such as omelets.

Head Cheese
Calf's Head

The rich are conservative in choosing what part of the animal to eat—only 20 percent of the beef of a steer is steak, yet steak accounts for over 60 percent of American meat purchases. The poor are by necessity less choosy, more daring, or if you wish, more refined in eating a greater variety of the meats of an animal—the "corners of the cow." Oxtail stew, calf's head, tripe, and chitterlings are delicacies made from parts of the animal too often disdained. Fine French cooking, which sometimes calls for meats like coxcombs and pig's feet, owes a large debt to the culinary adventures of the hungry man. The quality of the protein is consistent, and the taste more varied. Head cheese, known as braun in the British Isles and *daube* in France, is a prime example of the best innard cusine. Calf's head can be ordered from your butcher if it is not kept generally in stock.

    1 calf's head
    3 small onions
    ¼ lb. (125 g.) butter
    ½ cup (125 ml.) red wine
    Salt, pepper, nutmeg, and cloves to taste

Split the calf's head into 3 or 4 pieces. Take out the brains and eyes, cut off the ears and snout, and trim as much fat as you can. Cover with cold water, add onions, and boil for 2–3 hours until the meat falls from the bones. Meanwhile, boil brains in salted water until firm, about 20 minutes. Trim meat from the head and cut into small pieces. Combine meat with brains (which have been chopped up), butter, wine, and seasonings; place in a baking dish and bake for 30–40 minutes. This can be covered with a pastry before baking, or served with a gravy made from the reserved stock. It can also be chilled with a weighted cover and sliced before serving.

Chitlins'
Pig Intestines

Chitlins' or chitterlings are the small intestines of a pig and are a great delicacy of the American South. They are often found cooked up with hog maws or stomach of the same animal. They can often be found already cleaned, but if you get them fresh at slaughtering time you'll get a better flavor, and probably less smell. While still warm, empty them out by turning them inside our and scraping thoroughly. Remove the lining and as much of the fat as possible. Soak for 24 hours in cold salted water, then wash several times.

> 8–10 lbs. (4 kg.) chitterlings
> 1 large onion, quartered
> 1 clove garlic, sliced
> 1 tbs. (15 g.) salt
> Several whole peppercorns
> ¼ cup (60 ml.) vinegar, white wine, or apple cider
> 1 bay leaf
> 1 tsp. (5 g.) crushed hot chiles, or 3 dried hot chiles
> Optional: 3 hog maws, washed, parboiled, drained, scraped and cut
> up

Cover chitterlings with cold water and add remaining ingredients. Bring to a boil slowly and then simmer for 3 to 4 hours. Drain chitterlings, cut into 2 inch lengths and return to the pot. Serve with corn bread and greens.
Serves 10–12.

Haggis
Stuffed Sheep Stomach

1 smaller stomach bag
1 sheep's stomach
½ lb (250 g.) suet
Liver, kidney, other internal organs of sheep
2 cups (500 g.) rolled oats
2 – 3 onions, chopped
1 tbs. (15 g.) salt
1 tsp. (5 g.) pepper
Mashed potatoes with mashed turnips stirred in

Clean stomach bags and soak overnight in salted water. Cook together small bag and sheep parts for 1 or 2 hours, or until tender. Put this cooked meat through a food grinder along with the suet. Combine meat and suet mixture with oats, onion, and seasonings. Moisten mixture with a cup or two of the cooking liquid, then put into the large bag, not filling too tightly. Sew up the bag and prick it in several places to keep it from exploding. Place in a large pot of boiling water and simmer for 3 hours. To serve, make a large X in the top with a sharp knife. Spoon out over a mound of mashed potatoes and turnips.
   Serves 6 – 8.

Kok koretsi
Innards Brochettes

No Greek Easter feast is complete without the roasting of a Pascal lamb accompanied by these curious brochettes. The feast is prepared outside as the celebrants dance by the fire to the sound of the *santouri* and clarinet.

Lamb heart, liver, lungs, kidneys, brain, cut into 1 – 2 inch cubes
Lamb intestine, cleaned and washed
Chopped parsley, basil, and mint
Lemon

Skewer the cubed meats. Sprinkle with herbs and lemon. Wrap the intestines around the skewers in coils. Grill slowly.

Steak and Kidney Pie

1 − 2 lbs. (500 g.) lean round or chuck steak cut into 1 inch cubes
Flour
4 − 5 tbs. (60 g.) butter, suet, lard, or vegetable oil
1 lb. (500 g.) beef or veal kidneys, blanched, skinned, trimmed and
      cut into 1 inch cubes
1 medium onion, chopped coarsely
Enough pie dough to line and cover a heavy deep 2 − 3 quart cas-
      serole (about 4 cups (500 g.) flour, 1 − 1½ (250 g.) cups butter or
      shortening, salt, water)
3 − 4 cups beef (750 ml.) stock or beef stock and red wine
2 − 3 tsp. (10 g.) salt
1 tsp. pepper
1 bay leaf
½ tsp. thyme
1 − 2 tbs. chopped parsley
Optional: 1 egg, beaten

Dredge steak in flour and sauté in butter until browned. Remove from pan
and sauté kidneys and onions also (kidneys may be dredged also if you
desire). Line casserole with pastry, brush with a little butter, and transfer
meat cubes to casserole. Pour stock into the pan which has been used for
cooking the meat and onions, and simmer, stirring to incorporate bits of
flour, meat, etc. Add seasonings and stir together for a few minutes, then
pour into casserole. Cover casserole with remaining pastry (slashing in
center to allow steam to escape), crimp tightly around the edge, and bake
for about 1 hour, first 30 minutes at 450°F (230°C); then lower temperature
to 350°F (175°C). The crust will brown better if it is brushed with a beaten
egg.

Paella
Chicken or Shellfish in Rice

Paella is a familiar dish to tourists and patrons of Spanish restaurants. It is found in Spain in many variations, enriched with whatever ingredients are at hand.

> 1 chicken, cut-up
> Olive oil
> 2 onions, chopped
> 4 cloves garlic
> Salt, pepper
> 3–4 pistils saffron, crushed and soaked in a little water
> ¼ lb. (125 g.) *chorizo* (Spanish sausage), sliced
> 2 cups (500 ml.) chicken stock or water
> 1 cup (250 g.) rice

Brown the chicken in oil. Add onion, garlic, and seasonings, then the *chorizo*. Transfer to a seasoned clay *paella* dish. Add stock or water. Cover and simmer 40–45 minutes.

Add rice. Simmer 15 minutes until the rice absorbs all the juice.

PAELLA A LA VALENCIANA   Replace the chicken with cockles and mussels, both with shells removed. Poor Valencianos eat it Sundays and during local celebrations, both patriotic and religious, such as the festivals in honor of San Vicente Martír and El Cristo del Grao.

Arroz a banda
Rice and Fish

Spanish fisherman rice.

>   4 onions, chopped
>   Olive oil
>   1−2 lbs. (700 g.) tomatoes
>   2 qts. (2 l.) water
>   Bay leaf, peppercorns, sage
>   1−3 lbs. (0.5−1.5 kg.) fish heads and trimmings
>   2 lbs. (1 kg.) fish
>   2 lbs. (1 kg.) mussels and crayfish, mixed
>   3−4 pistils saffron
>   3−4 cloves garlic
>   2 cups (500 g.) rice

Brown the onions in oil. Add peeled tomatoes, water, and seasoning, then fish heads and trimmings. Simmer ½ hour. Strain.

Slice fish into chunks. Wash mussels and crayfish. Open the mussels and remove one of the shells. Lay fish, mussels, and crayfish in a big pot and pour in about half the fish stock. Simmer about 8 minutes. Season with saffron crushed with garlic. Simmer another 8 minutes.

Meanwhile cook rice in the remaining stock (there should be about 1 qt.). Cook until all liquid is completely absorbed.

Pile the rice on a serving plate and serve the fish and shellfish *a banda*— that is, on the side.

Serves 6.

Indonesian Fish

1 lb. (500 g.) fish with white flesh (haddock, flounder)
3 chili peppers with seeds removed
1–2 cloves garlic
Turmeric, lemongrass, salt
1 tsp. (5 g.) fresh, grated ginger
1 tbs. (15 g.) sugar
Juice of 1–2 lemons
Banana leaves (or corn husks or parchment paper)
2 onions, chopped

Filet or cut the fish into steaks. Crush the seasonings in a mortar and mix with onion and lemon juice then spread over the fish. Wrap in banana leaves and cook in an oven 15–20 minutes at 350°F (175°C).

Indian Koftas
Fish Balls

1 lb. (500 g.) filets of fish with white flesh (haddock, flounder)
1 onion, chopped
Chopped fresh coriander
1 tbs. (15 g.) cumin
1–2 hot chiles, fresh and chopped or dried and crushed
Salt, pepper
Egg
Bread crumbs
Ghee (see p. 31) or oil

Crush fish together with onion in a mortar, add herbs and spices. Bind with egg. Shape into balls and roll in bread crumbs. Fry in *ghee* or oil.

In vegetarian regions of India where no eggs are eaten, the binder for these balls is a paste made from *gram dhal* (*dhal* flour—see p. 28), water, salt, and a pinch of baking powder.

Kedgeree

This dish, a British adaptation of the Indian *kichri* (see p. 100), has been transmitted to British-influenced parts of the world from India. It was usually eaten for breakfast but is now generally served for lunch or dinner. You can also make it with leftover fish.

> 1 lb. (500 g.) smoked haddock (Finnan Haddie) or cod
> 3 cups (750 g.) cooked rice
> ¼ cup (60 g.) melted butter
> 1 tbs. (15 g.) curry spices: turmeric, cardamom, fenugreek, cumin
> ¼ tsp. cayenne pepper
> ¼ tsp. freshly ground black pepper
> 4 hard-boiled eggs, finely chopped
> 2 tbs. (30 g.) parsley, finely chopped

Poach the Finnan Haddie or smoked cod in water to cover for 10 minutes.

Remove fish from water and drain thoroughly; with two forks, break into bite-sized flakes, removing any bones. Mix into rice in the top of a double boiler; heat through while preparing sauce.

Stir together melted butter and seasonings; stir in eggs and blend thoroughly. Fold into rice and fish mixture. When well blended and warm, turn onto serving plate. Garnish with parsley.

Finnan Haddie
Smoked Haddock in Milk

> 1½ – 2 lbs. (700 g.) smoked haddock (Finnan Haddie) or cod fillets
> 4 – 6 cups (1 l.) milk
> 1 tsp. (5 g.) whole black peppercorns
> 1 small onion, sliced
> ¼ lb. (60 g.) butter

Wash fish in cold water; place in a heavy shallow pan. Cover with milk (add more or less as necessary). Add peppercorns and onion and bring slowly to the boiling point. Do not allow to actually boil; lower heat and simmer for 15 or 20 minutes, turning fish once, until the fish flakes easily. Lift fish from the milk to a plate and tear apart into bite-sized pieces, removing any stray bones. Strain peppercorns and onions from the milk and discard. Reheat milk to steaming if it has cooled by this time. Cut butter into small pieces, place in serving bowls and pour hot milk into each one, spooning fish in at the end.

Greek Fish

3−5 lbs. (1.7 kg.) whole fish (e.g. sea bass)
Salt, pepper
Lemon juice
2 minced onions
3−4 cloves garlic
Chopped fresh parsley
Olive oil
2−3 peeled tomatoes
1 cup (250 ml.) dry white wine
1 tbs. (15 g.) sugar
Tomato slices

Wash a big fish thoroughly. Sprinkle with salt, pepper, and lemon juice. Lay out in a baking plate. Slash skin in 2 or 3 places.

Brown onions, garlic, and parsley in olive oil. Add peeled tomatoes. Add a little water and a cup of white wine. Mix in sugar.

Pour sauce over the fish. Cover with tomato slices. Bake 30−45 minutes at 400°F (200°C). Test with a fork to see if cooked through. Do not overcook.

Seafood Gumbo

One of the important ingredients in any gumbo is *filé*, a seasoning made from powdered sassafras, available in herb and spice stores and some supermarkets.

1 chicken
4−5 qts. (4 l.) water
1 cup (125 g.) flour
½ cup (125 g.) bacon drippings
1 large onion, chopped
1 stalk celery, chopped
1 cup (250 ml.) tomatoes
1 lb. (500 g.) okra
2 lbs. (1 kg.) peeled, deveined shrimp
1½ tbs. (20 g.) salt, pepper
2−3 chiles with seeds removed, chopped, or 1 tsp. powdered chiles
1 pint (500 ml.) fresh shucked oysters, including juice
1½ tbs. (20 g.) *filé*

Simmer the chicken 1½ hours in water to cover. Drain, reserving the broth. Bone and skin the chicken.

Stir flour into hot fat and brown deeply. Add chicken broth and remaining water. Stir and let boil 20−30 minutes. Add onion and celery and simmer another 30 minutes. Add tomatoes, okra, shrimp, salt, pepper, and chili. Simmer 10−15 minutes until shrimp is tender. Add oysters and chicken meat. Simmer 5−10 minutes until oysters curl at the edges. Remove from heat and stir in *filé.*

Serve with rice.

Serves 6−8.

Sushi

Japanese Stuffed Seaweed

> 2 cups (500 g.) cooked rice, preferably sticky, wide-grained Japanese rice
> ¼−½ lb. (125 g.) raw fish (e.g. tuna, bass, octopus, or mackerel)
> Japanese hot radish paste or hot mustard
> Rice vinegar
> 6−10 sheets *nori* seaweed (purple laver)

All of these ingredients are available in Japanese markets and, with the exception of radish paste and fresh fish, at health food stores.

Form rice into long cylinders with strips of fish running through or along them. Daub with a little hot radish paste. Sprinkle with vinegar. Roll up in a sheet of laver, moistened with vinegar. Serve cut into 1 inch sections.

For a more economical version of sushi, replace the fish with vegetables, such as *daikon* or carrot, or a sliced, hard-boiled egg.

Peruvian Ceviche

This method of "cooking" fish cold in lemon juice is found not only on the Pacific coast of South America but also in the Pacific islands—in fact, *ceviche* could just as well be called Tahitian.

 1 lb. (500 g.) raw fish such as haddock or flounder
 6–10 lemons
 Salt
 2 cloves garlic, chopped
 1–2 hot dried chiles, with seeds removed and chopped, or ½ tsp. powdered chiles
 1–2 onions, cut into rings
 1–2 sweet peppers, sliced

Skin and fillet fish with firm, white flesh—haddock or flounder will do. Wash well. Dice the fish. Cover with lemon juice. Add salt, garlic, and chiles. Stir to make sure the pieces are well marinated. Cover with raw onion rings and sliced pepper. Let soak in a cool place for a few hours.
 Serve with boiled sweet potatoes.

VARIANT Replace fish with raw shrimp.

Bacalao

Portuguese Cod

Cod is the poor man's fish all over the world. Portugal, as a fishing nation, is noted for its large variety of cod recipes.

> 1 lb. (500 g.) dried salt cod (*bacalao*, see p. 36), soaked overnight and drained
> 3 onions, chopped
> 2–3 cloves garlic, chopped
> Black pepper
> Chopped parsley
> 1 lb. (500 g.) potatoes
> Olive oil

Soak cod overnight in abundant water. Drain.

Spread minced onions in a frying pan. Sprinkle with garlic, pepper, and chopped parsley. Cover with an even layer of cod, then of sliced potatoes.

Add oil to cover, or sprinkle generously with oil.

Cover and cook at least 1 hour over a low heat.

African Dried Cod in Tomato Sauce

Dried fish is an important resource when the catch thins out. This dish is served with *chi kuang*, the traditional manioc balls (also known as *fufu* and often made with yam or plantain paste instead of manioc). Leftovers may be shaped into sausages, wrapped in banana leaves, tied with vines, then poached. Cooked this way, they keep a long time. Fish and manioc are sometimes accompanied by *gombos*, or okra mixed into a plate of spinach or young manioc leaves, boiled and crushed to a paste, then thickened with ground up peanuts and seasoned with hot pepper. Boiled green bananas take the place of bread.

> 2–3 onions, chopped
> 1–2 cloves garlic, chopped
> Vegetable oil or peanut oil
> 2–3 fresh or soaked dried chiles with seeds and stems removed, chopped or 2 tbs. (30 g.) powdered chiles
> 4–6 tomatoes, chopped
> 1 lb. (500 g.) salt cod (*bacalao*, see p. 36) soaked overnight in cold water, drained, and cut into 2 inch pieces

Sauté onions and garlic in 1−2 tbs. peanut oil. Add chopped chiles and fry for a few minutes. Add chopped tomatoes and simmer 10 minutes before adding the salt cod. Serve with manioc balls:

> 1 cup (125 g.) manioc meal
> 2½ cups (625 ml.) water
> Salt

Add manioc meal gradually to boiling salted water, stirring constantly. Simmer, stirring, 20 minutes. Let cool. Shape into walnut-sized balls and serve.

Squid with Rice

Octopus and squid are eaten fresh or dried in many countries, such as Spain, Portugal, Turkey, Japan, the Windward Isles, and France. They can be dried by hanging on a line like laundry, but once dried they get tough and must be soaked well before use.

> 1 lb. (500 g.) small squid
> Flour
> Olive oil
> 2 cloves garlic
> Chopped fresh parsley
> 1 cup (250 ml.) tomato sauce (see p. 45)
> 1−2 onions, chopped
> 1½ cups (375 g.) rice
> 3−4 pistils saffron
> 3 cups (750 ml.) water or stock

Prepare the squid by removing the sepia hood. Young, small squid do not have the cuttle bone that must be removed in larger squid. Blanch 3−5 minutes in boiling, salted water. Drain. Wipe dry, dip in flour, and fry in oil 10 minutes. Sprinkle with garlic and parsley, and put into an aromatic tomato sauce. Meanwhile make a rice pilaf by frying onions with rice and crushed saffron in olive oil, then adding water or stock and simmering until absorbed. Combine squid, tomato mixture, and rice, and serve, with mussels on the side if wished.

Preserved Squid

> 2 lbs. (1 kg.) small squid
> Shallots or small white onions
> 1 cup (250 ml.) dry white wine
> 1–2 cups (250 ml.) water
> Bay leaf, peppercorns, thyme
> Salt

Prepare the squid by removing the sepia hood and pounding to tenderize. Simmer 15–20 minutes in a spicy court bouillon made with shallots, wine, water, and spices. Put in earthen pots or glass jars and cover with a marinade consisting of equal volumes of the court bouillon in which the squid cooked, vinegar, and water. Add more fresh spices (bay leaves, thyme, pepper, etc.)

Prepared this way in the early fall, squid will keep through the winter. It can be eaten in salads or cooked in stews.

Greek Octopus

> 1 octopus, weighing about 1½ lbs. (700 g.)
> ½ cup (125 ml.) wine vinegar
> ½ cup (125 ml.) olive oil
> 1 cup (250 ml.) water
> 4 onions
> 2 cloves garlic
> pepper

Remove head, eyes, beak, and ink sac. Cut across the tentacles to make ¼ inch slices, and pound with a wooden mallet or rolling pin to tenderize.

Put all the ingredients in a pot. *Do not salt.* Close tightly and simmer 2 hours.

Make sure to cover the octopus entirely with liquid and to close tightly—otherwise the octopus will be horny and uneatable.

Spanish Octopus

    1 octopus, weighing about 1½ lbs. (700 g.)
    2 onions, chopped
    Olive oil
    1 cup (250 ml.) dry white wine
    2−3 tomatoes
    2−3 cloves garlic
    Chopped fresh parsley, basil
    Salt, pepper, thyme
    ½ tsp. cayenne

Remove head, eyes, beak and ink sac. Cut across the tentacles to make ¼ inch slices, and pound with a wooden mallet or rolling pin to tenderize.

Brown the onions in oil. Add the white wine, tomato, garlic, herbs, and seasonings. Add pieces of octopus. Cover tightly and simmer 2 hours.

Serve, adding butter to the sauce.

DESSERTS AND DRINKS

Korean Melon

> 1 melon
> 1 cup (250 ml.) water
> 1 cup (250 g.) sugar
> 1 orange or lemon

Cube an oval melon. Prepare syrup by simmering water, sugar, grated orange or lemon peel, and orange or lemon juice together for 10–15 minutes.

Mix the cubes with the syrup and bring to a boil. Cover and simmer 10–15 minutes.

Candied Maduros

Maduros are a variety of plantains, tougher in texture than ordinary bananas, with a dark skin. You can find them in Hispanic markets.

> 6 *maduros* or bananas
> Lard or butter
> 1 cup (250 ml.) dry white wine
> ½ cup (125 g.) sugar
> ½ tsp. cinnamon
> 1 tsp. (5 ml.) vanilla

Slice ripe *maduros* and soak 20–30 minutes in salted water to remove excess moisture. Drain.

Sauté in lard and pour over white wine, sugar, vanilla, and cinnamon. Simmer 15 minutes or so.

Mexican Maduro Bananas

6 *maduros* or bananas
Lard or butter
½ lb. (250 g.) fresh cheese (farmer's cheese or ricotta)
½ cup (125 g.) sugar
½ cup (125 ml.) rum
Cinnamon
½ cup (125 ml.) heavy cream

Peel and slice the bananas. Brown in lard or butter. Place a layer of slices on the bottom of a greased baking tin. Beat together the cheese and the sugar, rum, and cinnamon, and cover the bananas. Build alternating layers of banana slices and sweet cheese. Pour cream over the top and bake 25 minutes at 350°F (175°C). The cream should be almost entirely absorbed. Serve hot.

Apple Sauce

2 lbs. (1 kg.) apples
2 tbs. (30 g.) butter
¼ cup (50 g.) brown sugar
Lemon juice
Cinnamon

Wash and core apples. Slice coarsely and simmer slowly in very little water until soft, for 10–15 minutes. Mix butter and sugar. Add lemon juice and cinnamon to taste. Puree in a food mill, if you prefer a creamy texture.

Serve hot or cold, by itself, or with cake as a dessert, or with potato pancakes.

Oriental Oranges

1 dozen mandarin oranges, tangerines or small thin-skinned oranges
2 cups (500 g.) sugar
1 qt. (1 l.) water
1 tsp. (5 ml.) vanilla

Scrape the oranges. Do not peel. Mix sugar and water to make a syrup. Add vanilla. Add the oranges and simmer at least 1 hour. Let cool and serve in their syrup.

If refrigerated, these oranges will keep for a month.

Camotes in Syrup
Latin American Sweet Potatoes

Camote is the Mexican name for a variety of sweet potato which is also known as *batata* and *boniato*.

> 2 lbs. (1 kg.) *camotes* (sweet potatoes)
> ½–1 cup (125 g.) sugar
> Water

Peel and simmer the *camotes* in a very little water for 10 minutes until half-cooked. Drain.

Put in a pot with sugar and enough water to cover. Simmer 20 minutes or so. The sweet potatoes should look glazed and almost transparent.

Serve cold in their syrup.

El mistouf
Sweet Couscous

> 2 cups (500 g.) *couscous* (see p. 89)
> 1 cup (250 g.) pitted dates
> ½ cup (80 g.) almonds
> ½ cup (80 g.) raisins
> 1/3 cup (80 g.) sugar
> ½ cup (80 g.) shelled, unsalted pistachio nuts
> Grated orange peel
> Butter

Prepare couscous according to recipe on p. 89, or use leftover couscous. Cover with halved dates before the last steaming (or resteam leftovers).

Meanwhile, crush almonds, raisins, sugar, pistachio nuts, and orange peel together in a mortar (you can grate the nuts first if that's easier). Mix with the couscous and sprinkle with melted butter.

Peanut Caramel

An African treat.

    1 lb. (500 g.) raw, unshelled peanuts
    3 cups (750 g.) sugar
    1 cup (250 ml.) water

Roast peanuts for 10−15 minutes in a 400°F (200°C) oven, and shell them by rubbing between your hands. Mix sugar and water and boil 10−15 minutes until you have a thick syrup. Add the peanuts and continue boiling, stirring until the caramel thickens and takes on color. Spread on a buttered plate or marble slab, like nougat. Cut when cooled.

Russian Candied Milk

    2 cups (500 ml.) rich fresh or raw milk
    2 cups (500 g.) sugar

Heat sugar and milk gently and simmer 2−3 hours, stirring frequently: the mixture will get very thick and take on a golden color. Pour into little pots or spread onto a marble or linoleum slab and cut into 1−2 inch squares when cool. This dessert will keep a long time.

Sarikauja
Malaysian Custard

    1 cup (250 g.) sugar
    4 eggs
    2 cups (500 ml.) coconut milk (see p. 47)
    1 tsp. (5 ml.) rose water

Beat sugar and eggs together. Add coconut milk and flavor with rose water. Pour into greased individual molds. Set in a pan half-full of hot water, cover and cook 45 minutes in an oven at 350°F (175°C).
    Turn out of the mold when cooled.

Tamina el béjauia
Semolina Pudding

Serve with mint tea, as in North Africa.

> 2 cups (500 g.) couscous (coarse semolina)
> 2 cups (500 ml.) honey
> ½ lb. (250 g.) butter
> Optional: chopped dates

Grill couscous over a moderate heat in a dry, heavy frying pan. Shake constantly so it will not stick. Cook 3 minutes.

Melt the honey and butter together to make a smooth cream.

Mix quickly with the hot couscous. If desired, add chopped dates. Pour onto a buttered plate or shallow pan.

Smooth. Cool and cut into squares.

Lukschenkugel
Noodle Pudding

On Rosh Hashanah, the Jewish New Year, it is traditional to eat sweet things like honey cake or this noodle pudding, in hopes of a sweet year.

> 1 lb. (500 g.) wide egg noodles
> ¼ cup (60 ml.) corn oil
> 3−4 eggs
> ½ cup (125 g.) sugar
> 3−4 apples
> ¾ cup (170 g.) raisins
> 1½ tbs. (20 g.) cinnamon

Boil and drain the noodles. Oil a shallow baking pan generously and put in the noodles, mixing so that they are coated with oil. Beat the eggs with half the sugar and mix into noodles. Peel, core, and slice apples finely and with raisins add to the noodles. Combine remaining sugar and cinnamon, and sprinkle over the surface. Bake at 350°F (175°C) for 45 minutes.

VARIANT: Mix ½ pound drained pot cheese in with the noodles.

Bread Pudding

½ loaf stale bread, sliced
Butter to cover each slice both sides
1 cup (160 g.) raisins
½ cup (100 g.) brown sugar
2 cups (500 ml.) milk or milk and cream
4 eggs
Freshly grated nutmeg

Butter sliced bread and layer in a deep, buttered baking dish with raisins and brown sugar. Beat together milk and eggs until very frothy, then pour over bread. Bake at 350°F (175°C) for about an hour, or until custard is set and tops of bread are slightly brown. Grate nutmeg over pudding and serve with fresh cream.

Bouza

Bouza is a delicious pudding served in parts of Africa, delicately scented with geranium water. The traditional way of preparing this dish includes pounding the sorghum dough, thinning with cream, and pressing through cloths, blanching and skinning the nuts, and pounding them into a fine powder. The method below takes only a short time to make, yet results in a good approximation of the original.

If you find it hard to locate sorghum flour (see p. 77), or you could try substituting millet flour.

1 cup (125 g.) very finely ground sorghum flour
2 cups (500 ml.) cold water
1 cup (150 g.) shelled filberts (hazelnuts)
1 cup (150 g.) shelled almonds
2 cups (500 ml.) milk or cream
½ cup (125 ml.) honey
1 tsp. (5 ml.) geranium water or rose water

Stir together flour and water. Put through a sieve, pouring liquid into medium saucepan and discarding any sorghum remaining in sieve. Shred nuts in a mill or blender until very fine. Stir into sorghum and water mixture; slowly add milk or cream, stirring constantly to prevent lumps. Bring to a boil over low heat, stirring often. When mixture has thickened, stir in honey and geranium or rose water and serve. Bouza may also be chilled thoroughly in small bowls and sprinkled with shredded nuts before serving.

Mazamorra
Uruguayan Corn Pudding

> 1 cup (250 g.) whole dried corn
> 1 tsp. (5 g.) baking soda
> Milk, sugar

Soak corn overnight. Bring to a boil and simmer 45 minutes. Add the soda dissolved in some cold water. Boil a few moments then remove from heat. Pour into a bowl and let cool.
  Serve with milk and sugar.

Indian Pudding

The key to making this classic American dessert is to cook it very slowly for a long time. If possible, use a stone or clay pot, such as a Boston bean pot.

> 1 cup (130 g.) cornmeal
> ½ cup (125 ml.) molasses
> ½ cup (125 g.) sugar
> ¼ cup (60 g.) lard or butter
> ¼ tsp. salt
> ¼ tsp. baking soda
> 2 eggs
> 1½ qts. (1.5 l.) hot milk

Mix together the cornmeal, molasses, sugar, lard or butter, salt, baking soda, eggs, and ¾ qt. (.75 l.) milk in a saucepan, and bring to a boil over a high flame on top of the stove. Pour mixture into a well-greased stoneware or clay pot, mix in remaining milk, and bake in a very slow oven 5–7 hours. The temperature in the oven should be so low that the pudding is just barely bubbling, without actually boiling—200°F (95°C) at the most. Bake until the pudding browns slightly and comes away from the edges.

Billila
Whole Wheat Pudding

This Greek dessert is a specialty on the feast of Saint Barbara. In Yugoslavia a similar dish called *jito* is prepared in honor of the household's patron saint's day. A priest traditionally comes to bless the *jito* as well as the *kolatch*, a festive cake.

> 1 cup (250 g.) whole wheat grains
> 1/3 cup (80 g.) sugar
> Anise or orange water
> 1 cup (125 g.) chopped almonds or walnuts

Boil wheat grains until they burst, as if preparing *bulgur* (see p. 81), but do not mill. Simmer 20–30 minutes more.

Mix in sugar, anise or orange water, and chopped almonds or walnuts. Pour into a bowl, chill and serve.

Bean Pudding

There is nothing unusual about multiple uses for beans, but one Indian tribe of North and Central America uses beans so much they earned the name Papagos—the bean people.

> 1 cup (250 g.) white or red beans
> 3 cups (750 ml.) water
> 1 cup (150 g.) dried figs
> ¾ cup (180 g.) sugar
> 1 tsp. (5 ml.) vanilla

Soak beans overnight. Drain. Add water, simmer 2½ hours and drain. Puree in a food mill or mash. Meanwhile, simmer dried figs ½ hour in a little water, drain, and chop. Add to the beans along with ½ cup sugar and the vanilla. Heat gently and stir so that it thickens evenly.

Melt the remaining sugar over a medium heat in a dry, heavy frying pan. Add 2 tablespoons water and stir until the caramelized sugar is dissolved. Pour into a mold. Then add the bean puree and chill. Turn out of the mold and serve.

Squash Pudding

A favorite in Latin America.

1 lb. (500 g.) calabaza or butternut or hubbard, squash
1 cup (140 g.) cornstarch
3 cups (750 ml.) milk
1½ cups (300 g.) sugar
Juice and peels from 5 oranges
1 egg, beaten
2 tbs. (30 ml.) water

Pare and cut up the squash. Steam for 5–10 minutes, then puree in a food mill. Mix the cornstarch with the milk and heat gently until it starts to thicken. Add the squash, most of the sugar, orange juice, grated peels, and the beaten egg. Heat gently, stirring steadily.

Meanwhile, melt the remaining sugar over moderate heat in a dry, heavy pan. Add 2 tbs. water and stir to dissolve the caramelized sugar. Pour into a mold.

Pour squash pudding into the mold and chill. Turn out of the mold and serve.

Sago Pudding

Sago is starch from the pith of the Sago palm.

1 cup (100 g.) sago
4 cups (1 l.) milk
Sugar to taste
4–6 cups (1 kg.) peeled, sliced apples
½ cup (125 ml.) water

Stir sago into milk in medium-sized saucepan; bring just to a boil and simmer slowly, stirring occasionally, until mixture thickens, about ½ hour. Sweeten to taste. Meanwhile, stew apples in ½ cup water (cover pan tightly and they will make their own juice) until tender. Sweeten to taste and sprinkle with a little cinnamon, then place in a serving/baking dish and pour sago over them. Bake together at 325°F (160°C) for ½ hour.

Scottish Carrageen Pudding

Carrageen, a seaweed also known as Irish moss, is available in many natural foods stores.

½ cup (15 g.) dried carrageen
Lemon peel
3 cups (750 ml.) milk
1/3 cup (90 g.) sugar

Soak the carrageen in water for 15 minutes and drain. Heat the lemon peel with the milk. Stir in sugar. Add the soaked carrageen. Return to heat and boil gently 20 minutes. Pour into a chilled, wet mold. Take out of the mold when cold and set.

Beet Halva

5 large beets
1¼ cups (300 g.) sugar
6–7 tbs. (100 g.) *ghee* (see p. 31) or butter
½ cup (80 g.) chopped raisins
½ cup (80 g.) chopped cashews

Wash and steam the beet roots for 15–20 minutes, until tender all the way through. Puree in a food mill or a blender and add sugar. Simmer gently for 20–30 minutes, stirring frequently. Gradually mix in the *ghee*, (see p. 31), raisins, and nuts. Pour into a wide plate and smooth. Serve cold.

VARIANT   Replace the beets with potatoes.

Egg Halva

In the strict vegetarian districts of India, this dish is made with cooked, pureed carrots or squash instead of scrambled eggs.

    4 eggs
    1 cup (250 ml.) coconut milk (see p. 47)
    ½ cup (125 g.) sugar
    ½ cup (80 g.) raisins
    ½ – 1 tsp. cinnamon
    ½ cup (80 g.) chopped almonds or diced fruit

Scramble the eggs. Meanwhile, gently heat coconut milk with sugar and raisins and cook 5 – 8 minutes, to thicken. Add to the eggs and simmer gently 5 minutes. Add cinnamon. Mix in grated almonds or diced fruit, and remove from heat.

Bunuelos
Mexican Sweet Fritters

All over the world, fritters are the easiest and quickest pastry to prepare.

    2 eggs
    2 cups (250 g.) flour
    2/3 cup (160 g.) sugar
    Oil
    2 tbs. (30 g.) anise seeds or 3 cinnamon sticks
    2/3 cup (160 ml.) water

Beat eggs with 2 tablespoons of sugar, then mix thoroughly with the flour, to get a loose dough. Let sit 20 minutes. Divide into walnut-sized balls, and flatten by slapping them between your hands. Deep fry in oil and drain.

   Bring anise or cinnamon and water to a boil and simmer for 20 – 30 minutes. Remove cinnamon or anise. Stir in remaining sugar, turn up heat and boil 5 – 10 minutes. Pour over fritters and serve.

Filhos
Portuguese Pumpkin Fritters

These fritters are treats at every *carnaval*.

> ½ lb. (250 g.) pumpkin flesh
> 2 cups (250 g.) flour
> 3 eggs, separated
> 2 orange peels, grated
> 1 cup (250 ml.) ruby port wine
> Oil for deep frying
> 1 cup (250 g.) sugar

Cut the pumpkin flesh into a few large chunks and steam 30 minutes, until tender. Puree in a food mill or blender. Pour off any excess liquid or drain in cheesecloth, if necessary. Add flour, yolks, and orange peel. Mix together and moisten with a little wine. The result should be a thick, smooth paste. Let sit.

Add stiffly beaten egg whites. The mixture should now have the consistency of normal fritter batter. If it is too thick, add a little more wine.

Drop by tablespoons into hot deep frying oil. Drain.

Stir sugar into remaining wine and bring to a boil. Boil for about 5 minutes to make a syrup, and pour over the fritters. Serve.

Jallabis
Indian Fritters

In India desserts are numerous and often very fine, but they are not generally served at the end of a meal. Instead, they are eaten like other sweets, all
through the day. The common people, of course, taste these sweets only on
special occasions, since luxury is not their everyday fare.

> 2 cups (250 g.) flour
> 1 tsp. (5 g.) yeast
> 3 cups (750 ml.) water
> 1 2/3 cups (400 g.) sugar
> *Ghee* (see p. 31) or oil
> Pistachio nuts, grated or crushed

Mix flour and yeast with 2 cups water, to the consistency of thick cream. Let
sit covered 6–12 hours.

Stir sugar into 1 cup water, bring to a boil and boil 5–10 minutes. Keep
warm.

Heat *ghee* or oil in a frying pan. Dribble the batter by tablespoonfuls
through a funnel into the oil. Fry until golden brown, drain. Soak in the
syrup 10 minutes. Drain and sprinkle with crushed pistachio nuts.

Brazilian Beer Biscuits

> 2 cups (500 g.) flour
> ½ cup (125 g.) sugar
> ¼ lb. (125 g.) butter
> ¼ cup (60 ml.) beer.
> Pinch of baking soda
> ½–1 tsp. cinnamon

Knead ingredients to make a thick dough. Divide into balls and flatten
between your palms. Lay out on a buttered baking sheet and bake 15
minutes at 350°F (175°C). Let cool on a rack.

Slavic Kolaches

½ cup (125 ml.) milk
2 tbs. (2.5 g.) active dry yeast
½ cup (125 ml.) warm water (110°F or 45°C)
¾ cups (180 g.) butter
½ cup (125 g.) granulated sugar
1 tsp (5 g.) salt
4 egg yolks
4½ cups (500 g.) sifted white flour
2 tbs. (30 g.) melted butter
2 tbs. (25 g.) sifted powdered sugar

Scald milk. Cool to lukewarm. Sprinkle yeast on warm water; stir to dissolve. Cream butter, sugar, salt, and egg yolks together until light and fluffy. Add yeast, milk, and 1½ cups flour. Beat well until batter is very smooth; scrape bowl frequently. Stir in remaining flour, a little at a time, making a soft dough that leaves the side of the bowl. Place in lightly greased bowl, turn dough over to grease top. Cover and let rise in warm place free from drafts until doubled, 1 to 1½ hours.

Stir down; turn onto lightly floured board and divide into 24 pieces of equal size. Shape each piece into a ball. Cover and let rest 10 to 15 minutes. Place 2 inches apart on greased baking sheets; press each piece of dough outward from the center to make a hollow with a ½ inch rim around the edge. Fill each hollow with a tablespoon of filling. Cover and let rise in a warm place until doubled, 30 to 40 minutes. Bake at 350°F (175°C) for 15 to 20 minutes or until brown. Brush tops of rolls lightly with melted butter and sprinkle lightly with sifted powdered sugar. Remove from baking sheets to wire cooling racks. Makes 24 kolaches.

PRUNE FILLING:
30 dried prunes
Water to cover
¼ cup (60 g.) granulated sugar
½ tsp. (2 g.) allspice

Cook prunes in water until tender. Drain, mash with fork, removing seeds, and stir in sugar and allspice. Filling will be very thick. Makes enough to fill 14 kolaches.

APRICOT FILLING:
25 dried apricot halves
Water to cover
¼ cup (60 g.) granulated sugar

Cook apricots in water until tender. Drain and press through food mill or buzz in a blender. Stir in sugar. Filling will be thick. Makes enough to fill 10 kolaches.

Hamantashen
Prune Cookies

On the holiday of Purim, Jews celebrate the downfall of the villain Haman. They eat these delicious cookies filled in memory of Haman's pockets (i.e., *hamantashen*), which he no longer needed after the Persian king hanged him.

DOUGH:
4 cups (500 g.) flour
¾ cup (200 g.) sugar
4 eggs, beaten
½ cup (125 ml.) oil
Juice and grated peel of 1 orange, if desired (if you do not use juice,
    replace it with 2–3 tbs., 30 ml., cold water)

LEKVAR (PRUNE FILLING):
1 lb. (500 g.) prunes
1 orange, sliced
Cinnamon, allspice

DOUGH   Sift flour and mix with the other ingredients. Knead into a sticky but firm dough. Chill 1 hour.

LEKVAR   Stew prunes with sliced oranges and spices for 15 minutes. Cool, remove pits, and chop. If desired, add raisins or chopped nuts.

Roll out dough on a floured board and cut into disks about 4 inches in diameter. Or, divide dough into 2 dozen balls and roll each one to make 4 inch disks.

Place a spoonful of *lekvar* on each disk and fold in the 3 edges to form the shape of a three-cornered hat, or perhaps old Persian pockets. Bake at 350°F (175°C) for 30 minutes. If desired, brush with egg white or milk before baking.

For a lighter crust, sift 2 – 3 tsp. baking powder with the flour.

Polish Kluskis
Poached Cakes

> 2 cups (250 g.) flour
> 1 tbs. (15 g.) yeast
> 2 eggs
> ½ cup (125 g.) sugar
> 6 – 7 tbs. (100 g.) melted butter

Make a pile of flour and put a hole in the middle. Mix yeast into a little warm water. Place eggs, sugar, and yeast mixture in the hole, and stir into the flour. Knead together well. Let sit 3 – 4 hours.

Divide into ½ inch balls, cover with a cloth, and let rise 20 – 30 minutes more.

Poach 5 minutes in salted water. Serve with melted butter.

Molinetes
Chilean Chocolate Roll

> ½ lb. (250 g.) butter
> 1 cup (250 g.) sugar
> 3 cups (375 g.) flour
> Orange peel, grated
> 1 tsp. (5 g.) baking soda
> 2 tbs. (30 g.) cocoa

Beat butter and sugar together until smooth. Add flour, orange peel, and soda. Mix well and divide dough into two halves.

Work cocoa into one of the halves.

Roll out each dough carefully with a buttered, floured rolling pin. Lay the light dough on top of the chocolate dough and roll up together to make a long cylinder.

Let sit in a cool place for at least 1 hour.

Cut into thick slices. Lay on a buttered cookie sheet and bake 10 minutes at 350°F (175°C). Cool on a rack.

Parkin

This dryish sweet bread is a favorite teatime snack in the north of England and is usually served on Guy Fawkes Day.

¾ cup (150 g.) brown sugar
½ cup (125 g.) butter
1 cup (250 ml.) molasses
1 egg
2 cups (500 ml.) milk
1½ cups (200 g.) rolled oats
1½ cups (180 g.) white flour
1 tsp. (5 g.) powdered ginger
1 tsp. (5 g.) baking soda

Melt sugar, butter, and molasses together over low heat. Beat egg well, blend with a cup of milk, and add to first mixture. Combine oats, flour, and ginger in a large bowl and stir in molasses mixture. Beat well, then add remaining milk in which baking soda has been dissolved. Stir until blended, then pour into a well-buttered 9 by 14 inch baking pan. Bake for 1 hour at 350°F (175°C). Cool slightly and cut into squares.

Tipsy Cake

The British people are experts at using up leftover pastries, breads, and cakes. This traditional dessert is one example of making do with stale remains.

> Remains of a large sponge cake
> Apricot jam
> ½ – 1 cup (125 ml.) dry sherry or wine
> 2 cups (500 ml.) milk
> 3 eggs, well beaten
> ¼ cup (60 g.) sugar
> ½ cup (125 ml.) heavy cream
> Sugar to taste

Slice stale cake horizontally and spread thickly with jam, then put pieces back together and place in a deep baking dish. Cover with enough sherry to soak well. Beat together milk, eggs, and sugar, and bring to a boil. Lower heat and simmer, stirring constantly, until thick. Cool to lukewarm. Pour custard over soaked cake. Whip cream until very thick and sweeten to taste. Spoon over pudding.

Creole Cake

> 2 eggs, separated
> ½ cup (125 g.) brown sugar
> 1 cup (125 g.) grated fresh coconut
> 1/3 cup (50 g.) flour
> 3 tbs. (50 g.) butter, melted
> Pinch of cinnamon
> 1 tsp. (5 g.) baking soda

Beat egg yolks with sugar. Add coconut, flour, melted butter, cinnamon, and baking soda. Mix in stiff beaten egg whites at the last moment.

Pour the mixture into a shallow buttered baking pan or mold and bake 25 minutes at 350°F (175°C).

Creole Corn Cake

2 eggs, separated
½ cup (150 g.) sugar
¼ lb. (125 g.) melted butter
¾ cup (125 g.) cornmeal
1/3 cup (50 g.) white or whole wheat flour
1 tbs. (15 g.) baking soda
2 tbs. (30 ml.) boiling milk

Beat together yolks and sugar, add melted butter. Mix in the flours and baking soda gradually, then the milk.

Fold in stiffly beaten egg whites and pour into a buttered baking pan or mold. Bake 30 minutes at 350°F (175°C).

Kalva
Greek Semolina Cake

In Greece, and in every country where a long Turkish occupation has left its mark, semolina cake is a popular dish.

4−5 tbs. (60 g.) butter
1 cup (200 g.) semolina
2 cups (500 ml.) milk
½ cup (125 g.) sugar

Melt the butter and add the semolina. Brown, stirring constantly. Then pour in the hot milk mixed with sugar. Cover and simmer 10−15 minutes or so. The semolina should absorb all the liquid.

Spread onto a wide plate. Cool and cut into squares.

Greek Yoghurt Cake

¼ lb. (130 g.) butter
3 cups (750 g.) sugar
4 eggs, separated
1 cup (250 ml.) yoghurt
3 cups (375 g.) flour
1 tbs. (15 g.) baking soda
1 lemon
Bread crumbs

Cream together butter and sugar. Add yolks, then yoghurt. Mix in flour and soda. Add the juice and grated peel of the lemon. Add stiffly beaten egg whites last.

Pour into a buttered baking pan or mold lined with bread crumbs. Bake 45 minutes at 350°F (175°C). Make sure it is cooked all the way through. Cool on a rack.

Sweet Potato Cake

Sweet potatoes are good alongside main dishes and in desserts. They have a fine dry flavor recalling that of chestnuts.

2 lbs. (1 kg.) sweet potatoes
2−3 tbs. (40 g.) butter
1/3 cup (80 ml.) rum
1/3 cup (80 g.) sugar
2 eggs

Boil or steam peeled sweet potatoes 20−30 minutes until tender. Drain. Mash and add butter, rum, sugar, and beaten eggs. Pour into a mold and bake 20 minutes at 350°F (175°C). Turn out of the mold when cooled slightly.

SWEET POTATO FRITTERS   Prepare a sweet mash as above, very thick. Fry by spoonfuls in oil. Dust with sugar and cinnamon and serve hot.

Montecaos
"Little Cakes"

These delicious Spanish cakes have made their way into North African cooking as well.

  4 cups (500 g.) flour
  1 cup (250 g.) sugar
  ½ cup (125 ml.) olive or other oil
  ½−1 tsp. (3 g.) cinnamon or 1 tsp. (5 ml.) vanilla

Mix ingredients, knead, and shape into little balls about the size of pecans. If desired, add a little brandy or water to bind the dough. The cakes are flakier if you use less liquid. Lay out on a buttered baking sheet. Start baking at 450°F (230°C) for a few minutes, then lower to 350°F (175°C); total baking time should be 15 minutes.

Spanish Cakes

This is a shortbread with a fine, delicate taste.

  1 cup (250 g.) sugar
  ½ lb. (250 g.) lard
  1 egg
  2 cups (250 g.) flour
  ½ tsp. (2 g.) cinnamon or ½ tsp. (3 ml.) vanilla

Beat sugar and lard together. Add egg and flour. Knead and add cinnamon or vanilla.

  Divide into balls about the size of walnuts and arrange on a baking sheet. Bake 20 minutes at 350°F (175°C). Cool on the sheet.

Bean Cake

A favorite in Latin America.

  1 cup (250 g.) white or red beans
  2 cups (500 ml.) water
  1/3 cup (100 g.) sugar
  ½–1 tsp. (3 g.) cinnamon
  2–3 eggs, separated
  Bread crumbs

Soak beans overnight. Drain. Add fresh water and simmer 2½ hours. Drain and puree in a food mill or puree cone. Add sugar, cinnamon, and egg yolks, then fold in stiffly beaten egg whites.

Pour into a buttered baking pan or mold lined with bread crumbs. Bake 30 minutes at 350°F (175°C).

Serve warm or cold.

Pecan Pie

A Bossier Parish, Louisiana, recipe.

  FILLING:
  3 eggs
  ¾ cup (180 ml.) dark karo (corn syrup) or molasses
  ¾ cup (180 g.) sugar
  Salt
  3 tbs. (45 g.) melted butter
  1 tsp. (5 ml.) vanilla
  1½ cups (200 g.) whole or coarsely chopped pecans

  CRUST:
  1/3 cup (85 g.) butter, lard, or shortening
  1 cup (130 g.) flour
  2–3 tbs. (40 ml.) cold water

To make the crust, cut half the lard or butter in with the flour, until evenly mixed and granular. Cut the rest of the lard or butter in very coarsely. Add the water little by little, just enough so that the ball of dough will stick together. Let sit covered, in a cool place for at least 1 hour. Roll thin on a floured board to make an even disk, 11–12 inches in diameter. Lift carefully by draping over a floured rolling pin and lay gently over a 9 inch round pie pan. Gently push the dough down into the corners and crimp the rim by pinching the dough into little peaks at regular intervals, cutting away any excess. Cover bottom with parchment paper, weigh down with dried beans and bake 1–2 minutes at 375°F (190°C). Remove beans and paper.

To make the filling, stir the eggs together gently. Mix in syrup, sugar, salt, butter, and vanilla. Then add the pecans.

Pour into crust and bake at 375°F (190°C) for 15 minutes, then lower heat to 325°F (160°C) and bake 30–35 minutes more.

Serve warm or cold.

Arahara
Millet Drink

The Tuareg, a people of the central and western Sahara, prepare this nourishing drink using *tikamarin* cheese, a hard goat cheese which may be replaced with feta or pecorino.

1 cup (150 g.) pitted dates
3–4 cups (750 ml.) water
¼–½ lb. (250 g.) dry goat cheese
1 cup (125 g.) millet flour

Chop dates very finely and add a little water to make a light paste. Crumble the cheese finely.

Mix the date paste and cheese with water and millet flour. The liquid will look like milk and when served chilled is very refreshing. This dish is also easily made in a blender.

Chicha
Corn Liquor

This is an adapted version of the more homey native brew (see p. 26) made by Mexican and other Latin American Indians.

2/3 cup (125 g.) dried corn kernels
½ cup (125 g.) barley
1 gal. (4 l.) water
1 stick cinnamon
1 lb. (500 g.) fresh pineapple, crushed
1 cup (250 ml.) orange juice
4 cups (1 kg.) sugar

Lightly toast half the corn and half the barley, then soak these with the rest of the grain in 1 qt. of water for 2 days. Grind the grain in a mortar and pestle or run through a food mill or meat chopper, and mix with remaining 3 qts. of water together with cinnamon, pineapple, orange juice, and sugar. Keep in a clay pot for 2 days. Strain and serve with ice.

Mexican Chocolate

A fine version of a good, stimulating drink.

2 – 3 ozs. (70 g.) unsweetened chocolate
1 qt. (1 l.) milk
½ cup (90 g.) brown sugar or 2/3 cup (160 ml.) honey
2 – 3 cloves
1/3 cup (50 g.) almonds
½ tsp. cinnamon or 1 cinnamon stick

Melt the chocolate in gently heated milk. Stir in sugar. Crush the cloves and almonds finely with the cinnamon in a mortar and mix with the hot chocolate. Whip with a *molinillo*, a wooden hand beater, or with an egg-beater. Or, melt the chocolate in gently heated milk, put in a blender, add the other ingredients and whip. The blender will chop the nuts and spices finely as well as make the drink foamy. Serve hot.

Clabbered Milk

A tangy drink of pioneer America, clabber was either naturally soured milk or residue from the butter churn (buttermilk). If you have unpasteurized milk available, place a little in a small glass dish or bowl, and set it out until it has turned, then refrigerate until ready to drink or use in baking. Since pasteurized milk will not sour properly, but simply spoils, you'll need to resort to cultured buttermilk, commercially available, to make your own clabber, if you have no raw milk of your own.

> 1 cup (250 ml.) skim milk
> 1 tbs. (15 ml.) cultured buttermilk

Scald milk and cool to lukewarm (about 80°F. or 25°C). Stir in buttermilk and cover. Let stand at room temperature until clabbered. Stir or shake until smooth; refrigerate until ready to drink.

Barley Water

This is an all-purpose curative in Britain.

> ½ cup (125 g.) barley
> 6 cups (1.5 l.) water
> 1 lemon, sliced very thinly
> 1/3 cup (80 ml.) honey

Cook barley in water for 2 to 4 hours. Drain, reserving barley for soups. Bring liquid back to a boil and pour over lemon and honey. Stir until honey is dissolved, then allow to sit 15 minutes. Drain once more and serve warm.

Ginger Beer

1½ oz. (60 g.) ground ginger
1½ oz. (60 g.) cream of tartar
4 qts. (4 l.) boiling water
1 lb. (500 g.) brown sugar
Juice and rind of 2 large lemons
1 tbs. (12 g.) yeast dissolved in ¼ cup (60 ml.) warm water with 1 tsp.
   (5 g.) sugar

Combine ginger and cream of tartar; pour in a little of the boiling water, and stir until well dissolved; then add sugar, lemons, and remaining boiling water. Cool to lukewarm, stirring often, then add the yeast solution, stir well, and bottle immediately in clean strong bottles. Cap tightly and store bottles on their sides for several days in a dark place (safe from curious animals or children; bottles have been known to explode). Store bottles upright after that, and chill before opening to lower chance of explosion.

Wassail

This is the traditional festival punch in Great Britain.

4 cups (800 g.) brown sugar
1 gal. (4 l.) claret or other red wine
1 stick cinnamon
1½ inch piece of ginger
10 whole allspice
¼ whole nutmeg
5 whole cloves
One dozen eggs, separated

Stir sugar into claret and heat slowly, simmering without boiling. Tie spices into a gauze bag and suspend them into the heating wine. Beat egg whites until stiff; beat yolks until thick and light yellow. Fold whites into yolks, place in punch bowl, and pour hot spiced wine into them, first removing spice bag. Whip wassail with a wire whisk until frothy.

Shopping Guide

Wheat flour, rice, corn, chicken, beef, pork, onions, and garlic are used in the recipes of all races, groups, and classes of people in almost every country; they present no problem to the Western shopper. Some exotic dishes are exotic to Westerners, only because familiar products are used in unfamiliar ways: coconut with chicken, chocolate with rice, or peanuts with barbecued ribs. Some products, like seaweed, *molokheya*, and dried malva flowers are harder to find. Every ingredient in this cookbook can be either bought (or grown or gathered wild) in North America or Europe. It may, of course, take some adventuring which, apart from being enjoyable, is a lot easier than the kind of adventuring that most of the world's people have to undertake to procure the same products.

The best and most interesting stores in which to find the ingredients in this cookbook are ethnic markets. Peoples from the overpopulated Third World often emigrate, bringing their cooking and necessary ingredients with them. Emigration does not change tastes quickly. One of the best uses of this cookbook, in fact, is as an excuse to go into Chinese, Latin, Italian, Middle Eastern, and Indian stores with appropriate requests and questions. Aside from the satisfaction of sophistication, learning how to distinguish *bamias* from chick-peas and *chayote* from *calabaza*, you literally get the flavor of foreign countries and their peoples without the cost of a plane ticket and hotels. The utensils used in many of the recipes—the *tawas*, woks, *comals*, *molcajetes* and associated paraphernalia, are often quite beautiful to look at and practical and can usually be found alongside the foods. Using authentic utensils should not, of course, be an obsession. The kind of fire you use to cook the foods affects the taste and texture, but stoves are hard to duplicate. A stone mortar, such as a *molcajete*, is, on the other hand, easy to find and hard to beat when grinding small quantities of spices or making a chili paste out of soaked chiles. Do not, however, disdain a blender when grinding large quantities of chiles and spices for *mole*, or chick-peas for *hummus*.

Another major, and often more convenient, source of peoples' products are the health or natural food stores. The relation of these foods to health apparently depends on the greater simplicity of unprocessed foods. Most Third World peoples, who eat only such foods as are found in health or natural food stores, are anything but healthier than are Westerners with their impressively complex system of processed foods. Still, they do avoid the high incidence of cardiovascular disease and other ailments of affluent societies, and there is much Western man can learn from them.

Although supermarkets usually carry a great variety of bottled spices, it is worth the effort to find a herb and spice store where you can browse through the even greater variety, educating your nose to the various types and subtypes of aromas. Loose spices must be bottled or they quickly lose their pungency, and even bottled they fade, so spices should if possible be bought in regular visits or for the occasion rather than in rare, grand expeditions. Herb and spice wholesalers, such as Aphrodisia in New York, are good suppliers of some rare products such as dried malva flowers for soup.

If you are not careful, shopping for unfamiliar products can be expensive, especially if you buy huge quantities of a spice you only intend to use once or twice. The best advice is to be prudent; become aware of which products do and do not stay fresh (dried foods generally keep indefinitely; dried herbs loose their flavor; whole grain flours turn rancid rapidly); try to consult with the shopkeeper when possible (admittedly this is difficult in some ethnic markets, but it is worthwhile trying to communicate with people from foreign cultures especially those who share your city); and most of all, use your own common sense. At any rate, you will not find yourself spending exorbitant amounts on expensive cuts of meat or prepared imported delicacies when you use this cookbook. Also remember that experimentation and learning will save you a lot of money in the long run. Some of the products you buy may interest you enough to want to make you grow or make them from scratch—the cheapest and most satisfying "shopping" of all.

One good way to organize a meal using this cookbook is to try to feature one or two unfamiliar foods. Or try recipes all from one region or nationality. That way, you simplify preparation and really get to taste the food. Also, if you are cooking for guests, remember that people tend to be more conservative about what they eat than how it is prepared, so it may be confusing to try too much at once. There really is little reason to be squeamish or afraid—people's stomachs vary less than their religions. It is worth the effort to challenge your habits of taste. Once upon a time, populations in easy reach of despised herring starved to death in Europe.

Indian Markets

The cooking of India varies tremendously from region to region. Indian markets, such as the group on Lexington Avenue between 26th and 28th Streets in New York City, stock many of the items needed for the different regional foods. They always stock *ghee*, which along with coconut milk, garlic and curry spices, is largely responsible for the taste of the most familiar kind of Indian cooking. Indian markets also stock mustard, sesame and peanut oils, and sesame seeds which are characteristic of other regional styles of cooking. These stores are the best source of staples like *dhal*, *dhal* flour, lentils, beans, rice, rice flour, *atta* (wholewheat) and *maida* (white wheat) flours. In our supermarkets we are used to very little variety in staples, which in our well-organized nation are nationally and consequently homogeneously marketed; but in these Indian markets, *dhal*, lentils and even rice are available in a surprising diversity of colors, shapes, and taste.

Curries are subtler and more delicate if you mix the spices yourself instead of using blended curry powders. Indian markets stock all the spices that make up a curry blend: fenugreek, turmeric, cloves, cinnamon, hot peppers, cardamom, cumin, coriander, bay leaves, saffron, black pepper, and fennel. This is an area for imagination—using the above spices selectively, you can develop a complex aroma that matches the dish, instead of the blended single taste of curry powder. Note too that spices get stale slower when bought whole instead of powdered so that whole cardamoms and cumin seeds ground specially for a recipe have a fresher taste than shelf-dead curry powders. These spices are also available in herb and spice stores.

Other flavorings, such as rose water, tamarind paste, sesame seeds, sesame paste (*tahina*), raw sugar, and coconut cream are usually in stock in Indian markets. If you do not feel like making Indian curds or *panir* (drained curds), which are generally not available at these stores, you can replace the curds with soured milk, sour cream, or yoghurt (see p. 29) and use farmer's cheese in place of *panir*.

As for utensils, you can buy a *tawa*, a concave griddle, but not an *enghati*, a wood stove, for making Indian breads. Banana leaves are not generally available, although some Chinese and Latin markets have them; but these too can be replaced without detriment by corn husks, parchment paper, cheesecloth, or even grape or cabbage leaves, depending on the recipe.

MAIL ORDER

Kalustyan Orient Export Trading Co.
123 Lexington Avenue
New York, New York 10016

Bazaar of India
1331 University Avenue
Berkeley, California 94702

Chinese Markets

Chinese markets have the widest variety of foods available anywhere.
Besides the great number of foods and styles of cooking they owe to their
immense country and developed culture, the Chinese have mastered so
many techniques of preserving food that they can routinely supply very
unusual products. Moreover, the Chinese stick to their traditions, even in
foreign cities, and continue to cook and sell the same foods they eat in
China.

The assortment of vegetables available in Chinese markets is very rich,
including: (1) familiar vegetables such as tomatoes, cabbage, bananas, fresh
ginger, watercress, radishes, mustard greens, raw peanuts, and potatoes;
(2) unfamiliar varieties of familiar vegetables such as yard beans (long string
beans), celery cabbage, black radishes, long white radishes (*daikon*), snow
peas, Chinese melons, kumquats, *calabazas* or pumpkins and long cucumbers; and (3) unfamiliar vegetables such as *bok choy*, water chestnuts, bitter
melons, winter melons, *taro* (Chinese potato), arrowroot, yam bean, fresh
coriander, kohlrabi, and bean sprouts. The selection of dried vegetables is
even richer, including: mushrooms and fungi, water chestnuts, lotus root,
bamboo shoots, grasses, taro, arrowroot, banana and lotus leaves, beans,
lentils, and soy beans. The markets also stock many pickled vegetables,
such as *kimchi*.

All the familiar staples and then some are available: rice, rice flour, wheat
flour, cornmeal, water chestnut powder, millet, and tapioca. It should be
noted in passing that the Chinese commonly use water chestnut powder
instead of cornstarch or flour to thicken soups and sauces. Wheat, rice, and
soy bean noodles come in many shapes and textures. Bean curd, another
Chinese staple, comes fresh, fermented, dried, and canned, but most of the
recipes in this book are best made with the fresh.

The important flavorings sold include: soy sauce both thin and salty and
thick and sweet; sesame oil, which with soy sauce, garlic, and ginger, is

responsible for the familiar taste of Chinese food; ginger, and hot peppers both dried and fresh; rice vinegar, Szechuan pepper and star anise. Peanut oil is the most important cooking oil.

Some of the most picturesque sights of Chinese markets are the dried seafoods used for dishes, sauces and stocks: shrimp, scallops, and squid of all sizes, fish ranging from tiny sardines and anchovies through eels to 6 foot sharks and cod, and exotic shellfish like sea cucumber, whelk, and abalone. Fish such as sea bass, eel, and shark are also sold fresh—even here the selection differs from that in familiar fish markets, although the fresh fish come from familiar waters. Dried and smoked pork joints and ducks, hams and sausages ornament Chinese stores. Fresh meat is not butchered in the familiar manner in Chinese butcher shops but comes in different shapes. The ears, feet, tails, and other parts of pigs, fowl and beef used in soups are important items, as well as organ meats.

Chinese utensils, particularly the wok, are extremely useful cooking tools. Others available include: steamers that fit into woks, clay soup pots for slow cooking, chopsticks, frying ladles, and chopping knives.

125 Mott Street, N.Y.

Some Chinese products can be found in regular supermarkets: soy sauce, bean sprouts, some frozen vegetables such as pea pods, and canned vegetables such as water chestnuts and bamboo shoots. Frozen Chinese vegetables are tasty, but canned water chestnuts, bamboo shoots, and noodles often leave something to be desired.

Chinese products are at their best in Chinese markets in Chinatown in no matter what city. Although it may be difficult to make yourself understood, and some of the foods appear strange, the experience of shopping alongside people for whom lotus root is a more familiar taste than potatoes adds to the taste of the dishes and the appreciation of their importance.

Some markets commonly found in urban Chinatowns are maintained by other Oriental peoples and emphasize other Asian cuisines such as Vietnamese, Thai, and Indonesian. They usually also stock most of the same staples as the Chinese markets in addition to their national specialties.

MAIL ORDER

Wing Fat Co.
35 Mott Street
New York, New York 10013

Wing Chong Lung Co.
922 South San Pedro St.
Los Angeles, California 90015

Japanese Markets

Japanese markets are not quite as common as Chinese markets but are another excellent source of oriental products. Dried seaweed is a true Japanese staple and available in great variety, including sheet laver for sushi and kombu. Dried fish, such as flaked tuna (bonito), dried shrimp and rice, especially the fine, wide-grained Japanese rice, and rice flour are other important staples.

These markets also stock soy beans, miso (soy bean paste for soups), fresh and fermented bean curd, soy sauce and tamari (a heavy soy sauce); fresh vegetables such as daikon (Japanese radish), Chinese (celery) cabbage, bok choy (like broccoli), ginger, and bean sprouts; and often carry fresh seafood including octopus and tuna. Dried Japanese mushrooms are very fine. Hot radish powder for sushi and sashimi (sliced raw fish), and rice vinegar, as well as prepared foods like rice biscuits with seaweed (kakimotchi sembei), many different vegetables preserved in brine or vinegar, including kimchi (see p. 159) and other Japanese specialties are available.

Japanese markets also stock utensils, including the noble wok with its accompanying steamers and paraphernalia, and good knives.

MAIL ORDER

Katagiri & Co.
224 East 59th St.
New York, N.Y. 10016

Uwajimaya Inc.
519 6th Avenue South
Seattle, Washington 98104

Pacific Mercantile Co.
1925 Lawrence Street
Denver, Colorado 80202

Latin Markets

There are many Latin markets of varying nationality—Puerto Rican, Mexican, Cuban, Dominican, Brazilian, Portuguese—in most major cities. They routinely stock wide assortments of staples like dried beans of all colors, green bananas (platanos and maduros), yams (ñames), sweet potatoes (batatas or camotes), taro (dasheen and yautia), breadfruit, manioc (yuca), manioc meal, dried corn, many grades of corn meal, prepared tortillas, rice flour, dried cod (bacalao), dried beef (carne seca), chorizo sausage, fresh and hard cheeses, dried chiles, chocolate, and spices like epazote. Latin markets also carry fresh tropical fruits and vegetables such as chayote, calabazas, mangoes, papayas, coconuts, and fresh coriander (culantro). Canned chiles, tomatoes, and mole sauces are also available. Some stores stock utensils as well as foods, including metates (stones for grinding grain), molcajetes (mortars), clay dishes for paella, comals (griddles), and tortilla presses. Butchers in these markets carry wide selections of pork products including sausages, lard, heads, tails, and feet.

MAIL ORDER:

Casa Moneo
210 West 14th St.
New York, N.Y. 10014

Casa Esteiro
2719 West Division
Chicago, Illinois 60622

Middle Eastern Markets

The markets of the nations on the eastern shores of the Mediterranean stock many products in common, reflecting the still strong influence of the old Turkish empire. For example, Greek markets carry many of the same items as Syrian markets.

Relatively unfamiliar staples like bulgur, chick-peas, and couscous are commonly available in different grades in Middle Eastern markets, as well as familiar staples like beans, rice, and lentils in uncommon variety. Middle Eastern markets are the best source for grape leaves, *tahina* (sesame paste), sesame oil, dried *bamias,* and mint. Nuts, ground lamb, olives, and dried fruits are central elements of Middle Eastern cookery available even in supermarkets.

Middle Eastern markets carry the same spices as those available in Indian markets, but with a different balance: cumin dominates, especially in Arab markets; and anise, a favorite of Mediterranean France as well as Greece is important. Cardamom and cinnamon are commonly used in teas and desserts. Middle Eastern markets also carry other flavorings for sweets, such as honey, tamarind paste, orange water, and rose water.

The large, heavy metal mortars sold in these markets are useful and handsome utensils.

The best Middle Eastern markets in New York City are on Atlantic Avenue in Brooklyn near Borough Hall, where stores such as Sahadi and Beirut even stock *molokheya,* which even herb stores do not.

MAIL ORDER

Malko Brothers-Cassatly Co.
197 Atlantic Avenue
Brooklyn, New York 11201

Italian Markets

Many Italian products, such as spaghetti and Parmesan cheese, are familiar supermarket items, but you can find greater variety and better quality in Italian markets. For instance, pasta varies greatly in quality—fresh fettucine is delicious, and even spaghetti bought by the pound in one of these markets generally tastes better than the mass-marketed brands. Nothing of course tastes better than home-made. Parmesan comes in many grades and is best bought in chunks and ground just before serving.

Italian markets are scattered in most urban centers and stock fine goods like polenta, chick-peas, chick-pea flour, pignoli nuts, Piedmontese rice for risottos, excellent canned tomatoes that are better in sauces than "fresh" tomatoes out of season, mozzarella, ricotta, Parmesan and other cheese, dried mushrooms, and pork products (which, incidentally, are a major source of protein throughout Europe for rich as well as poor, and also a major pleasure). Chestnuts are available fresh in season, dried all year round, and sometimes ground for polenta. Italian greengrocers often carry fresh fava beans, fennel, dandelion leaves and other greens, not to mention tomatoes and garlic, the appreciation of which we owe to the Italians.

Health or Natural Food Stores

Health or natural food stores are increasingly common. They owe their name and some measure of their popularity to the whole grains and flours they stock. Supermarkets, unless they have extensive health food sections, do not stock important staples like whole wheat, millet, rye, oats, buckwheat, and corn but usually carry only a narrow range of refined flours and meal. Refined flour is a luxury to poor people—white bread is eaten as a treat in parts of Eastern Europe—but it is not as nutritious as coarser grains. The protein rich germ of the grain is milled away in refining because it spoils relatively quickly when ground into flour. The superior nutritive quality of whole grains confers a right to the title "health" food store. The superior nutrition is important if the whole diet consists of little else but grains. Perhaps more important here, in a country where varied fresh fruits, vegetables, and meats are generally available, is the fact that these whole grains have their own tastes and textures, unrelated to white bread and cakes. The taste and textures of the grains used give much of the character to simple peoples' cooking

The title "natural food" stores depends on a metaphysical distinction. Almost all food is processed before eating, if only by cooking. Some processing is necessary to bring out the nutritive elements of some foods, or to remove poisons. Many natural peoples' staples, such as manioc, bread-fruit, and acorns, go through long processing before they are considered edible. *Popoi*, the staple of Tahitians, the most natural of people according to some writers, is made by a fairly lengthy process. What is natural and what is not is a cultural decision. Perhaps the closeness of human hands to simpler processes make those processes more natural. More to the point here is that native people do in fact eat these "natural" foods, if only because they lack the technology to produce any other kind.

Health food stores are invaluable sources of: whole grains, including wheat, rye, oats, millet, barley, brown rice of several kinds, and buckwheat; excellent flours made from all the grains; oils including sesame, coconut, and nut oils; beans, soy beans, lentils, raw nuts, and dried fruits. They also stock oriental products such as bean curd, soy sauce, *tamari*, *miso*, bean sprouts, dried fish, and dried seaweeds such as *kombu*, laver and non-oriental Irish moss (carrageen). They usually carry a wide assortment of spices and herbs, including herbs for infusions such as camomile; and yeasts.

One final note: "organic" foods are more expensive and not necessarily better quality. There is also no control on the use of the word, so all depends on the honor of the producer and the reliability and selectivity of the retailer.

INDEX

Note: Page references to illustrations are in **boldface.**